# In Search of
# the
# Pangolin

The
Accidental
Eco-Tourist

First published in 2006 by New Holland Publishers (UK) Ltd
London • Cape Town • Sydney • Auckland
www.newhollandpublishers.com

Garfield House, 86–88 Edgware Road, London W2 2EA,
United Kingdom

80 McKenzie Street, Cape Town 8001, South Africa

14 Aquatic Drive, Frenchs Forest, NSW 2086, Australia

218 Lake Road, Northcote, Auckland, New Zealand

ISBN 1 84537 259 X

Publishing Manager: Jo Hemmings
Project Editor: Gareth Jones
Editor: Liz O'Donnell
Design: Adam Morris
Cover Design: Ian Hughes
Pangolin Artwork: Zena Deretsky
Production: Joan Woodroffe

Reproduction by Modern Age Repro House, Hong Kong
Printed and bound by Replika Press PVT Ltd, India

Satyajit Das
& Jade Novakovic

# In Search of
## the
# Pangolin

The

Accidental
Eco-Tourist

# CONTENTS

# PREFACE

In 1991, we trekked in Zaire to see mountain gorillas. The inspiration was a photo in a colleague's office. The hours that we spent with two families of gorillas in the Kahuzi-Biega Park in the Virunga Mountains had a profound impact on us. Since that time, we have been fortunate to travel to many eco-travel destinations in the world. *In Search of the Pangolin* is about these journeys.

We would like to thank our publisher, Jo Hemmings of New Holland, for believing in the idea of the book, and her support. We would like to thank the production team at New Holland, including Liz O'Donnell and Gülen Shevki-Taylor, for their help in preparing the book for publication. Special thanks to Gareth Jones, our editor, who worked closely with us to improve the book. We thank Pat Quinn-Boas, Cindy Statts, Christine Hartgill and Vic Kline for their suggestions and reading of previous drafts.

The book recognizes the commitment of the rangers, guides, conservationists and ordinary people who shared the experience and beauty of wild places with us so generously. Without the selfless and passionate devotion of these people many of these places would not survive.

The book is dedicated to the wild places and wondrous creatures that inhabit them.

Satyajit Das and Jade Novakovic
Sydney, Australia

# IN SEARCH OF THE PANGOLIN

I know the precise moment when the question occurred to us. It was during breakfast at Ranthambore.

Ranthambore is in Rajasthan, south-west of Agra (famous for the Taj Mahal). We were in Nepal and India visiting a number of national parks and wildlife sanctuaries. Some would be more accurately described as wildlife-less sanctuaries. Eco-tourists travel to India to see the royal Bengal tiger, a magnificent member of the cat family. Decimated by hunting and loss of habitat, the tiger survives only in a number of parks, like Ranthambore.

Ranthambore is a small park, around 155 square kilometres (60 square miles) in size. A reminder of the great virgin forests that once covered central India, it was once the centre of a Hindu kingdom. The ruins of Ranthambore Fort overlook the park. The fort, with its old defensive walls and other structures, is largely overgrown, and tigers can occasionally be seen in the ruins. In actual fact, Ranthambore is famed for its tigers. It was used in 'Project Tiger', started in 1972 by the World Wildlife Fund and the Indian Government to save the animal from extinction. Numerous wildlife documentaries have been filmed at the park, researchers work in and around it, and it is a magnet for foreign tourists and amateur wildlife photographers. We had seen two tigers at Ranthambore. But that was not the subject of our discussion at breakfast...

We were staying near the park. Our hotel was once the hunting lodge of the Maharaja of Jaipur. Queen Elizabeth and Prince Philip had been there at a famous hunting party in 1961 – the British Raj and Indian nobility had delighted in the slaughter of tigers as a strange, inexplicable form of entertainment. We took daily drives in jeeps with guides in the park, in the morning and afternoon. After breakfast, at around 6.30–7.00am, we left the lodge to join the queue to enter the park. Being early in the queue was an advantage. You entered the park while the wildlife was still active and before the animals found a place to settle until the heat of the day had passed. You had the chance to see them before other jeeps scared them away.

At breakfast that day, there was a BBC crew: Mike, the genial, bearded producer, along with a cameraman and a sound person. There was Valmik Thapar, famous for his work on a series about Indian wildlife, *The Land of the Tiger*. The BBC was in India on a 4–6 month project to film a documentary on tigers. The crew spent all day in the park, having a special dispensation to enter the park early, stay all day and leave late. Tourists were only allowed at fixed times in the morning and late afternoon, so we usually saw them at breakfast on their way out. Our breakfast conversation was about the pangolin. Both Jade and I wanted to see one.

A pangolin is a scaly anteater that is prehistoric in appearance. Its name comes from the Malay language, and refers to its ability to curl up into a ball. The pangolin feeds on ants, termites and other insects. It is small, about the size of a cat, with a long tail and is covered in large yellowish-brown scales. The scales are two-sided elevations of skin flattened from the back towards the stomach. It has small eyes with thick lids to protect it from ant and termite bites, and its snout is long, ending in a round disc that is wide at the sides. The pangolin hunts with the aid of its long tongue and sticky mucus produced by its salivary glands. Ants and termites get stuck in the mucus and are eaten. It is mainly nocturnal. All this was, by the way, based on guidebooks and natural-history books. We had never actually seen a pangolin...

Why did we want to see a pangolin? The reasons are complicated. By the time of our visit to India, we had been travelling as eco-tourists for about 7–8 years. We had seen many of the 'hallmark' species that eco-travellers want to see and photograph. But never a pangolin. Nor had we ever met anybody who had. On the whole, eco-tourists want to see cuddly or fierce creatures with charisma. In Africa, we were bemused by the frantic desire of tourists to see the 'Big Five' – a common term used to denote lions, leopards, elephants, rhinoceroses and cape buffaloes. The tourists' eagerness to see these species (preferably as quickly as possible) was fascinating.

Just as these tourists had lists of what they wanted to see ('tick-a-box' travel), we had our list. Our list was made up of obscure creatures, such as the pangolin. In conversations with serious eco-travellers, there is one-upmanship, and you must be able to offer something remarkable. We have seen an aardwolf – a strange cross between a hyena and a jackal that feeds on termites – and a giant eagle owl – a species of large African owl. These sightings can be offered up and will be accepted as evidence of club membership. A sighting of a pangolin would be special. We also really wanted to see this exotic creature out of a sense of curiosity.

'Wonder if they have ever seen one?' Jade mused about the BBC crew. It was early in the morning. Sensible people on holiday would be fast asleep. 'I mean they must have seen one, don't you think?' She was making conversation over the 'pukka' English breakfast (cornflakes, eggs, toast, etc.) in the lodge's dining room.

'Why don't you ask them?' I replied, half asleep.

'I couldn't,' Jade said.

My ears perked up. This was now a contest.

'Dare you,' I said.

'I couldn't,' Jade said again. Imminent victory in this dare was making me feel more awake. 'Why don't *you* ask them?' This was not good. Jade had reversed the dare. 'Yes, why don't you?' She was more strident. 'You are the one who wants to know.' This was a clever reversal. *We* wanted to see a pangolin. Now, I had no choice.

I pushed back my chair and walked over to the table where the BBC crew was sitting. They were chatting.

'Have you ever seen a pangolin?' I blurted out, aiming for an air of nonchalance and cool. It sounded like a stupid question in school. I would just kill Jade later.

Mike looked up, startled. This clearly was not a question he was asked often – at least not recently and not at breakfast. He blinked several times. 'I haven't, no,' he said slowly. 'But I will ask around.' 'Must go,' he added, standing up.

The BBC crew was getting ready to go out. Mike walked off with a cheery wave, though I detected a perplexed look on his face.

I wandered back casually to our table and sat down. 'He hasn't but he'll ask around,' I said. Jade smiled, an ironic look on her face. I didn't care – I had won the dare.

'There *are* pangolins here,' he began, when I next saw him. 'Hard to see... nocturnal. David has seen them.'

'David..?'

'Attenborough,' he said.

'Of course.' I felt like a right dork.

'He has seen them in Papua New Guinea. I sent him an e-mail.'

Someone had seen a pangolin. I was excited and full of questions...

'Sorry, must run, cheers,' he said and moved off to join the BBC crew at the other end of the veranda.

We got to know the crew vaguely after that. We chatted about what they were doing, other documentaries. Chuck was doing brown bears for David in Kamchatka. We had no idea who Chuck was. We left Ranthambore a few days later on the next stage of our travels.

## Inspiration for eco-travel

In the 1980s, Chris, one of the people I worked with, travelled through Africa in the pioneering days of overland travel. He got out slides of his journey along with some souvenirs. I remember him showing us a circumcision tool from the Pygmy tribes.

Later, I worked with another man, Peter, who had two photos in his office – a mountain gorilla and a big male elephant with huge tusks. He showed us photos of his African travels. Somehow the photos worked a magic spell on us. We made our first journey to Africa in 1991, trekking in Zaire's Virunga

Mountains to see gorillas. The moment we saw our first mountain gorilla we were hooked. The two hours we spent with two separate family groups in the mountain forests remain intensely special to us. It changed our lives.

Eco-tourism or eco-travel is defined as 'travel to unusual destinations specifically to admire and enjoy wildlife and undeveloped, relatively undisturbed natural areas, as well as indigenous cultures'[1]. Devoted eco-travellers are mad. They have a genuine love of nature and appreciate the beauty of flora and fauna, especially in wild and often remote places. They possess an almost childlike wonder, an obsession with ecology, a righteous zeal in defence of conservation, a tendency to misanthropic behaviour. These are some of the behaviours that Jade has pointed out in me. The devoted eco-traveller incessantly watches nature documentaries, studies the credits on most *Discovery Channel*, *National Geographic* and *Animal Planet* programmes, seeking out new destinations, and reads *National Geographic* and books on the biology of the reed warbler. They can be found memorizing bird-identification guides and taped birdcalls.

I recognized the aardwolf in Namibia's Etosha National Park instantly. It was at a latrine site. Aardwolves are primarily termite eaters. They hunt by smell. Their diet means that their scat (faeces) smells of termites. To avoid confusion with real termite odours, the aardwolf uses established latrine sites in its territory. This aardwolf was using one of these sites, giving us a rare opportunity to see this wonderful creature. I had rattled off all I knew about aardwolves under my breath while watching the animal through my binoculars. Our companions, Judith and Ian, were a little stunned. Ian pulled out his animal guidebook, locating the entry on aardwolves.

He turned to Judith in amazement and said: 'You know, he's right.'

I had never seen an aardwolf before that moment; I had seen photos and read a lot about them.

## The search for the pangolin

What stays with us throughout our travels is the idea of chancing upon rare creatures, the unusual ones, the ones that people know very little about and most people, even eco-tourists, have not seen. We want to see a pangolin. Why? What's the point? Why do we travel at all? Why do we spend our holidays in the wilds, full of mud, forests and exotic (usually untreatable) diseases? Why do we get up before dawn and traipse through jungles for a momentary fleeting glimpse of a wild creature?

Alain de Botton, in *The Art of Travel*, wrote that 'perhaps few activities reveal as much of the dynamics of this quest [for happiness] – in all its ardours and paradoxes – than our travels'[2]. What do our travels reveal about us, about our world?

The wildlife that the eco-traveller comes to see is frequently in danger of extinction. Many will not survive, despite the best efforts of dedicated conservationists, beyond the next few decades. Douglas Adams immortalized this in his book *Last Chance to See*[3], recording his journey in search of threatened wild species. This is the paradoxical appeal of eco-travel, to glimpse a dying world before it is gone.

The pangolin has become our private joke, a metaphor for our travels: *The Search for the Pangolin*. This search is about the elusive and rapidly disappearing natural history of our world. It is also a metaphor for the absurdities of our journeys. It is a way of explaining our strange holiday destinations and answering friends who don't quite know what we do on our holidays. We never expect to actually see a pangolin. But then again, if we are really lucky, we just might.

This book records our travel to eco-tourist destinations. We are interested in the people, the places and the process. We want to record a little of the unearthly beauty and splendour of the wild places and magnificent animals that we were lucky enough to see. We want to record the joys and despair, the sanity and the absurdity of our journeys. We want to bear testament to the right of wild creatures to live and for human beings to learn to share this planet with them.

# CHAPTER 1

'The Guidebook Says...':
Planning The Eco-
adventure

*...In the rainforest, we
chatted to our guide,
Rachel, an American
biologist. 'Why do people
come to the Amazon?'
She replied carefully,
'They have been every-
where else...'*

# CHAPTER 1

## Travel and eco-travel

Travel is a form of recreation, a palliative to the ordinariness of our everyday lives. People travel to discover new worlds. Once these were real voyages of exploration for science or for plunder. Today, people travel to visit foreign countries and exotic locations. Travellers seek out worlds outside their own range of experience. Eco-travel isn't new. People with a love of nature and wild places have been undertaking what is now called 'eco-travel' or 'adventure travel' for a long time. It is all about discovering the natural history of the world we live in: the natural places, the animals that inhabit them and the people who live there. Well, that's the theory! Some eco-travellers have different motivations.

In the rainforest, we chatted to our guide, Rachel, an American biologist. 'Why do people come to the Amazon?'

She replied carefully, 'They have been everywhere else.'

For some travellers, the African savannah or the Amazonian rainforest is not that different from a visit to Rome or Paris – just a twist on leisure travel. 'This year we thought we'd do something a little different.' 'Our friends did it.'

In reality, there are a few common eco-travel destinations. There are the plains of Africa and the rainforests in South and Central America, Asia and Australia. There is Alaska and parts of the USA and Canada. Increasingly, there is interest in travelling to the Arctic and Antarctic.

Jade and I have visited some of these destinations. In 1991 and 1995, we travelled in Africa to Zaire, Kenya, Tanzania, Zimbabwe, Zambia, Botswana and Namibia. In 1994, we did a semi-circumnavigation of the Antarctic. In 1997 and 2004, we travelled to Central and South America, visiting Peru, Ecuador, Venezuela, Costa Rica and Guatemala. In 1999, we travelled in India and Nepal. In 2001, we travelled in Alaska and Canada. In 2005, we travelled to Borneo. Each journey was to see the natural history of the destination. And, of course, in recent times, we have been looking for the elusive pangolin.

Each of our journeys requires extensive preparation. A Das holiday has a day-by-day itinerary (Jade insists it's minute-by-minute), rigorously planned after extensive research and expert consultation. On normal holidays, it is accepted that you sleep and eat a lot, lounge about the pool, get sunburnt and, if the spirit dictates, see the local attractions. Eco-travel is different. The question is 'How do we know where to go and what to do?'

There are different philosophies on holiday planning – detailed planning versus just winging it. Jade is prepared to decide on the course of a journey using a set of dice. I am more from the Einstein school that refuses to believe that the Gods play dice with the world. It is not clear which of the two positions is more likely to yield us a glimpse of the pangolin.

## Fellow travellers

Friends are sometimes useful sources of information. In polite society, travel is a safe topic. The host might say, 'Jade and Das have just been to [insert suitable destination].' Another guest might respond, 'Really? We were there recently/We have always wanted to go there/We know someone who has been there/We are going to [destination] for our holidays.' The routine riffs its way around the table. Depending on interest, this banter may continue for any length of time. A critical factor is the ability to tangentially develop the conversation. Someone may introduce accommodation: 'My God, have we ever told you the story of our stay in [name of hotel]?'

Travel conversations rarely provide useful information. This is because they are a form of display. Travel to out-of-the-ordinary (read 'expensive') destinations is consistent with wealth. Travel to remote, unheard-of places demonstrates a sense of adventure. Travel to a distant eco-travel hotspot or to work with a NGO (monitoring some endangered species) speaks of your social credentials. A trekking holiday or walking safari demonstrates your vigour if you are not young. Who said only birds and animals have interesting display behaviours?

A conversation with a hard-core fellow eco-traveller is different. I spotted Alan in a supermarket in Sydney. We had first met him in Africa. He was nice in that way Canadians are nice. You could attack them physically and they would smile and say, 'Take care, don't hurt yourself.' He was on holiday in Australia and had recently been in South America. Here was a chance to get first-hand information... I invited him to our house for a drink. Jade looked at me with a mixture of humour, disdain and pity. She knew what he was about to endure.

Alan showed up. We served drinks, and then I was away. The nature of the conversation, loosely described, can be seen from the dialogue set out below:

DAS: So, you have been to South America.
ALAN: Yes.
DAS: Where did you go?
ALAN: I spent a fair bit of time in Peru.
DAS: How long?
ALAN: About three weeks.
DAS: What were the highlights?
ALAN: It was very interesting generally.
DAS [*annoyed*]: No. Which were the best? Did you go to the Peruvian Amazon?
ALAN: Yes.

DAS: Was it via Iquitos or did you go to one of the smaller tributaries?
ALAN: Through Iquitos. A lodge about 80 kilometres outside of Iquitos.
DAS: What was the wildlife like?
ALAN: Okay.
DAS: How many bird species did you see? See any jaguars or tapirs?
ALAN: Didn't see any of them.
DAS: How many in the camp? How many guides? What was the guide–guest ratio? Any of them trained biologists?
ALAN: Don't remember the exact number of guides. They were okay.
DAS: Any Indian guides?
ALAN: I don't think so.
DAS: Did they use motorized boats or paddled canoes?
ALAN: Motorboats, I think.
DAS: Didn't the noise disturb the wildlife?
ALAN: I suppose so.
DAS: What about night activities? Can you go out at night?
ALAN: I am not sure. We didn't.
DAS: What about river dolphins?
ALAN: We didn't see any that I can remember. Someone told us about a place you can swim with them.
DAS [*interested*]: What was the name of the place?
ALAN: I think it was called [name of lodge]. I am not sure.
DAS: Can you try to remember? It is kind of important.
ALAN: Sorry. I can't remember.
DAS: Never mind! Did you use a local agent? Who are the good ones?

It had all the charm of an interrogation by the secret police. Alan probably would have preferred that.

## Reading the paper

Most newspapers have a travel section, which may provide some information about potential eco-travel destinations. In Nepal, we came across a travel writer. We had come to Bardia National Park hoping to see tigers, Asian elephants and, in particular, the one-horned Indian rhinoceros. We also thought there may be a chance to see a pangolin if we were very lucky. It was listed as one of the animals inhabiting the park.

The travel writer stayed for one night. He went out on elephant back with us. We saw very little that day, a hazard of viewing wildlife. The mahout used a metal rod, the *trisul*, to control the elephant and administered fairly hefty clouts.

The travel writer asked us in a serious voice after the ride, 'Was that an unusual amount of discipline that was used with the elephant?' Jade and I were puzzled. Trying to control even a domesticated elephant requires coercion.

The man was a freelance writer and also a location scout for motion pictures. He knew nothing at all about the wildlife of Nepal and was not particularly interested. He was keen to return to Kathmandu, the capital of Nepal. He wanted to shop for 'local items'. His story was for an English newspaper. His flight had been paid for by a Middle Eastern airline. The accommodation and activities were free. I never saw the article but can imagine it.

It would start with the flight from London to Kathmandu via some Middle Eastern city. The excellent service on the plane would be referred to in terms of Arabian hospitality. The aircraft would be described in detail: spacious interior, interactive entertainment system. Nepal would be exotic. There would be a sentence or two on the history of Nepal, (but no mention of politics, especially not the Maoist insurgency). There would be a little on travel through the picturesque and green countryside. Villagers would be busily working in the fields. They would be in touch with the earth and happy (albeit only as happy as you can be without food, plumbing, education, health services or hope). The lodge would be rustic, built from local materials in the local style (Swiss-style chalets now being part of indigenous Nepali architecture). The accommodation would be comfortable, European (no exotic native sleeping arrangements), and with private facilities (no sharing of bodily functions with other guests). The food would be simple, delicious and abundant (it was). The lodge staff would be well-trained and English-speaking (they were). The weather would be described as fresh (Jade frequently reminds me that she associates freezing cold and Indian rhinoceroses with Nepal). The local guides would have an exceptional ability to track wildlife using their native skills (they *were* exceptional but that he could have picked this up in the course of an uneventful visit will remain testament to his extraordinary skill). The unusual game-viewing from the back of an elephant would be the highlight. He would describe the wildlife present in the park (the fact that he saw little will not need to be mentioned). There may also be a conservation angle – the disappearing natural world.

I imagine there will be a photo of a tiger, elephant, Indian rhinoceros or travellers on an elephant. It will be from a photo library. If the sub-editor knows his or her natural history, then the photo will match the text. If an incongruous shot of a penguin or a lion is used, then there will be the inevitable letter to the newspaper from a reader pointing out that the species featured is not found in Nepal.

# CHAPTER 1

## The guidebook says . . .

There are now travel guides and guidebooks to most destinations. There will soon be meta-guidebooks – a guidebook to guidebooks. I have always wanted to write a guidebook to an imaginary destination. In recent times, such a book has been written[4]. It would be interesting to see if anybody tried to book a flight to the non-existent destination.

There are general and destination guides. There is a guide to North America. There is the guide to Canada. Then there is the guide to British Columbia and one to Vancouver. I am waiting for the street-by-street travel guides. There are guides focused on the budget of travellers: the Shoestring or Rough Guides. There are guides based on a specific monetary level, such as $10 a day. That '$10 a day' shows my age; with inflation it must now be $100 per day at least. There are guides on more comfortable travel experiences (read 'more expensive'). They are rarely marketed in the same way. There are no travel guides for when cost is no concern or is $10,000 a day.

There are guidebooks that focus primarily on activities. One provides exquisite detail about bungee jumping. The guidebook lists the choice of platform: bridges, fixed towers, helicopters, hot-air balloons. It lists the options available for a jump from a bridge over a river: 'wet' (your head goes into the water), 'damp' (you barely touch the water) and 'dry' (you stop short of the water).

There are few guidebooks focused on eco-tourism. The market is small and eco-travellers are an eclectic and opinionated lot. Many do their own research. Those available look exactly like a normal guidebook to the broader destination, the only difference being that there are a few pictures of wild animals and some details of national parks and eco-travel operators thrown in. Oh yes, and the price is double that of the normal one. Eco-travel guidebooks use the word 'eco-' a lot. They also use the word 'green' repeatedly. They are incantations. If they are repeated often enough, then the natural world will be saved. Eco-travel guidebooks also include long lists of animals that you are meant to be able to see or that someone has seen once, fleetingly, in the past 10 years. You are meant to tick these off as you see them. Most of the lists include a pangolin.

Guidebooks are all done to a certain formula. There are facts about the country: basic history, geography, economy, social structure and people. There will be information on visa requirements, money matters, local currency and health. The guidebook provides information about travel to, from and within the country. It covers air, train, road and water travel. In some countries, it would be useful to include information on other modes of transport: ox-cart, camels, donkeys and Sherpas. In the Himalayas, many intrepid mountain climbers find themselves riding to the top of the peak on the backs of Sherpas.

The section in guidebooks on tipping behaviour is always interesting. Travellers may be unaware of the fact that in some countries you are actually responsible for employing the waiter and paying his or her wage. A person from a non-tipping culture may place his or her life at risk in a tipping culture. The reverse is also possible. In an emerging market country, a traveller may tip a waiter the equivalent of a year's salary, creating unexplained changes in the nation's current account balance.

Guidebooks are written in cryptic code. An eco-lodge may attract the following entry: 'Many travellers speak highly of [name of establishment], characterized by its good location, reasonably sized rooms (some with private facilities) and friendly/helpful guides'. The following linguistic guide may be helpful:

good location: it is above water, at least most of the time.
reasonably sized rooms: if you hire several rooms you and your luggage might just fit in.
private facilities: there is no difference between private and public, and the facilities are an open field behind the lodge.
friendly/helpful guides: there were some when the writer was there a long time ago.

Food descriptions are also insidious:

an ample buffet: the food makes up in quantity what it lacks in edibility; the staff just keep topping up the piles of rotting food.
local delicacies: only the locals, who are immune to the bacteria, can eat this food.
serves Western food: serves what the locals think foreigners eat, based on Hollywood films – for example, hamburger with fries.

Guidebooks are a great business. The information is cheap and easy to obtain: old primary-school books, government information, a few maps, local restaurant guides and, of course, other guidebooks. Descriptions of local sites are identical to free guides available from the tourist information service. It is hard to be original in these matters.

It is all marketing. The same data is repackaged constantly. New editions are published at regular intervals; the traveller wants up-to-date information. I generally buy old, remaindered editions at discount bookshops. I assume that the destination hasn't changed in between the two editions. Jade buys the latest version, not noticing the price difference.

Guidebooks also sometimes contain amazing errors. In 1991, we travelled to Zaire's Virunga Mountains to see the mountain gorillas. When we arrived at the airport, we waited for our guide to arrive. Thirsty, Jade and I contemplated the offerings at the modest airport kiosk. There was a sign advertising the prices of the drinks. I opened the guidebook and located the exchange rate. According to my calculations, a beer in these parts cost US$200. Zaire was experiencing hyper-inflation. No guidebook – not even the new edition, as opposed to the remaindered ones that I buy, could have kept up with the alarming rate of devaluation. The beer was actually US$2. I worked out that a local beer in Africa was always priced around US$2 for foreigners. You could use the price of a beer as a way to establish the current exchange rate in any country.

Guidebooks fatally shape our expectations of travel. They create a peculiar traffic pattern in tourist destinations, the guidebook waltz. Guidebooks suggest walking tours of points of interest. At the appointed hour (guidebooks are specific about times), tourists descend on the place and begin to perambulate along the suggested paths. They are easy to spot by the guidebook that they carry. The procession is a little ragged. Progress is uneven. Some (Jade and I, for example) commence at the wrong place or make tangential journeys off the prescribed route, causing traffic hazards. Order is restored by the arrival of the German or Japanese tour group marching with drill-ground precision.

I hold the map like a book so I can read the text. Jade turns the map to align it with the direction she is facing. Jade's method leads to the text being sideways or upside down – making it, in my opinion, difficult to read. This usually leads to arguments. Many relationships have floundered on this doctrinal dispute. Eventually, you just follow a tour group. There are frequent stops, such as the orientation stop to ensure that you are going the right way or to look up the next object of interest. At each stop, someone reads aloud the guidebook entry on the site to a deaf companion. Our knowledge of certain destinations is derived entirely from such overhead conversations.

The guidebook allows locals to know the areas to avoid in peak tourist season. The people you meet at tourist sites are fellow travellers and those that cater to or prey on visitors. The guidebook describes these people as 'authentic' locals. In the end, the guidebooks strip the adventure and surprise that we crave from travel. They create a bi-polar world: it is either in the guidebook or it is not. If it is not in the guidebook, then it does not exist. Guidebooks channel people to the same places and contribute to the increasing homogeneity of travel. You can always go beyond the end of the road. But how do you do that? There are no guidebooks to that destination. There are definitely no guidebooks to searching for pangolins.

'THE GUIDEBOOK SAYS...': PLANNING THE ECO-ADVENTURE

# Travel writing

Another source of information is travel writing. Homer's *Odyssey* is the original travel book. Marco Polo recorded his journey on the old silk road to China in the 13th century in the modestly titled *Divisament dou monde* (*Description of the World*)[5]. Marco Polo's writings read like *The Arabian Nights* or a hybrid between a Boy's Own story and a Gothic novel. The description of the Andaman Islands in the Bay of Bengal includes sightings of dog-headed men.

A personal favourite is George Nathaniel Curzon's *Travels with a Superior Person*[6]. (Curzon was not prone to self-doubt.) He had travelled around the world extensively by the time he was 30. He writes of climbing at night to Mount Etna's crater and witnessing the sunrise over snow-capped mountains. He writes of the beauty of Asian countries considered mysterious at the time. He describes meetings with kings and beggars; bargaining for unusual items; the difficulty of travel, on horseback, on foot or by whatever other means available. He meditates on the philosophy of travel, its essential meaning and significance, and writes movingly of the experience of travel as well as the scenery, the fragrance of the lands, the peoples and the exotic wild animals that he saw, his humility at seeing the remains of ancient civilizations.

There is also a more literary form of travel writing in which destination is context and the subject is the author. Bruce Chatwin's *In Patagonia*[7] uses a journey to Tierra del Fuego, the southern tip of South America, to present carefully crafted stories of characters and events. His writing is devoid of a firm sense of location. Paul Theroux, another well-known travel writer, was critical of Chatwin's writing in that he does not explain how he gets to destinations. Theroux's travel books frequently focus on transport: trains (*The Great Railway Bazaar, Riding The Iron Rooster* and *The Old Patagonian Express*) and kayaks (*The Happy Isles of Oceania*)[8]. In Theroux's writing, each and every logistical step of a journey is painstakingly described.

There is little literature on eco-travel. One notable exception is the work of Peter Matthiessen, who recorded many expeditions to the wilderness of Alaska and the Canadian north-west, South America, Africa and Asia. His sparse, haunting prose records the continuing loss of the natural world to human greed, stupidity and incompetence[9].

Travel writing does not encourage the reader to travel and so is the opposite of a guidebook. In the documentary travel writing tradition, journeys are to difficult locations that few readers would visit. In the literary travel writing tradition, there is little about the location. In modern travel writing, there is also a sense of discomfort; the journeys are difficult and arduous. Theroux's railway journeys discourage rail travel. Matthiessen's expeditions are exercises in sacrifice. Travel writing speaks mainly of the difficulty of

CHAPTER 1

travel and the discomforts, such as cramped conditions, poor food and primitive sanitary conditions that must be borne. The reader is left to experience
everything vicariously.

## Picture perfect

Pictures are the ultimate source of information on eco-travel. It was, after
all, photos of a gorilla and an elephant that were our own inspiration. Once
photography developed, it became a way both to record and to communicate
the natural history of the planet. In 1858, David Livingstone used a camera
to record his expedition to the Zambesi. In 1878, William Henry Jackson
photographed Mammoth Hot Springs in Wyoming, publicizing the beauty
of Yellowstone's wilderness.

BG (formerly British Gas before the fad for alphanumeric names) sponsors
a worldwide photography contest on natural history. The winning photo in
2002 was shot in South Luangwa National Park in Zambia, a place we have
visited. A family of African elephants stops momentarily while crossing the
Luangwa River to watch a grey heron in front of them. A baby elephant on
the left looks quizzically at the bird. The photo is in shades of blue, studded
with the solid brown, muddy shapes of the African elephants, the world's
largest living land animals. The elephants' opaque reflections are etched
across the water. The scene is timeless and tranquil. It speaks of a natural
order far removed from my normal existence. You could be in Africa...

Pictures provide inspiration but are a strange means for planning actual
travel. They can provide the list of the things that you want to see when you
arrive at your destination. You may want to see groups of elephants, or
gorillas or tigers – just like in the pictures. This can be difficult to achieve in
reality, though clearly it seems others have been able to do it. What the photo
doesn't tell you is that the photographer or filmmaker has spent hours, days
or even months in dreadful conditions waiting to catch the magic moment.

Then there are wildlife films and documentaries. *Gorillas in the Mist* is
about the life of Dian Fossey and her efforts to study and protect the mountain
gorillas. The film has inspired thousands of people to travel to see them. *Out
of Africa* is the story of the life of Karen Blixen, who published Gothic fiction
under the name Isak Dinesen. Blixen lived in Kenya. In one scene in the film of
the book, thousands of flamingos take off into the African sky. The result is an
ethereal pink cloud. The flamingos have little to do with the story, but the
scene with the flamingos is part of the collective romantic vision of Africa.
Travellers to the Rift Valley Lakes frequently mention the film. They hope that
they too will be able to see the flamingos take off.

In the early days of television, *The National Geographic Show* and *Zoo Story* launched the career of David Attenborough. In the 1970s, Attenborough, then in charge of BBC2, produced two hugely successful series: *Civilisation* and *The Ascent of Man*. The success resulted in a series on natural history. Attenborough's passion and enthusiasm and the BBC's renowned natural history unit created *Life on Earth*. This was the 'sledgehammer' series. A huge success, it opened up the large and lucrative US market, despite concern that Attenborough's English accent was incomprehensible to American audiences[10]. *Living Planet, Trials of Life, Private Life of Plants, Life of Birds, Life in the Freezer, The State of the Planet, Blue Planet* and *Life of Mammals* followed. Competing broadcasters created programmes, such as *Wild South America, Wild Africa* – basically anything with 'Wild' stuck on the front.

Wildlife documentaries favour splendid images of exotic and far away places that allow us to escape the humdrum daily reality of our existence. The exotic made palpable is an affirmation of the value and meaning of our lives. This is especially so, as we can do this while munching away on our take-away pizzas in the comfortable surrounds of our homes on our brand new home-entertainment system.

Wildlife programmes are an intoxicating mix of soap opera, action films and drama that even Bollywood can't match. One scene in the *Life on Earth* series alone probably assured its success. Attenborough was filmed with the mountain gorillas. The gorillas were being studied by Fossey and were habituated to humans. Attenborough reclines in the grass and talks, very close to a female gorilla. Suddenly, the female stretches out a hand and touches Attenborough and looks at him. Attenborough's words still resound in my memory: 'There is more meaning and mutual understanding in exchanging a glance with a gorilla than any other animal I know.'[11] The scene has an electricity and drama that is astounding.

Wildlife documentaries seem to be beyond censorship. They are violent. We are rarely spared the slaughter. One documentary records chimpanzees systematically hunting and killing a black and white colobus monkey. The colobus is much smaller than the chimpanzees and they use teamwork to ambush it. Once they have caught it, the killing is merciless. Mad with blood-lust and whooping loudly, the chimpanzees tear apart the colobus that fought to try to save its troop. The chimpanzees begin to eat its flesh almost before it is dead. There is also sex everywhere: erect penises, nudity and mating abound. There is probably more sex in a wildlife show than in hard-core pornography. Animal sex is clearly more acceptable than human sex on the television.

Wildlife documentaries are good business, the main reason being that you don't have to pay the stars. The languid giraffe flowing through the Serengeti

# CHAPTER 1

is cheaper than Julia Roberts. There are no unions, agents or revenue per-
centages. You don't have to pay the writers or presenters much. Academics
and scientists happily turn out reams of information and text for a pittance,
excited that someone is interested in their life's work. The documentary also
provides a chance of an expenses-paid field trip to actually see and research
their subject.

Wildlife footage can be used over and over in different works. It is possible
to make most wildlife programmes entirely with existing footage. You can't
take bits of footage of Julia Roberts to splice together a new *Pretty Woman*.

There is some rare footage of electric eels using their high-voltage bodies
to kill a young caiman – a crocodile prevalent in South America – that unwisely
strays too close. The eels throw themselves repeatedly over the body of the
hapless animal, triggering a charge of several thousand volts each time. It is
nature's electric chair. The young caiman's body twitches helplessly as it is
killed. I have seen it used in at least five or six programmes. There is rare
footage of a shoebill stork – a prehistoric wading bird with a huge shoe-
shaped beak – as it catches a lungfish. Likewise, I have seen this footage in
several programmes.

In using a combination of various bits of existing film to make a new
programme, you have to be careful that the bits both make sense together
and are also appropriate. There is a film on leopards, *The Night of the
Leopard*, which follows a female of the species.

We watched this with an African guide.

During a scene in which a leopard is shown climbing down from a tree,
the guide fell about laughing.

'He has batteries,' he hooted, referring to the leopard's large and clearly
visible testicles.

The film's producers had probably spliced library tape into the documentary. They may not have known the difference between male and female
leopards or maybe they had no other film available that fitted the plot. They
hoped that people would not notice.

Nature documentaries are organized around a 'theme'. This might be
the type of animal, such as mammals or birds, or a specific species, such
as lions. It might be the place: a continent, country or a reserve. It might
be organized around habitats: wetlands, savannahs, rainforests. The theme
might be animal behaviours such as breeding behaviour – sex again. *Blue
Planet* is organized around the planet's oceans and different habitats such
as shoreline, reefs and deep oceans. There is the seasonal plot: the cycle
of the seasons. We watch the changes driven by the climatic conditions and
the effects on life. Then there is the life cycle of an animal. Animals follow a
highly predictable lifestyle: hunt, eat, drink, urinate/defecate, sleep, groom,

mate and, if you are female, give birth to and bring up young. Lions in the Serengeti do not discuss Wittgenstein. There is 'the spirit of a place': the natural history of a location through its geology, botany, animal- and bird-life. There is the natural history lesson: a specific argument such as evolution or human impact on the environment. The wildlife scenes are spliced into sequences where they support or contradict the thesis.

The script can make soap opera dialogue look Shakespearean:

'The sun rises majestically across the [ocean/forest/plain], bringing with it a new day in [wherever the hell we are].'
'As darkness falls in [insert place], a whole new world begins for the creatures of the night.'
'There is food aplenty for now, but times are getting tougher.'
'The seasons drive the creatures of the forest.'
'Life is harsh in the [wherever]. Death is never far away.'
'The ancient laws of nature continue as they have for millions of years. The animal of the [wherever] live as they have done through the millennia.'
Et cetera.

Attenborough is the Emeritus Professor of wildlife presenters. He is knee-deep in bat guano. He lies in the forest next to a gorilla. He is on top of a kapok tree, face to face with a howler monkey.

The cut-away shot, where the camera captures the animal and the presenter simultaneously, is the staple of documentaries. The purpose is to establish that the presenter was there. There is no other point to standing up to one's chest in cold slimy swamp water in the Everglades talking about 'the unique eco-system'.

Other networks have focused on creating Attenborough clones. There are a lot of herpetologists (reptile biologists). There is a man who specializes in catching anacondas with his bare hands after feeling them in the swamp with his unshod feet. There is Steve Irwin, the Australian crocodile 'expert', loud and possessed of an interesting if limited vocabulary. (He is trying to trademark his characteristic 'Oh crikey'.) Irwin is hugely successful at lurching from one continent to another, grabbing snakes and displaying them with highly technical commentary. 'He's not happy. I mean he's not happy.'

Many of the presenters on wildlife programmes whisper – Jade's pet hate. I have assured her that it is simply reverence for the scene described. There is also a technological marvel called the volume control if the whispering continues to bother her. It is impossible to watch a wildlife documentary with her these days. She rails continuously at the whispering.

In the end, pictures of wildlife – still and moving – inspire a lot of eco-travel. Captivated audiences want to see the 'real thing'. They want to sit next to the gorillas, handle snakes, cuddle an orang-utan or koala. They have seen people do this. There is an expectation when you plan your trip that you will see the migration of the wildebeest; you will see the turtles laying eggs on the beach; you will see the wild animals you have come to see, even if you are only there for a short period of time. Planning will get you to the location and may even get you there at the time that certain events are meant to happen. But you cannot be aware of local conditions and local events. More than once we have been caught out. In Bardia we arrived when the local farmers were undertaking burning-off activities that impacted the wildlife that we had come to see. In Zambia we arrived just after a large cull of hippopotamuses had taken place and the animals were all affected. In the end there are no guarantees in eco-travel.

## Das planning

I collect travel information of all sorts and have lists of possible journeys. Jade would say that I have lists for everything. I have been gathering information on the Ndoki, a remote part of the Congo, the Kalahari Desert, and Kamchatka in Russia. There are piles of brochures. I must be on every eco-tourist operator's mailing list – I hope so. I read magazines, newspapers and travel writings with the passion of an addict. I watch wildlife documentaries and scan picture books. I correspond with people who may have useful information about the best time to go, how best to see the things of interest and about guides.

Our trip to Manu, a wildlife reserve in the Amazon in Peru, began with an article in *Time* magazine. I tore it out and kept it. It took six years, but eventually we went and it was wonderful. A torn-out page from an airline magazine on grizzly bears was the inspiration to travel to western Canada to see them up close and personal. One day we decide on a particular place. I re-read the material, update the facts and get additional information. It all starts taking shape in my mind. Jade and I discuss it. Then we book the trip.

## The travel agent

Psychiatrists only interpret dreams. Travel agents have the more difficult task of turning dreams into reality. The travel agent sometimes advises on destinations. I have heard conversations in England where the only specification is 'somewhere warm!' 'A good heater placed in your lounge room would be just the shot for you, Sir.' The travel agent advises on a range of different transport options ('Does Sir have several years or several hours to get to Somalia?'), accommodation, activities. I wonder what the travel agent would do if the only criteria was 'We wish to see a pangolin.'

The travel agent develops an itinerary of your dream within the budget that you have specified. Lindsay, our travel agent, tells me that there are two types of client: 'clueless' and 'impossible'. He tells me that I am a 'perfect' client. (He says it to everybody.) The clueless client doesn't know where they want to go or what they want to do when they get there. They change their mind frequently. Wherever they go, they will be disappointed. The impossible traveller is over-researched with highly fixed opinions (the words are Jade's – she is also writing a book *Living with an Obsessive Man*). In the end, they too are disappointed.

There is the actual travel agent, the person in the shop front who sits with you, exploring various options. They hand you various brochures, prepare your itinerary, and give you your tickets, visas and the tacky travel wallets and bags in an unlikely combination of colours stamped with their name. This is the person you complain to when things do not turn out as you expected. There is the travel wholesaler, the person the travel agent deals with. The wholesaler arranges tours or packages. They have a lot of inside knowledge on what is available and, in the new economy, buying power. They market to the travel agent. Then there is the local agent, the person at the destination that the wholesaler deals with. The local agent provides local knowledge: that is, whom to bribe and how much to bribe them. They make the local arrangements. Finally, there is the operator, the person you see holding up the sign with your name misspelt at the airport. They drive you to the eco-lodge and take you on the 'birding trip'. They are the people who make your adventure a reality.

You are paying for all these mouths. You are the sole source of revenue in this food chain. You pay the travel agent. They take their cut and pass the cash down to the wholesaler. The wholesaler takes their cut and passes on the rest to the local agent. The process is repeated and the operator gets the remainder after commissions on commissions on commissions. The local operator is the person or business providing the service. They are going to make the trip a success or failure. You don't know who they are. You don't deal with them. They get what is left.

You pay the travel agent. The travel agent sits on the cash for a while and only pays after the other side issues a legal claim or well after the payment terms allowed. It is capitalism, making money from other people's money. It is no fun being at the wrong end of the alimentary canal.

Travel agents are businesses. The airline, hotel and tour operator pay the travel agent. Is there a conflict of interest here? The game is maximization of revenue and minimization of input. Maximization of revenue equals booking you on to tours and activities that pay the highest commissions. Minimization of effort dictates the ubiquitous 'packaged tour' or 'standard itinerary'. The incentive to favour particular operators is driven by commissions. There are also 'freebies'. Airlines give you free flights. Hotel operators provide free rooms. Operators entertain groups of travel agents in order to ensure custom.

Most travellers actually want the same thing. Like Oscar Wilde, they fear 'originality'. Some pay lip service to being different, but in practice, they want the same trip that their neighbour, friend or family member went on. They want to repeat the experience. This is the standard trip that wholesalers package up and market through travel agents. They may modularize it, allowing the marginally more adventurous travellers to add and subtract bits. Just pick up any brochure at a travel agent. There are tours with dashing names: The African Wildlife Experience, The Amazon Discovery Tour, The Reefs and Rainforest Tour – all much the same. The travel agent listens to your requirements and fits them into a pre-packaged trip sold by a wholesaler or a combination of pre-packaged trips. Commerce has met and conquered dream and hope.

Specialist eco-travel agencies do exist. They sometimes specialize by geography: Africa, South America, the Polar Regions. A few specialize in bird-watching trips. Some do 'expeditions' into uncharted reaches of the Congo. This is true Old-World exploration. You really might never come back. These travel agents are keen eco-travellers pursuing personal passions. Eco-travellers hold strong opinions about where to go, what to do, what is interesting. For instance, we have a special interest in pangolins and other obscure wildlife. If you are lucky, you find someone who knows what you mean and you have a great trip. If you are unlucky, then you end up waist-deep in mud or slimy water dragging a canoe with the team leader screaming at you to keep moving as it is going to be dark soon. You are starving, haven't had any sleep and are being bitten to death by things you can't see. It is all part of the adventure. The person next to you has a stupid grin on their face as if they are really enjoying it all.

In 2001, we travelled to Alaska and western Canada to see grizzly bears. After we returned, I received a newsletter from an eco-travel operator. The owners had just returned from a lodge that we had stayed at. They wrote of their astonishing experiences when, on a kayaking expedition, they came very close to a grizzly bear. I know exactly where the encounter took place. The guides are careful not to allow guests to get anywhere near that close to bears as it is not safe, but they make every effort to give eco-travel travel agents an unforgettable experience. Eco-tourism operators get the best guides and the best opportunities. It is good business sense. Their adventure is sold to you as what you can expect. In reality, yours is only ever likely to be a lesser experience.

Our dealings with travel agents have been quite mixed. In 1995, we travelled to Africa for about five weeks. The travel agent was knowledgeable. Zambia and Botswana went well. The lodges were excellent, the wildlife and nature spectacular. The guides were great. In Namibia, things went out of control… The accommodation was sub-standard. The guide, a woman from rural Australia, knew very little. Her commentary was straight from the guidebook. I had the book open and followed every word carefully. The travel agent had booked us with a local operator based on price (read profit margin). It was unforgivable. We were being 'impossible'. We still managed to enjoy Namibia's extraordinary wilderness, but it could have been so much better and less aggravating.

In 1999, we travelled to India. We used a travel agent that specialized in Indian wildlife. They effectively subcontracted everything to the Indian operator. The trip was fine barring the occasional disaster. It is not easy to know whether the problem was the operators or simply India. We had asked whether January/February was a good time to go. March/April would have been better. The timing coincided with public holidays when the parks were crowded. If we had known this then we would have planned our trip a bit better. We wrote to the agent. It was not a complaint. We made suggestions for improving the information given to travellers. She wrote back, annoyed. She found fighting the 'negative energy' of our letter 'disabilitating [sic]'.

In 2001, one agent, Maryanne arranged our trip to Alaska. Her love of the place was profound. She advised us to change several aspects of our trip. We travelled to the Katmai coast instead of the more famous Brooks Fall and were rewarded by a series of amazing days. The amount of care she took was extraordinary. She tracked us and made sure things were okay, especially when things went wrong because of the weather. It was an extraordinary effort on her part.

## The itinerary as script

The typical itinerary comprises a covering letter and a few pages listing dates and activities. There is information on weather, clothing and the places that you are visiting. It comes with airline tickets and vouchers to evidence bookings. This modest collection bears the full burden of your expectations.

The language is extraordinary. The covering letter is mercifully short. It talks about your forthcoming trip to the 'ancient' land. It entreats you to enjoy your trip and gain an understanding of the country and people you are about to visit. It says you will return refreshed and revitalized from your trip. (You haven't even begun the journey and here you are already back.) The day-by-day description of travel is fascinating:

Friday [date]: you will join [flight number] at [airport] to fly to [destination]. Saturday [date]: you arrive in the gateway city of [name] to begin your wonderful journey. You are met at the airport and transferred to [name of hotel]. Your hotel is centrally located [near name of some city highlight]. The hotel is an old colonial mansion set in large tropical gardens, and a favourite with international visitors for its relaxed and friendly ambience.

The itinerary starts with a vacuum. The description of the flight misses the time taken to get to your destination. You do not so much arrive as fall from the plane in an expectant but disoriented way. Circadian rhythms hammer away to a distant tune. The most common memory of the start of a holiday is a blur of meals, snatched sleep sitting upright in a plane and immigration formalities at the destination. The itinerary is more Chatwin than Theroux.

The description of locations is baroque. You fly to mysterious [place] whose culture has secretly evolved and whose people have a unique way of life. The buildings are original, stately or historically significant. The landscape is beautiful and magnificent. The journey will be along a picturesque route. The markets will be full of exotic and authentic local products. The people will be descendants of the original inhabitants of [name of place and/or civilization].

In eco-travel, the destination will have the most unique natural history of the [universe/world/continent/etc.]. The area will be full of wildlife. It will be a haven for nature lovers. The national park will be remote and wild. You will be staying at the [name of lodge], which combines highly personal service with a unique way of enjoying the wildlife. [Name of lodge] will be located on a sweeping bend of river or [name of vantage point] with a commanding view of the reserve, offering magnificent and unique game-viewing opportunities. You will be able to sit on your own private [patio/veranda] watching the peaceful feeding of [type of antelope].

The place may well be stunningly beautiful. It is hard to say that about the description. The activities are described in superfluous and excessive terms.

Your tour of the city becomes a trip through the historical city centre with broad boulevards and large well-laid squares, where you will visit the world-famous and marvellous [name of museum], where you will see the golden treasures of [name of civilization]. You will be taken to see the spellbinding [name of monument], one of the wonders of the [ancient/ modern] world.

The sentences are long – you need to hold your breath for several minutes to read them. Everything seems to be the same. All museums are 'historical'. All sites are 'important'. Everything is a 'wonder' of some age. The description of the natural history is subtler. The park will be home to a vast number of animal species. The list of these will always run to many lines – who says less is more? There will be the 'potential' to see animals. The park may be 'noted' for its primate population. The bird species will include the 'rare' or 'elusive' [name of animal or bird]. There will be flexible game-viewing activities... Game drives in open vehicles, walking safaris, canoe trips, bird hides. Naturalists and guides with a vast and detailed knowledge of the wildlife and its mysterious ways are on hand at [name of lodge]. Activities are designed around the special individual needs of all guests.

There is no mention that you will actually see any of the animals or birds mentioned. But they will be there. I am sure that there have been hundreds of pangolins in places where we have been. It's just that we didn't actually get to see them.

The descriptions are sometimes short on essential detail. An older couple we met went trekking to see mountain gorillas in Uganda.

The itinerary said 'After an early breakfast, depart for your day of tracking gorillas in the park with picnic lunch.'

Sounds pleasant, doesn't it? The combination of undergrowth and dense vegetation make it difficult to walk in the forest. Frequently, it is necessary to cut your way through. You walk on thick leaf litter and vines. It is not easy. This is one case where the name – the Bwindi Impenetrable Forest – provides a reasonable indication as to what to expect. The older couple had almost given up, but persisted. The description in the itinerary did not provide an accurate or detailed guide to the actual activity.

Depending upon where the gorillas are, it can take several hours of difficult walking. When we went to see the mountain gorillas in Zaire, the vegetation was not that dense and there were clear trails – made by elephants, we were told. The gorillas proved to be quite close, but we had to walk for about two hours.

Itineraries include helpful travel hints. My favourite instructions relate to travel in Costa Rica:[12]

> More people have to change their vacation plans because of sunburn than for any other reason. [There follows advice as to how to avoid sunburn.] If you are a person who does not burn in the temperate zone and want to know what sunburn feels like, don't follow this advice.
>
> Much of what is interesting in the tropical forests is up in the trees and much of what is dangerous is on the ground. Two simple safety rules, then, are: when you are looking up – don't move your feet. When you are moving your feet – look down.

31

It also seems that getting on and off buses and vans is a lot more dangerous that [sic] one might think. Please be careful!

Although very few tourists have been bitten by poisonous snakes in Costa Rica, they do exist. Without becoming paranoid, a few precautions are advisable. Small snakes can be just as deadly as big snakes.

While a snakebite is not a common incident, falling down is. A very common accident is slipping and falling while walking the steep slippery edge trying to avoid a puddle. In tropical forests, you will probably get your feet wet sooner or later. To avoid the suspense, and perhaps a nasty fall, we suggest that you walk through the first puddle you see.

## The journey: inspiration and reality

The idea of travel starts with an inspiration: why don't we go *there*? We find out as much as we can about the place. The research builds excitement. There are pangolins there. The anticipation fills us with joy. The process engages with the pragmatic business of travel. We talk to the travel agent. The choices narrow. We prioritize, trying to exclude things that are too time-consuming, too difficult, too expensive. Then, one day, everything is fixed. There are some final details, but we are on our way. The only tangible part of our dream is the itinerary. It is where we are going, what we are going to do, the script of our adventure.

We have noticed a trend. It used to be that shortly after we went somewhere, chaos and mayhem ensued. In 1991, we visited Rwanda and Zaire. A short while later, Zaire collapsed into civil war. Rwanda witnessed a terrible genocide. We used to leave death and destruction in our wake. These days we bring death and mayhem if we contemplate travel to a particular place. Weapons of mass destruction indeed. We only have to consider a particular destination and something awful happens. Madagascar is one example. In 2002, we were ready to go there. Civil war and then a flu-like disease broke out on the island. The Australian Government recommended cancellation of all non-essential travel to Madagascar. The insurance people wouldn't cover us. We cancelled.

The author Joris-Karl Huysmans, in *A Rebours* (Against Nature)[13], describes the anticipation of and preparation for a journey to London by the protagonist, Duc des Essientes. First, he decides to travel to London. This is against his instincts as he has steadfastly spent his life in a cloistered existence at home surrounded by books. His desire to travel is aroused by reading Charles Dickens. He also reads Baedeker's travel guidebook to London. He greatly anticipates the atmosphere of London as gleaned from his reading. The anticipation is replaced by concerns about the reality of the trip. He becomes anxious about the train journey, the hotel room and getting around in a strange city. Besides, from his readings, he already has experienced London vicariously. At the last moment, he abandons the trip to London. He goes home and never travels.

It is surprising that more people never leave home. Planning the journey contains the greatest excitement. It is the anticipation of travel that provides a sense of exhilaration. But just occasionally, the real thing lives up to and exceeds that anticipation. Seeing a pangolin would be right up there. It is this possibility that makes travel to distant and unusual destinations exciting for us.

# CHAPTER 2
## 'Rushing And Waiting': The Journey

*...The itinerary had precise instructions. The pilot would meet us at Harare Airport. 'How high do you want to fly?' he asked. I have never before been asked to nominate altitude. Seats, menu choices, but never flying height...*

# CHAPTER 2

## Rushing and waiting

In modern travel, the journey is a boundary marker. It catapults us into the exotic and foreign world of our destination. The journey is pure transformation. Alain de Botton wrote that he found 'few seconds in life are more releasing than those in which a plane ascends to the sky'[14]. It is conducive to 'internal conversations'[15]. It is the displacement of our relationship to time and space. It is also about our relationship to a lot of other less ethereal things.

There is an essence of the journey. We learnt what it was in Africa. There were two Americans staying at the eco-lodge with us. The husband was a small, wrinkled and unhappy man. He looked like he had spent the past month under a sun lamp. He had talked a lot about HIV/AIDS. It was apparently a 'social disease'. A large part of the population in eastern and southern Africa are HIV positive. He was travelling with his own impressive personal kit of syringes. This was to avoid any risk of using a contaminated needle in case of the need for an injection.

She was a small, blonde American, the trophy second or third wife. She was metallic in appearance and thin in an 'X-ray' kind of way[16], and dressed in a bright neon tracksuit – obviously, in the colours of season. She was talking about travelling.

'Rushing and waiting; it's all rushing and waiting,' she intoned. 'You rush to one place and then you just wait. Rushing and then waiting.' With those parting words, she proceeded to commence her daily jog around the camp fence. The camp was encircled with electrified wiring to keep elephants out. It was about 38.5°C (100°F). By God, we thought, she's right...

The rushing and waiting in eco-travel is much the same as in any travel. You have to get to wherever you are going. But there are differences. Eco-travel will frequently take you off the normal beaten track. You may have to travel to isolated places that are difficult to get to. Frequently, your destination is a developing country (political correctness means you can't refer to them as 'under-developed').

This means that your method of travel and the surrounding infrastructure is often different to normal journeys. For example, a herd of elephants on the runway rarely interrupts air traffic at London's Heathrow airport. In Africa, in remote wildlife areas, it is a relatively common occurrence.

Your journey to your eco-travel adventure starts off in normal, familiar ways. At each stage of your journey, there are changes. The nature of the airport is different. The planes get smaller and more cramped. You find yourself in a car where you can't tell if you are on or off the road. You feel the changes as you go deeper into the wilderness away from civilization. It is a strange mixture of the familiar and the unfamiliar. It's all part of the adventure.

## Temples of travel

The journey usually starts and ends at a familiar place: an airport. Getting into and out of certain airports leaves an indelible impression about the destination. In developed countries, the home of most eco-travellers, airports are all gleaming steel and glass. They reek of award-winning monumental architecture and efficiency. Developing countries are different. For example, Indian airports always give the impression that they are designed to ensure that any traveller who gets there is unlikely to repeat the mistake. There is the smell: urine mixed with disinfectant. Then there are the hours spent in the immigration queue, the wait for baggage and the fight for a baggage trolley. All this takes place between the hours of midnight and dawn, the preferred time for flight arrivals and departures. Finally, you emerge into the wider chaos that is India.

Airports in many eco-travel destinations, especially in Africa and South America, are a throwback to a previous age of travel. Crowds wait for flights with erratic schedules that seem to leave only when there are enough passengers. The airports are more like town squares or markets. The impersonal nature and clinical efficiency of modern airports is replaced by a curious feeling of community. People seem to have settled in for a long stay. There is no certainty when the flight will arrive or leave.

In 1997, we travelled to Zambia's South Luangwa National Park. We flew from Harare in Zimbabwe to Mfuwe, a small village close to the park. Mfuwe airport is tiny: a short grass runway, a radio beacon and a small building. Our single-engine Cessna landed. We disembarked and wandered off with our bags in the direction of the building. The pilot came with us. There seemed to be no one around. Eventually, a man appeared.

'Welcome,' he smiled. 'Welcome to Mfuwe in Zambia.' He was pleased to see us. There weren't many flights to Mfuwe – maybe one a day. We broke the monotony of his wait. He processed us slowly, with great care. We filled out immigration and customs forms. He stamped our passports. 'Welcome and enjoy your stay.' It was the most personal and welcoming entry into a country that we have ever made.

## Passport/visa olympics

All airports come complete with rites of passage. There are attendant priests and acolytes – immigration and security officers charged with conducting the ceremonies. At each stage, the traveller's motives are questioned and their worthiness is tested. If you satisfy the examiner then you pass to the next stage. Travellers must be suitably penitent and supplicant in approaching these gatekeepers to the other world. They must pay the tithes and make the ritual offerings demanded in order to smooth their way.

You cannot get anywhere without a passport. A person without a passport has no country. I keep mine strapped to my body at all times when travelling. I have 'passport' rash. My passport smells badly. Immigration officials handle it with suspicion.

The passport has little in it: a photo, minimal information and a signature. The passport photo bears little resemblance to its holder. The immigration official glances frequently at the passport photo and then at you. You stand sweating. Incontinence is a real possibility. This is how they get their kicks. Your passport is passed under an ultra-violet light. As a child, I learnt to write in ink only visible under certain lights. Is there something written in my passport? Is it like Rosencrantz and Guildenstern in Shakespeare's *Hamlet* – 'Execute the bearer of this passport'? If your papers are in order, the official then stamps your passport and hands it back, sending you on your way. They may tap on a computer keyboard. This is to continue the game of solitaire.

You must fill in an embarkation card. Each country has a different set of questions that you must answer: name, address, occupation, date of birth, passport details, destination and reason for travel. Most of the information is in your passport. The sole purpose seems to be to trip you up. The reason for travel has also caused me problems. Should I state the real reason: 'Searching for a pangolin'?

Mistakes are easy to make. I occasionally fill in my date of birth as the day of departure, accidentally. If prone to vanity, this lowers your age significantly: 'Sir, you will be giving me a lie. You will be declaring that you were born today, this very same day. How is this possible? I do not believe that this is possible. I will be having to have my superior review this matter.' Thus spoke the Indian immigration official.

The alternative is the dreaded command: 'You have filled in the form incorrectly. Please correct your form and rejoin the queue.'

If you are in the USA, there is the second dreaded command: 'Please fill in the entire form from the beginning. The form can have no errors or anything crossed out on it.'

You may require a visa to enter a country. In the age of globalization, most developed countries have now dispensed with visas. Many eco-travel destinations continue to require expensive visas. It is a way of making money from the visiting traveller. Getting a visa usually involves going to the embassy or consulate of the country. The Consulate for Paraguay in Australia has closed. The nearest offices are in Tokyo, Santiago and Buenos Aires. You probably have to apply for the visa in person.

# 'RUSHING AND WAITING': THE JOURNEY

Getting visas for eco-tourist destinations can be fun. Many are small, poor countries without the normal bureaucracy of immigration. The embassy is the 'honorary' representative's house. You find yourself in a living room. The official apologizes for the pet or child. They scramble to find a stamp and a receipt book. Your visa is stamped without the formality of bureaucracy. You are invited to have a cup of tea or coffee. There is conversation about the country. There is a nostalgic strain to the conversation if the honorary counsellor is an emigrant from the place.

The visas are sometimes extraordinary in themselves, full of vividly coloured stamps. They speak of the excitement of travel and adventure. Sometimes, the stamps depict a country's national animal or flower of the country... No, I have not to date encountered any country that has the pangolin as its national animal.

Visas and passports present many obstacles for the traveller. I have a bad record with visas and immigration, probably because my passport photo makes me look like a terrorist. In my passport, my place of birth is Calcutta. Many immigration officials don't know where Calcutta is, so I helpfully put – Calcutta, India – on the disembarkation/entry form. My stated birthplace and the one on my passport don't agree. If I put Calcutta then they argue that there is no country called Calcutta. Calcutta has also changed its name to Kolkata, the Bengali version. My birthplace no longer exists.

India always presents immigration challenges. I was born in India, but I am an Australian citizen. I am an NRI, 'non-resident Indian'. Frequently, the following exchange ensues at immigration:

IMMIGRATION: Why is your address in India a hotel?
DAS: I am staying at a hotel.
IMMIGRATION: Why is it being that you are not staying with your family?
DAS: I have no family in India.
IMMIGRATION: That is impossible. You are Indian!
DAS: Yes, but my family are in Australia.
IMMIGRATION: Sir, you must be having some family in India. Why is it that you
            are not staying with them?

Jade and I needed tourist visas for India. I have an existing business visa, but that wouldn't do. I had to pay for a new visa for 'tourism purposes only'. We were going to be in India for six weeks with a single entry and exit. The standard single-entry visa is only for one month. The three-month visa requires multiple entries and exits that must be listed. We could not meet the conditions for either visa. In the end, we falsified an additional entry and exit to get the visa.

Multi-entry visas are cunning traps. In 1991, we used Kenya as a base for various trips in east Africa. The visa allowed three entries and exits. We had not counted the number of times we were going to be leaving and re-entering Kenya. We struggled to stay within the visa conditions. Luckily, in developing countries, a bribe generally fixes most visa problems, although you have to hand your passport to someone and they keep it for a while. As you will recall, a person without a passport has no country.

We were planning a few trips to the USA to see various wildlife parks. I decided to get a five-year unlimited entry visa. My employers swore to my good character, despite my appearance in passport photos. They certified that I was not an impecunious individual who would be begging or stealing shortly after arrival. Eventually, I was granted the visa. I went to the US Embassy to collect it. I handed over identification: my driver's licence, my credit cards. The room was very dark. The official was wearing dark glasses. He must have been a 'spook', a CIA operative. He looked carefully at my passport photo and then at me several times. He checked signatures with great care. Then, with a slight sigh, he handed me my passport with the US visa. I have rarely felt such relief.

Getting the visa was not the end of my problems.

The immigration official in New York looked at my visa. 'It's too perfect. It's just too perfect!' I was going to be charged with trying to enter the USA using false papers. Suddenly, he stamped the passport and flicked it casually to me.

Then, to confuse matters, America included Australia in the visa-waiver programme. Visas would be issued at the point of entry. My visa still had not expired. Should I fill out the form for 'You have a visa' or the form for 'You are a resident of a country not requiring a visa'? There was no form for 'You are a resident of a country not requiring a visa but have one anyway.'

'Sir, you must fill in the form for "You have a visa", not the form for "You are a resident of a country not requiring a visa".'

'Sir, you must fill in the form for "You are a resident of a country not requiring a visa", not the form for "You have a visa".' Handing over two completed forms simultaneously caused even more problems.

There is a bewildering array of rules. Your passport must be valid for at least six months beyond your stay. South Africa, a popular eco-tourist destination, introduced a new rule where your passport must have at least two empty pages when you seek entry. If your passport does not have the required two pages, you are refused entry and held in custody (jail) pending deportation. In Brazil, students and self-employed people must supply a bank statement when applying for a visa. I always travel with bank statements when I am about to enter a foreign country. Franz Kafka's protagonists would have understood immigration.

## Immigration inquisitions

Dealing with immigration can have a lighter side. We arrived in Ecuador. The flight appeared to be totally unexpected. Immigration officials finally arrived. There were no entry forms. We were given exit forms. We duly filled them in. On the way out we filled the same form in again. We left Ecuador twice without ever arriving.

On another occasion, my flight to New Zealand was several hours late. The airline had forgotten that the flight required a functioning aircraft. We arrived at Wellington in the early hours of the morning. On the flight, I had filled out the entry form. At the immigration counter, a woman looked at my completed form. She kept looking at the form and then glancing at me.

She placed the form in front of me. 'Did you mean to answer "Yes" to all these questions?' It seemed that I had admitted to being a terrorist, having convictions for capital crimes, a variety of serious diseases, previous travel to New Zealand under a different name and previous denied entry. She looked amused. Nobody had confessed to all this simultaneously. She changed all the answers to 'No', stamped my passport and handed it back to me with a smile: She would be dining out on this story for some time to come.

'Could you please show me a return ticket?', 'Who do you work for?', 'Why do you work for yourself?', 'What monies do you have?', 'How are you going to pay for everything?' These are civilities that are sometimes extended to me at immigration counters. I have learnt to be patient. I have learnt to supply personal details and irrelevant information politely. Jade rarely has any difficulties. I don't know why.

I remember seeing a black African man at immigration in an airport. The immigration official was questioning him. He appeared nervous. A policeman joined the immigration officials. Eventually, he was led away. I remember the look on his face. It spoke of failure, pain and dashed hopes. It spoke of desperation. The pleading eyes still haunt me. Was he trying to enter the country illegally? Was he seeking asylum? People from poor countries sell everything to finance a journey in the hope of gaining entry to some country. Often a family sells all they own so just one member can gain entry into a country. They pay unscrupulous 'people smugglers' to arrange 'passage'.

Every time I feel the anger rising in my body as immigration officials question me, I remember this man and the look in his eyes. I think of those who are trapped, who are not free to travel, to enter and leave countries at will. I think of those unable to escape poverty or tyranny and their exclusion by the cruel application of processes that we learn to negotiate as we travel. I think of those desperate to escape poverty or persecution, who scrape together the money for a ride in a cramped lorry or an unseaworthy boat, and those miserable

41

journeys that end so often in failure or a lonely death. Our journeys are indulgences. We are fleeing nothing except boredom. We travel in search of new experiences. For us, it is easy to negotiate the formalities of travel. My annoyances are so minor, so irrelevant in the scheme of things.

## Are you safe?

If immigration officials are the high priests, then security personnel are the acolytes. The acolytes ensure your purity and cleanliness for the journey. The traveller undergoes the security ritual alone. You abandon your possessions for the ceremony. You pass through the metal detector. The detector may sound the alarm. Acolytes rush to you. You are beckoned to one side and made to stand on a raised platform. A wand is passed over your body. Items are checked. Your purity verified, you are admitted.

In some developing countries, there is no metal detector and no X-ray machine. The ceremony is performed nonetheless. You walk through a wooden frame. You are searched manually. Like all rituals, only the form matters.

Sometimes you have to make a security declaration as part of your embarkation or disembarkation form. The entry form for one country asked whether we 'were completely safe?' Experienced travellers, we answered 'yes'. To this day, we have no idea what it actually meant.

I understand that security staff undergo 'an incredibly rigorous training regime' including the following multiple-choice examination question:

**Why is it important to screen bags for improvised explosive devices ('IEDs')?**
(a) The IED batteries could leak and damage other passenger bags.
(b) The wires in the IED could cause a short to the aircraft wires.
(c) IEDs can cause loss of lives, property and aircraft.
(d) The ticking timer could worry other passengers.

A fellow traveller observed with caustic wit: 'At US$4 an hour, you get US$4 of security'.

In the aftermath of 9/11, security and hysteria were hard to differentiate. You were searched when you entered the airport, searched when you entered the departure lounge and searched when you boarded the plane. Pocket knives, scissors, nail clippers, tweezers, knitting needles, any sharp objects and sporting equipment were all weapons now.

Eco-travellers like to go equipped with many tools and gadgets. One never knows what one could encounter. One European man had a super-duper

Swiss Army knife, suitable for brain surgery. The knife could not be carried onto the plane. The man argued that this was ridiculous. It was, but it was the rules. He gave up and asked if the knife could be put in the hold. It could not. In the end, he gave it to the security person.

'It is a gift,' he said ironically. The security person accepted without hesitation. He probably had a nice little business trading second-hand Swiss Army knives.

Shoes and belts also became a problem. After Richard Reid tried to blow up a plane with explosives concealed in a shoe, shoes became the centre of attention. At some airports you have to remove your shoes and put them through the X-ray machine. At other airports you have to take off your belt. This led to the increasingly bizarre sight of men in their socks holding onto their trousers and hobbling through the metal detector. On the other side, they would try to locate their belts, shoes and bags. This wasn't rushing and waiting, it was dressing and packing. The security area of airports resembled a changing room. The risk of indecent exposure was greater than the risk of terrorism.

The CIA instruction manual must detail how a belt is used as a weapon of mass destruction. I was asked to take off my belt at one airport. Aware that belts were weapons of mass destruction I had not worn a belt.

'You don't have a belt,' the security official said suspiciously. It sounded like this was an offence that would automatically lead to indefinite detention.

In 1991, Jade noticed a sign at an African airport proclaiming a dire warning:

Persons making inappropriate comments concerning hijacking, carriage of weapons or explosives will be prosecuted; imprisonment 24 months and/or $2,000.00 fine.

They had anticipated US Homeland Security by many years.

Security was also tightened on planes. Airlines implemented a policy of ensuring the cockpit door was locked at all times during the flight. Some airlines installed bullet-resistant Kevlar doors. Others installed CCTV cameras to monitor activity in the cabin. For the pilots, watching the passengers was the flight entertainment. On an Indonesian airline during a flight within Asia, the cockpit door was open throughout the flight. This was the new company policy. Previously, on another flight operating under the locked-cockpit-door policy, both pilots had somehow managed to be outside the cockpit at the same time. They had locked themselves out, following the locked-door policy a little too literally. Fortunately the plane was on autopilot. The pilots used fire axes to break down the door and get into the cockpit. The Indonesians had decided that the risk of pilots locking themselves out of the cockpit was far greater than the risk of terrorists taking control of the aircraft.

# CHAPTER 2

The drama of tightened security didn't affect most developing nations or smaller eco-travel haunts. Bored, listless staff still played at security. We walked through wooden frames and were patted down. Our luggage was rolled into a wooden tube that masqueraded as an X-ray machine. Sometimes, the staff shook us down for change for a drink or a bribe. It was business as usual. Once we left the so-called airport, we understood why. Malnutrition was rampant. Clean water was non-existent. The rates of infant mortality from simple preventable diseases were sky high. Malaria, dengue fever and TB killed thousands every year. Then there were the real nasties: ebola and marburg virus. Snakebites also resulted in numerous deaths. The road toll from overcrowded buses and poor roads was astonishing. Why would anybody worry about terrorists?

## Strange customs

At the start of your journey, you go through a security check. At the other end, customs officials wait for you. They are there to prevent you from bringing things into the country. Who knows what foreigners could bring in? Disease, pestilence, guns, slaves, weapons of mass destruction? Residents returning home may be bringing back booty – exotic things bought overseas on which they have not paid the tithes that the ruler of their home country decrees.

In the developed world, customs are designed to primarily keep out disease. On the trip to New Zealand where I admitted to terrorism, having finally passed through immigration, I collected my bags. It was now about 2.00am. A beagle approached my bag. New Zealand uses sniffer dogs to detect food, agricultural items or narcotics. If the dog smells something, then it sits by your bag. The beagle sniffed my bag, then sat down contentedly next to it. It has never happened to me before or since. The New Zealand customs agent asked me whether I had any food items in my possession. I did not. She asked me to see her colleague who would thoroughly search my bags. The search revealed nothing. The customs official apologized for detaining me. I left the airport around 4.00am. Our much-loved and spoilt cat Alice B. Toklas may have been the problem. She often sleeps on the bag, especially on return from interesting smelling places. Maybe her scent attracted the attention of the beagle.

In the developing world, customs are a mixture of employment creation, harassment and taxation. A bribe, described generously as a facilitation or agency fee, ensures free movement of your chattels and person. The tax system in developing countries is egalitarian and fluid. The customs officials decide whom to check. They also decide what can and can't be brought into the country and the duty to be levied. Once the tax is collected in hard currency, they decide how to spend it. It may be on improvements on their villa or on a new appliance. Their sister may be getting married so they are facing a period of heavy expenses. It is a microcosm of government: legislation, regulation, inspection, enforcement, revenue collection and government expenditure all rolled into one.

You enter a country. As an eco-tourist, you are carrying the obligatory amount of camera equipment. Who knows? You might see a pangolin. The equipment costs in excess of the annual customs budget of the country. The customs official sizes you up early. You look lost and helpless. He asks to see your customs declaration. Oh yes, did I forget to tell you? When you arrive in a country, you have to fill in a customs declaration. You protest, in your ignorant imperialist Western way, that nobody gave you a form. The customs official smiles knowingly. You must have a form. It is mandatory. It is your responsibility. You are fuming. He smiles.

As you have not lodged a form, he must inspect your luggage. The contents are strewn across the dirty table. Your partner's skimpy underclothes seem, in his mind, to be the obvious place to conceal contraband. He 'finds' your camera. It was around your neck, like the albatross that it will become. He has found your traveller's cheques and US dollar bills, that the guidebook recommended you carry. These items are against regulations. You protest vehemently. You are only bringing them into the country and taking them out again – re-exporting. The customs official asks how he can be sure of that. You should have indicated this in your customs declaration, the one that you failed to fill out.

The customs official wanders off. You wait for him. He takes his time. You are now very anxious. He eventually reappears. He has spoken to his superiors. You will have to pay some fines and taxes. He itemizes the fines and taxes carefully:

Fine for failing to fill out customs declaration: US$25
Fine for bringing in items without declaration: US$25
Fee for importing items above customs limit (to be re-exported): US$25
Inspection fee: US$25

The total (US$100) is payable in cash only. It is the annual income of the president of the country. If you are sensible, you pay. Life goes on. If you are more sensible then you have arranged for a local travel agent to meet you, who knows who to bribe and how much. The price for the transfer from the airport seemed exorbitant to you? There are so many people to bribe.

If you protest, then things can take a nasty turn. In a border crossing in Africa, a traveller protested. The customs official produced an AK-47 (a Russian-designed semi-automatic rifle, for readers who are not members of the National Rifleman's Association). 'You don't have a gun. I have a gun. *I* know the law.'

## Class warfare

Somewhere sandwiched in between the strange processes of immigration, security and customs is the journey itself. It is a case of planes, trains and automobiles. Planes first. Aeroplane travel is proof that the glamour of travel is not dead. Privileged passengers have just appropriated it in a counterpoint to the democracy of mass travel. They call it First Class or Business Class. The rest of us are of course in Economy.

In Economy, you are packed in like sardines in a tin. In a jumbo jet (a Boeing 747) the normal configuration is 10 across: three seats, aisle, four seats, aisle, three seats. Each seat is about 90 centimetres (36 inches) from the one in front – the 'pitch'. Each seat is about 45 centimetres (18 inches) wide – known, very descriptively, as 'width'. The amount of space would not meet minimum occupational heath and safety standards. I have seen planes that are 12 across: six seats, aisle, six seats.

The nature of class warfare on planes is easily seen from the ATTPP measure (Available Toilet Time Per Passenger). Planes have insufficient toilets for the numbers of Economy passengers. Assume 350 Economy passengers and eight toilets. On an eight-hour flight you have a permitted amount of toilet time of nine minutes 36 seconds each (calculated as seven hours [assuming the seat-belt sign stays on for about one hour during take-off and landing] x 60 minutes x eight toilets / 350 passengers). This assumes that they are all functional. It does not take into account meals, sleep periods, films or turbulence when the 'seat belts fastened' sign is on. It does not take into account the passenger who needs 30 minutes to perform their ablutions.

In First Class, there are two reserved toilets for 12 passengers. Flight attendants guard access to these with the ferocity of Cerberus at the Gates of Hades. Rather the poor unfortunate Economy passenger soils their clothes than gain access to these hallowed shrines. The toilets of one airline have gold-plated fittings. There are designer-brand toiletries to maintain your supple skin texture. On an eight-hour flight you have a permitted amount of toilet time of 70 minutes! You have time to give yourself a complete beauty treatment. As a matter of fact, some airlines actually provide these as well for their well-heeled 'premium' customers.

Billy Connolly, the Scottish comedian, noted that he had been poor and now he was rich. In his opinion, rich was better. Terry Thomas, the English comedian, remarked that he was very easy to please. The best of everything pleased him very well. First Class is like that. I got upgraded to First Class once. I enjoyed the comfort and space. I found my fellow travellers boorish and arrogant. I was not one of them. In *The Sound of Music*, a talent agent at the Von Trapp estate remarks: 'I like rich people. I like the way they live. I like the way I live when I am with them.' I definitely like to see how the rich fly.

Business Class is somewhere in between the extremes of travel. In First Class you get vintage French Champagne, smoked almonds and cashew nuts. In Business, you get sparkling wine and peanuts. It is full of business executives enjoying perks of position. 'I am travelling Business Class as an example to everybody.' 'I am travelling with one of my assistants.' 'I normally travel First.'

Many airlines have upgraded their Business Class so that they are superior to what First Class used to be. A rich businessman rang an airline with a query. Given that the airline had installed fully reclining beds in Business Class, he wanted a reason why he should continue flying First Class. The answer was 'because you wouldn't be seen dead in any place other than First Class.'

Despite the congestion and limited space, Economy remains the most interesting cabin in the plane. It is the unity of the suffering and condemned.

I asked a flight attendant which cabin she preferred.

In a long-suffering voice she said, 'You might find this odd but I prefer Economy. Back there they actually say, "Thank you" and appreciate anything you can help them with.'

Travellers from developing economies have flying really worked out. You will see this in the course of your eco-wanderings. It is glorified bus travel. On flights in China, Africa and South America, the experience is chaotic but enjoyable. The passengers bring their belongings onto the plane, not trusting the airline with their baggage. You sit in a seething mass of humanity. If you are a foreigner, there are openly curious looks. You smile helplessly. They smile at you. They have brought food with them and offer to share. You hold their children if you want to. They disregard all instructions. When the plane lands safely, they clap joyously and beam at you and each other. Even before the plane is anywhere near stopping, they are out of their seats and running towards the exits, just in case they accidentally get left on board.

## Air mad

If you are class conscious, then travelling in exotic countries or to eco-travel destinations may create indescribable suffering. They have communist tendencies. There is no First Class. If there is then booking it does not guarantee a First-Class seat. A local dignitary may be on the flight and may avail himself of your seat. There may also be no seat allocation system at all. Getting on first entitles you to the First-Class seats irrespective of what seat you actually booked. This is called 'free seating'. It is the airline equivalent of the proletarian revolution. On the small bush planes that you fly on frequently in eco-travel there are definitely no classes. There are just seats. In the ultimate indignity, you and your bags are weighed publicly as there are severe limitations on weight. People used to First-Class air travel and extra baggage allowances may find this a trial.

The airlines in developing countries have curious nicknames: Mexicana (a Mexican airline) is Air Cactus, Air Madagascar is simply Air Mad. Bush planes are usually just owned and operated by the pilot – 'Air Bob?'. It is the price of getting off the beaten track. The planes themselves are old and battered. They are cast-offs from First World airlines that have moved onto the newest and latest best thing.

There are other strange goings-on. One flight in Africa was crewed by pale, blonde and tall Scandinavians. The plane had been 'wet leased' from a Scandinavian airline complete with crew. We sat on the tarmac for some time. It was hot. Most planes have air vents that can increase the flow of air to passengers. This plane did not have any; there is not much call for air vents in cold climates. On the same trip, we flew from Nairobi to Harare. All the taps in the toilets were missing. They were gracing someone's dwelling in Kenya.

Safety gear on planes in eco-travel is sometimes optional. In 1994, our flight between Santiago, Chile and the Falkland Islands was over the sea. During the safety demonstration one passenger discovered that the plane did not have the required life vest under the seat. The chartered plane was not normally used for flights over the sea. Most of us didn't care. If the plane crashed, we would probably be dead or the cold water of the southern Atlantic would mean that we only survived for a few minutes. The man, a European Union bureaucrat, was insistent. We spent several hours at Santiago awaiting the arrival of life vests. In the process, we lost our planned day on the Falklands Islands.

In 1991, at Nairobi airport, we were trying to check in for the flight to Zaire. Our travel agent suggested a transfer service. We were younger then and less experienced in travel routines. We decided that we were perfectly capable of travelling to the airport and checking in by ourselves.

We arrived to discover chaos. Most of the airport was closed – the President was flying in or out. Eventually, we found the check-in counter. We joined what seemed like the queue. Others kept jumping the queue. A football team arrived and the players pushed their way to the front of the queue. Time passed. We were no closer to checking in for the flight. Things were getting desperate. We made the flight due only to the kindness of two black African women. They were large, loud, garrulous and dressed in the most amazing combination of bright colours.

They were going back to Brazzaville, which, we learnt, is across the Congo River from Kinshasa, the capital of Zaire. They took pity on us. Jade believes that I have a peculiar magic that works with old women and young children. The two women pushed and barged to the front. They screamed and bantered with others in the queue, they threatened and cajoled. They were magnificent. Most importantly, they dragged us forwards with them. Miraculously, our bags were checked in and boarding passes issued. Left to our own devices, we would have spent our entire holiday in that queue.

Sometimes getting the right seats can require Machiavellian manoeuvres. In 1994, for the flight between Santiago and the Falkland Islands via Punta Arenas (at the southern tip of South America), we were desperate for seats on the left-hand side of the plane. I had met a man on another plane who travelled to South America regularly.

'Left-hand side,' he had advised. 'Sit on the left-hand side of the plane from Santiago. You fly along the Andes. It's a great view.'

We demanded seats on the left-hand side of the plane. None were available. In an act of mutiny, we got on the plane and took possession of seats on the left-hand side. We were converts to 'free seating'. There was much confusion and then anger. We were immovable. Eventually, we won. It was worth it. The view of the Andes Mountain chain was spectacular.

In normal air travel, the behaviour at the boarding gate suggests that passengers are in mortal fear of being left behind. The airline staff tries to ensure orderly boarding. First to board are 'families with children' and 'older passengers or people who may require more time to negotiate the aero-bridge'. Then, they board First- and Business-Class passengers and their frequent flyers. Finally, they board the 'main' cabin in row number from the back of the plane.

At the first announcement, all passengers surge forwards towards the gate. No women, children and aged first here. It is remarkable how many people are members of families with small children. The level of infirmity and disability escalates to epidemic portions. The level of dyslexia among the passengers rises alarmingly. They are unable to distinguish numbers at all, leading them to instinctively attempt to board the plane upon any row being called. Then there are other individuals who need to be called by name before they deign to board.

In developing countries, the chaos is even worse. It is open warfare to get on-board. It helps to be small, so you can get on your knees and crawl on board between the others' legs. On small planes, it is first in by size. Passengers are asked to sit in specific seats according to their size so that the pilot can balance the load carefully. On small planes, I always go for the

49

seat next to the pilot. Anyone worried about flying doesn't need to know there is only one pilot. Other passengers may take comfort from my presence. I have an excellent command of Flight Simulator and have been dying to try out my skills in a real emergency.

## Delayed reactions

There are airlines in the world whose flight schedules are merely invitations to negotiate, rather than a basis for actual flight planning. That is before the airline's planes encounter mechanical difficulties. A Chinese airline, CAAC, came to be known as China Airlines Always Cancels.

When we were scheduled to fly from Kathmandu, the capital of Nepal, to Varanasi in India, we turned up at the airport. The flight was cancelled. We re-booked on the next available flight that was the next day. We arrived at the airport the next day and checked in. I overheard a conversation; the words 'flight cancelled' attracted my attention. The flight had been cancelled again. Two successive cancellations were beyond our allowance for emergencies. We never made it to Varanasi. In 10 days in Nepal, we visited Kathmandu airport no less than five times – surely a record?

The flight that had been cancelled normally flew from New Delhi to Agra to Jaipur to Khajurao to Varanasi and, finally, to Kathmandu. It then turned around and flew back the same way in reverse. The passengers were mainly foreign tourists. If there were any delays then the airline just shortened the journey. The flight got as far as it could and then turned around and went back. As Kathmandu was the last stop, the flight frequently did not make it there. No one had told us this, of course.

Aeroplanes are complex machines. It is not surprising that sometimes there are mechanical problems. Twice we were delayed because the cargo door would not close. Once the igniters, the spark plugs in the jet engines, refused to work. On another occasion, the pilot couldn't tell whether he had gas or not, the fuel gauge was faulty. Delays mean that you miss connecting flights, causing a complex chain reaction. It is an integral part of the dislocation or displacement of travel.

Travel in Alaska and Canada involved a series of delays – rushing and waiting. Flying from Los Angeles to Anchorage, we arrived late into Seattle. The connecting flight we were on to Anchorage had closed. They re-opened the gates to let us on the plane. Our baggage arrived on a different flight. Flying back from Dillingham to Anchorage we missed our flight due to fog and bad weather. We were 'no shows'. What we did not grasp was that once we were a 'no show' on one flight, all subsequent flight bookings were wiped from the airline's systems. We were 'no shows' and now had 'no hope'. When we showed up for our next flight, there was no record of our bookings.

The last flight on Alaskan Airlines was from Vancouver to Los Angeles where we would connect to a flight to Sydney. We had double-checked to make sure that we were in the system. We checked in. I tempted the Gods by saying, 'we've made it'. The flight was delayed. There was the real possibility of not making our connection to Sydney. We arrived in Los Angeles with about 20 minutes to go before our flight departed. There were other connecting passengers. The purser on the Alaskan Airlines flight was a laconic American with a dry sardonic sense of humour. His safety briefing had included the deadpan comment that if you failed to follow instructions during the flight 'you would be asked to step outside.' He had contacted the other airline and ensured that the connecting flight waited.

At Los Angeles, he ensured that the connecting passengers got off first. 'These folks are travelling to some place called New Zealand [the flight to Sydney was via Auckland]. It takes about a week or so to get there.'

A large black African woman gathered us together and quickly shepherded us through the terminal. She kept urging us to run. Several people were elderly and could barely walk let alone run. One woman in her 80s was about to have a heart attack. She found out she wasn't on that flight anyway but on one leaving two hours later. We made our flight. Even our baggage made it.

Flight delays in eco-tourism are common. A major factor is the weather. The combination of fickle meteorology and small planes can lead to long delays. In Alaska, we discovered that delays of one or more days due to fog and rain were normal. Sometimes the delays are the result of very odd factors. In Africa, one flight was delayed because hyenas ate the plane's tyres. On another occasion, baboons tore the fabric of the plane's wings. In one national park, the only airport was closed because a pair of extremely rare ground birds was using the runway for their mating rituals and as a nesting site.

## Baggage madness

Every eco-tourist has baggage, even if it is just several books on the biology of the pangolin. Your baggage is tagged to its final destination: MAD for Madrid; the incongruous SIN for very orderly Singapore. When you travel, your bags develop an independent streak. Frequently, you will be in one destination and your bags in another. If fortunate, then you will be reunited. It will be an occasion of great and tearful celebration. I once travelled from Asia to Amsterdam. It was winter in Europe. I decided to put my winter coat in my hold luggage. I arrived in Amsterdam. My baggage did not. I spent two

CHAPTER 2

days feeling cold and miserable. There were no clothing shops open on Sunday. My bags eventually arrived just as I was leaving Amsterdam returning to the tropics.

I had gone to 'baggage services' to track down my luggage. I said to the man behind the counter that my bags were lost.

He immediately corrected me: 'The bags are not lost, I know precisely where they are. They are in Singapore.' I was in Amsterdam.

One advantage of bush planes is that in theory you can personally check that your luggage is on board. This is because frequently you have to load it on the plane yourself. In the Amazon, one of our group arrived at the lodge to discover that his bag had been left behind. There was no flight again before the end of our stay. The advantage in the rainforest is that you can wear the same clothes in perpetuity. No one will notice. Everything is wet and smelly within a few minutes in the heat and oppressive humidity. Our fellow traveller had to make do with clothes provided generously by staff at the lodge and spent most of the week looking a little more odd than the rest of us.

## Wings and prayers

Eco-travel requires travel on small exotic airlines and small aircraft like bush planes. The pilots fly mainly by sight. Few planes have GPS (global positioning satellite) systems. We frequently flew in planes dating from the 1950s, from a more adventurous era of flight – closer to the Wright brothers than Concorde.

For the flight from Harare to Mfuwe, the itinerary had precise instructions. The pilot would meet us at Harare airport. We arrived at the airport and waited. Nobody showed up. I decided to go up to the control tower. Harare Airport's security is not the same as other airports.

The two air-traffic controllers were bemused to see me. 'You are not allowed up here,' one of them told me.

I explained our predicament. 'Do you know of any flight to Mfuwe?' They did not.

About two hours late, a pilot appeared. We must have looked like we were waiting for a pilot. The scheduled pilot was ill. Our pilot had been drafted to fly us to Mfuwe. He escorted us through immigration. We walked across the tarmac to a small single-engine Cessna. He didn't do much flying these days and had never been to Mfuwe.

'How high do you want to fly?' he asked. I have never before been asked to nominate altitude. Seats, menu choices, but never flying height.

'Low,' I said.

'Fine.'

52

# 'RUSHING AND WAITING': THE JOURNEY

We took off in the general direction of Mfuwe. As we flew across Harare, the pilot pointed to neat houses on rectangular blocks of land. 'The best suburbs of Harare,' he screamed to make himself heard over the engine noise. Small planes are not pressurized or soundproofed. We flew at a height of around 305 metres (1,000 feet) over the African bush. We crossed a river and could see hippopotamuses. We crossed the border with Mozambique, marked by a fence with cleared areas on either side.

'Mined,' he shouted, pointing down, 'there are minefields on both sides.' At one point, I asked him whose air-traffic control area we were in.

He looked puzzled. 'Nobody's,' he shouted.

I was sitting in the cockpit next to him, watching the fuel levels steadily moving towards zero. I was relieved when he reached over and switched to the other fuel tank.

After two hours of flying, he said that we must be close.

'Look out for the airfield,' he shouted. 'It's around here somewhere.'

Jade and I began to look around earnestly. A grass strip in a clearing eventually appeared. We had arrived in Mfuwe.

Travel in and out of Botswana's Okavango Delta is exclusively by small single-engine aircraft. One day, as the plane took off from the grass airstrip, we could see two large male elephants at the airport fence stripping leaves from a tree and eating them contemplatively. They were not disturbed by the noise of the plane in the least. Later in the trip we transferred between camps in the delta. We were waiting for our flight when a large herd of elephants appeared. They made their way slowly across the airport, pausing to eat along the way. When the plane finally arrived, the elephants had gone. The pilot flew low over the runway to make sure it was clear of animals before he landed.

In the Amazon, travel is by small aircraft or boats along the rivers. The airports are clearings in dense jungle near villages. The runway is rolled mud. You can't land or take off after rain.

Travelling to one lodge in Peru, we were dropped off and picked up at a small village. From there we travelled upriver to the lodge by boat. At the airstrip, the plane made a slow low turn on its final approach. A number of roseate spoonbills took off, displaying their bright red colours that contrasted vividly with the green of rainforest. On the way back, we waited at the airstrip. It was raining and foggy. An Indian man used a two-way radio to communicate with our destination, the city of Cuzco. We waited for 3–4 hours in the steamy heat with little shelter. The Indians weren't concerned with waiting. They were used to waiting. After a week or so in the Amazon you get used to the pace of life.

In another part of the Amazon, there were two 'airports'. The weather, state of the runways and level of the river dictated the airport used. We arrived and

CHAPTER 2

left by boat. The boat pulled up on the bank. We hopped out, trying not to get too wet, and scaled the muddy bank. We strolled past the village and onto the runway to wait. Then, the plane was there. We got on and the plane took off, clearing the trees by a few feet. Children from the village gathered around as we waited. They looked at us shyly. We were from a distant galaxy as far as they were concerned. If we looked at them or smiled, then they would smile back hesitantly. In those days there weren't many Western tourists. One of our party went back a few years later. The Indians had digital cameras. They were also savvier about Western tourists and were asking for money and gifts.

On the return trip, a villager going to the city hitched a lift with us. He had walked to the lodge to catch the plane over two days through undisturbed jungle. He had not been on a plane before and looked terrified. At our destination, one of the lodge staff met him. He looked scared of the airport and the city, although he had been unafraid walking alone for days through the rainforest.

In Alaska, rivers and lakes serve as airports. Lake Hood in Anchorage is the world's largest floatplane base. Hundreds of floatplanes are tied up at jetties like a marina for pleasure craft. You go to the plane base and wander around until you find the floatplane operator. You go up and say who you are or where you are going. The flights are charters. Eventually, the pilot saunters in and you follow him out to the jetty. You board and then you are away. At the other end, you set down in a river or lake. The pilot manoeuvres the plane to a gravel beach or jetty and sets you down. Sometimes you have to help tie up the aircraft. You help with luggage and other supplies. Once we carried fresh eggs to the lodge.

In Alaska, flying is difficult because of unpredictable weather conditions. Fog is common all year round. Winds can be violent. The planes fly low – usually under 150 metres (500 feet) – using landmarks as navigational aids. Landing is often difficult. The major problem is getting sufficient visibility to make the approach. Many flights, particularly late in the season, return, unable to land. The pilots rely on detailed knowledge of the lakes and rivers. A pilot set his floatplane down a little further along the lake than was usual at a lodge where we were staying. The staff rushed out, fearing the worst. He was fine. At another lodge, the winds were blowing hard. The pilot managed to land but couldn't get close to the jetty. The plane just kept being blown across the lake. It took several minutes of careful manoeuvring to tie the plane up.

Floatplanes are a key transport link between the communities in Alaska. We gave people lifts. We picked up a mechanic to work on an outboard engine. On the way back, we dropped a member of staff back at the same village. The pilot, Willie, landed the plane and beached it on a steep gravel beach.

He imparted an essential piece of floatplane folklore: 'You can land a floatplane anywhere – once.'

Earlier on the same trip, we were on Kodiak Island waiting to fly to Katmai Wilderness Lodge on Kukak Bay on the Katmai coast. The weather was bad. In the late afternoon, it was decided that we would try again the next day. The next day the weather was still bad, with low cloud and rain. But we would try. The weather on the Katmai side of the Shelikof Strait was fine; there was just a fog bank on this side. I asked how they knew. Willie said casually that one of the pilots had taken off to try to get through and had reported that it was possible to fly across.

On the way, we saw tight rafts of sea otters drifting along the coast and a pair of humpback whales in one inlet. On the way back, we arranged for Willie to fly us over the Valley of the Thousand Smokes. We flew west over the active volcanoes of the Katmai Peninsula. We flew over a glacier where Willie said he had noticed a new fissure. It is named after him.

'Do you want to see it?' he asked us.

He banked the aircraft in a tight turn over the fissure so we could see it 150 metres (500 feet) below us. Through a gap in the rock and ice we could see into the dark recesses of the earth and the valley's steaming geysers.

These journeys have a freedom and informality that modern travel lacks: there is a sense of wildness and adventure that is absent from the sanitized and efficient modern version. They remain fond memories.

## Flight magic

The view of the Earth from the planes is sometimes magical. This is the true mystery of flight. One of my favourite sights is the Hindu Kush Mountains in northern Afghanistan. I saw them first in the 1980s. The plane reaches the area about five hours after leaving Singapore on its way to Europe. Most passengers were asleep. I had woken up thirsty and asked the flight attendant for water. Bringing me a glass, he asked whether I was interested in seeing the mountains. He took me to the cockpit. The plane was over the Hindu Kush Mountains. All around were snow-capped mountains. We were at 9,500 metres (just over 31,000 feet). The peaks seemed to be within touching distance. The view was magnificent.

Whenever I fly that route, I try to see them. Peak upon peak, more than 6,100 metres (20,000 feet) above sea level, as far as you can see. I have seen them in the light of a full moon through scattered clouds. The moonlight on the ice and snow created a soft diffuse light. It was spectacular.

On our flight from Santiago to Punta Arenas in South America, when we saw the Andes from the left-hand side of the plane, we had a lesson in geography and geology: glaciers, moraine (terminal, lateral and median), ice sheets and volcanic craters. Some crater lakes were spectacularly blue, others a chemical green. We flew across Tierra del Fuego and the Straits of Magellan. I remembered the long and hard search for this route through from the Atlantic to the Pacific Ocean.

To get to Round Island, off the coast of Alaska, we flew by floatplane to a point on the coast. We landed in a small lake. We then walked across the dunes to a beach. The boat on which we were going to stay and travel to Round Island was moored off the beach. The skipper came to get us in a zodiac (a small, inflatable rubber boat). On the way back, we transferred to the beach and waited for the flight from Dillingham to pick us up. The skipper went off for a walk. A bear was fishing in the river. We spotted movement above the grass. It was a short-eared owl. Owls generally hunt at night but this species hunts during the day. We could see the owl but couldn't hear it – their wings are soundless in flight to prevent their prey from detecting them.

Flights across Australia are also extraordinary. During the day you can see the vast dry Australian landscape – dusty reds, yellows, greys and patches of brown and green. The scrubby landscape has a desolate beauty. The Earth speaks of its ancient history, its fragility and its harshness.

## Train travails

Train travel remains a staple in developing countries. To discover true train travel, you need to travel in India. We travelled a lot by train during our visit there. The statistics of the Indian railway system are mind-boggling: 60,000 kilometres (about 37,000 miles) of tracks; over 7,000 stations; 1.5 million employees. Each day, more than 12,000 trains carry in excess of 10 million passengers, at least, that's the known amount. Indian trains rarely run to schedule or on time. In 1947, India gained independence from Great Britain. With independence came many things: a train system that runs on time was not one of them.

Indian trains have wondrously evocative names: The Golden City Express or The Kolkata Mail Express. There is the 'toy train' from Jalpaiguri to Darjeeling in the foothills of the Himalayan Mountains, which is famous for its tea. I remember travelling on it as a child. It runs on a very narrow gauge of 0.762 metres (2.5 feet), a normal gauge being around 1.67 metres (5.5 feet). The eight hour train journey is about 90 kilometres (56 miles). When I first took the journey, steam engines were used. The little train climbs fairly steep inclines. There are constant switchbacks. At one point, the train reverses up a zigzag slope that is too steep even for switchbacks. There is another point where it goes up a sort of corkscrew spiral. I remember the train having to stop on several occasions to take on more water to fuel its precarious climb.

# 'RUSHING AND WAITING': THE JOURNEY

In India, no matter how early you go to book tickets, the train will be full. Seats, especially in the better classes, are reserved for ministers and government officials, in case they want to travel. You have to bribe the poorly paid railway ticket-office clerk. Foreigners unused to the subtle nature of Indian railway commerce find this incomprehensible. Then, there are the acronyms of train travel – First; AC 2 (Second-Class air-conditioned); Non AC 2 (Second-Class non-air-conditioned) and Third.

You have your ticket. The day of travel has arrived. You make your way to the station (or *thana*, in Hindi). Indian train stations are grand. Mumbai's Victoria Terminal, known to locals as VT, dominates Nagar Chowk square. The building is ornate, resembling a Gothic cathedral complete with spires, stained-glass windows and gargoyles. When you arrive at the station, there are people everywhere: travellers, those who have come to see people off and those who have come to meet arriving passengers. Several generations of the family, complete with servants, are milling about. People are asleep on the floor, cooking on open fires, gathered around public taps washing clothes and bathing. You are startled to see people performing private bodily functions near or on the tracks. Do these people live here? Probably. An Indian train station is a small town.

Freight is everywhere – boxes and jute bags full of who knows what. Porters with loads several feet high on their head stagger past. The noise and smell overwhelm you. You find your train. Your name and seat number is posted outside the carriage. Passengers push and shove their way onto the carriages. Compartments generally have four berths. If you are alone or with your partner then you share. Other people are already there, taking up all the space. You must be in the wrong compartment as they have booked all four! It is just a try-on. Eventually you slide in and take up a position in a warehouse surrounded by bags, trunks and suitcases. Indians like to travel equipped for anything. The carriage is stifling hot. The fan gently circulates the dust. You can smell the lavatory. It is not sanitary, hygienic or salubrious. Welcome to Indian trains.

Western women find themselves in compartments with crotch-scratching, farting and belching Indian men. Some Indian trains now have special compartments for women only. The sign says: 'Ladies only for all the 24 hours'. If you are seated with a family or women then there are different issues. You will be questioned in a confronting direct personal manner. Jade and I don't have children, creating endless scrutiny. 'Why will it be that you are not having children?' 'How long have you been married?' 'Will you then be having tried IVF?' 'Will you then be infertile?' 'Pray to [insert name of goddess] and you will blessed with children.'

A bell clangs. A whistle blows. The train leaves the station. If you look, you see the Third-Class carriages overflowing with humanity. There are people on the roof of the train. You remember the sign urging people not to travel on the roof. Outside, crowded, poorly built houses give way to shantytowns, then to countryside. The train never travels at a great speed. Every so often you pass a level crossing where cars, trucks, motorcycles, bullock-drawn carts, bicycles and people wait. The trucks and carts are piled high with farm produce. Men, women and children with large baskets on their heads watch the train rattle past. What are they thinking?

The ticket inspector comes and checks your ticket. He checks it many times, just in case. The bed-roll wallah comes by with bedding. It is frayed, smelly and none too clean. The *chai wallah* (tea seller) is doing his rounds. For a few rupees – about US 15 cents – he pours tea out of an urn into plastic cups. In the old days, they were clay cups. The tea is hot, strong and sweet. At stations, vendors run to the trains selling samosas, puris or parathas and nuts. Omelette sellers mysteriously conjure up an omelette in an instant and serve it on a plastic plate or bit of banana leaf. Vendors get on at one station and work the train, carriage by carriage, and get off at the next station. They work a train going in the opposite direction back to the station where they boarded. There is a sign: 'Steward is instructed to repel hawkers/vendors and beggars/urchins from the carriage.'

We were on an overnight train from New Delhi to Jabalpur, the access point for Kanha National Park. The train journey was meant to take about 10 hours. As the hours ticked by, we did not seem to be getting any closer. I got out the map and my compass. We were travelling east. We should have been going almost due south. In an eccentric routing, the train went east and then changed direction completely travelling south-west to Jabalpur. The train stopped frequently, often between stations. Passengers living near the train line pulled the emergency-stop cord and got off when the train stopped. This was a highly personalized form of transport. We arrived at Jabalpur late in the afternoon after 18 hours.

I asked two besuited men, who were sitting in the compartment whether or not the train was late.

'It is always late,' they said, unconcerned. It was Indian fatalism at its most magnificent. After India, train travel elsewhere is an anti-climax.

Sadly, the delay cost us dearly. We had been scheduled to arrive early in the morning. This meant that we would have been able to go out for a wildlife-viewing drive in the afternoon. The delay meant that we missed our scheduled afternoon drive. On that drive, the guides and eco-tourists saw a large male tiger very close up. We of course missed all that because of our train travails. If it had been a pangolin that they saw, then I would have slit both wrists.

Another common train journey for eco-travellers is the trip between Nairobi and Mombassa. The train was once the jewel of the Kenyan railways.

The train pulled out from Nairobi in the late afternoon. We travelled along
the boundary of Nairobi National Park. There were two white rhinoceroses
grazing by the side of the train tracks. The Mombassa train was full of
tourists. We ate in the dining car, curry and rice. There was an aura of decay.
The waiters were dressed in formal attire: white jackets and bow ties. The
jackets were threadbare and shiny with wear. There were holes. The uniforms
spoke of past luxury and elegance. The train crosses a river just before
Mombassa. The train crossed the bridge, travelling very slowly, and we
hung out the window looking at the view. Years later, the bridge collapsed
under a crossing train. Hundreds died. We had joked about the condition
of it when we crossed.

## Autobahns

The final leg of your journey will probably involve cars. It may be not quite the
motorway or autobahn of your native land. Major roads are well maintained,
but once you get off the beaten track, which is inevitable if you are serious
about searching for pangolins, the condition of the road infrastructure is
parlous. Roads are tarred but poorly maintained from lack of money. The
soil is soft and foundations too shallow for the weight and traffic of vehicles.
Small cracks turn into large potholes. Repairs are rarely successful. After
rain, the potholes reappear, bigger and deeper.

Most roads to eco-tourist lodges are dirt tracks.

A young guide in Zambia defined a main road: 'You can tell a main road
by the fact that it doesn't have grass growing down the middle of it.'

Dirt tracks are fine in dry climates. In equatorial Africa, it rains frequently
and hard. The red laterite soil turns into impassable mud.

Cars, buses and trucks travel along the roads. The trucks and buses
can be huge – 18-wheeled monsters. The buses and trucks must have high
ground clearance. Buses in some parts of Africa are actually lorries with a
bus body mounted on top. The large vehicles mangle the poorly designed
roads. Road accidents are common. In some countries, you cannot move the
wrecks until the police complete their investigation. As the police are relatively
unhurried in their work, the roads are littered with wrecks. You have to avoid
wrecks as well as the potholes.

To see the mountain gorillas, we had to drive from Burundi to Zaire. Our
journey was complicated. We were going to Zaire because of civil war in
Rwanda. As it turned out, we would have to drive through Rwanda in any
case, as the only 'decent' road available went through there. The trip was
along a tarred, single-lane road about 4.5 metres (15 feet) wide. Large pot-

holes covered the road. Some were large enough to entirely swallow up small cars. Part of the road had been washed away or was covered by mudslides. It was hard to see whether we were driving on or off the road. It took us about six hours to travel the 100 kilometres (62 miles).

Another hazard in developing countries is the roadblock. This is usually made up of some oil drums placed across the road, a flimsy wooden-boom gate or a plank of wood studded with nails extended across the road. The 'official' roadblocks have policemen or soldiers dressed in something resembling a uniform. Their job is to ensure compliance with the variable laws. You need a special permit that you do not have. Your car or mini-bus is not certified to carry passengers. Your vehicle may be missing vital equipment, a fire extinguisher or an axe. You pay them to let you through. The official simply asks for money, food, cigarettes, medicines, or whatever, directly. 'Entrepreneurial' roadblocks are the work of unemployed youth. Young men stand around in postures learnt from the latest films.

In Africa, I watched the local kids make an existing pothole bigger. They filled it with water, making it difficult to negotiate. A car pulled up. The kids explained the problem. More cars arrived, causing a traffic jam. For a small fee the kids agreed to repair the road. The drivers had no choice. Planks of wood and sand magically appeared. The hole was filled in. Planks were laid across the pothole. The fee was paid. After the cars had passed, the pothole mysteriously reappeared.

Driving in developing countries is memorable. The drivers seem to be maniacs, but everybody just drives like that in these countries. The driver generally motors along at high speed down the middle of the road. When he approaches a village, which is frequently, he doesn't slow down. He just puts one hand on the horn and keeps it there until he is through. People and animals scatter out of the way. At night, some will drive in almost complete darkness. The driver turns on the lights only briefly when traffic is approaching.

In India our driver carefully folded back the side mirrors of the vehicle. The roads were narrow and congested with cars, bullock carts, motorcyclists, bicyclists, pedestrians and cows. It was bedlam. Frequently, the distance between our car and the next car was about 8 centimetres (3 inches). It was easy to understand the need for streamlining. We were going through a small town. Jade and I noticed almost simultaneously that there was a car on the same side of a divided road speeding towards us. The driver had not noticed. We were both about to shout when suddenly our driver swerved and avoided the other car.

For our trip to Bharatpur near Agra to visit Keola Deo National Park, famed for its bird life and huge pythons, we started early in the morning. There was heavy fog. It was impossible to see more than 3 metres (10 feet). The road was officially a two-lane national highway; in reality, it had one lane. The traffic was heavy – mainly buses and trucks. On the verge of the road, there was a steady stream of people on foot and bicycles and an occasional herd of cattle or goats. The lack of visibility did not affect driving habits. Our driver ploughed on as fast as he could go. Trucks and buses going in the opposite direction emerged suddenly through the fog. We swerved, trying to avoid people, animals and a head-on collision. Both drivers pressed their horns creating a shrieking loud noise. Somehow, the vehicles missed each other and the assorted people and animals on the roadside. It wasn't for the faint-hearted. Yes, we saw many species of birds and the famed pythons.

We don't hire cars and drive ourselves very often. In Namibia, we ended up with a hire car after a disagreement with the operator. We had a small sedan. The roads in Namibia aren't bad by African standards – they were designed primarily for South African tanks and armoured personnel carriers travelling to oil-rich Angola. The roads, particularly in national parks, are gravel or dirt. We shredded two tyres in the course of our travels. One was shredded while driving around the Etosha Pan. We had to get out and change the tyre not far from where we had recently seen rhinoceroses and lions. While we were changing the tyre another car approached. We must have seen some interesting wildlife. When they found out we had not seen anything but had a flat tyre, they quickly drove off. They did not ask whether we needed help. The car was a Volkswagen with a 'temporary' spare tyre resembling a bicycle wheel. We used it to get to the next service facility where they fixed the main tyre. At one point, we had to drive about 100 kilometres (62 miles) on the temporary tyre across very rough roads. We saw almost no other traffic.

We hired a car in Alaska. When not avoiding collisions with huge motor homes driven by short-sighted residents of more southerly states, we concentrated on staying on the right side of the road. In Australia, we drive on the left side of the road. In the USA, they drive on the right side. Our long habit of driving on the left created problems. We shouted at each other a lot. 'Look left, look right, stay right, stay right to stay alive.'

Driving in South Africa posed different challenges. They drive on our side of the road. The road-users were polite and helpful. But 'car-jacking' is common and involves gangs armed with semi-automatic rifles. AK-47 Kalashnikovs, are cheap: these are the developing world's weapons of choice. The stolen car is stripped for its spare parts. Certain makes of cars are more popular with the organized gangs. People consulted suggested hiring a Porsche or Audi. The more unusual the car the less likely it was to be stolen. In the end we settled on a non-descript and fairly battered Japanese model. The insurance was exorbitant. The car came complete with instructions. In case of a car-jacking, you cooperate and always keep your hands visible to the hijackers. If you reach for something under the dashboard the hijackers might think that you are reaching for a gun. South Africans have high levels of gun ownership. The hijackers might shoot you. If you have a child or pet in the car then you politely inform the hijackers and ask for permission to get the child or pet, making sure that your hands are visible at all times. This advice was in matter-of-fact language. Our car was fitted with a satellite tracking device where it was being monitored at all times. If we went into areas where we were not expected to be, then an armed security team would respond, assuming that we must had been car-jacked. How this would work when we were simply lost was not clear. I was relieved when we handed the car back to the car hire company after two weeks.

Car breakdowns are common in developing countries. An Englishman we met in India had been travelling between two cities. The car broke down – a broken axle. Asking his passenger to wait, the driver walked off in the direction of the nearest village. The Englishman waited for his driver on the side of the fairly isolated road in the night. Some hours later, the driver reappeared on top of a bullock-drawn cart accompanied by another man. They hitched the car to the cart. The Englishman got on to the bullock cart. The cart moved off slowly with the car in tow. In the early morning, they reached a village. The bullock cart pulled up at a hut near an open fire. A man emerged – the village blacksmith.

The blacksmith and the driver dismantled the broken axle. There was much animated discussion. It dawned on the Englishman that the blacksmith was proposing to manufacture the broken part and reassemble the axle. It was the next morning when the blacksmith finished. The driver paid him, the Englishman got into the car and they continued their journey.

Eco-travel is focused on seeing wild animals in their natural environment. The process of getting to and from the eco-tourist destination is fascinating in its own way. Sometimes it is as alien as the wildlife that you are going to see. Some of the experiences probably rival the strangeness of the pangolin itself. It is all part of the experience. It too transforms us in various ways. That is, if you survive, of course.

## The meaning of the journey

I think often what our journey means to the local people we encounter along the way. I think about the men, women and children on the road and the people waiting patiently at the railway crossing as the train goes past. I think about the faces I have seen.

In Africa and India, I have sat in trains, cars and buses that travel through villages and towns. I have seen men and women standing by the side of the road waiting for a lift or a shared local taxi to arrive. If they don't have money, then I have seen them walk stoically and without complaint for miles to their destination. Children barely old enough to walk carry heavy loads on their heads along the side of the road. They walk in all weathers. They rarely ask for a lift. If they ask then we generally refuse. It is for security reasons. The people are always polite and uncomplaining, bearing their fate with equanimity. There is no resentment as we rush past in our train, bus or car. Where the road is narrow, they stand aside to let us pass and are sometimes splashed with mud or water. They breathe the toxic fumes of the exhaust from the vehicle.

I remember a man standing on the road in Namibia. He was dressed incongruously in a suit. It was very hot and he was sweating profusely. We stopped. He asked for water so we gave him some. I wonder where he was going? How long did he have to wait in the middle of nowhere before some-one gave him a lift?

A New Zealand woman I know went to Uganda to see the mountain gorillas. She was on the return leg of her trek to see them, and heading back to the place where she was staying. As she got into the mini-bus, she spotted a woman by the side of the road. The woman was in great distress. She was crying soundlessly, sitting and rocking gently in total inconsolable despair. Her face spoke of her pain and suffering. Her child had just died of a minor disease. If she had been able to take the child to the clinic in the nearby town, then the child may have lived. There was no transport available. She was poor so could not afford it. The woman from New Zealand described the strange combination of exhilaration and sadness she felt at that moment. She had flown halfway around the world to see the gorillas. The child had died because of the inability to transport her 20 kilometres (12.5 miles) to the nearby town. I think of all the space-age technologies that we have and of our journeys that rely on complex machines and planning to enable us to span large distances quickly and effortlessly, the same technologies that failed a tiny helpless child in this forgotten and poor part of the world.

# CHAPTER 3
## 'No Place Like Home': Travel, Food And Accommodation

*...The surgeon gasps. As Jade is lying face down, the cause of his reaction is not immediately obvious. 'You won't believe this,' he says. 'Something just looked at me.' An insect had thrust its head out of one of the incisions...*

# CHAPTER 3

## Room-service oxygen

We used Cuzco as our base when we were travelling in the Peruvian Amazon. We flew from Lima, the capital of Peru, to Cuzco. Lima is at sea level; Cuzco is high in the Andes Mountains, approximately 3,050 metres (10,000 feet) above sea level. The result was instant altitude sickness. Altitude sickness is the body's inability to generate sufficient oxygen from the increasingly thinner air above certain altitudes. Climbers refer to the highest peaks as the 'death zone'.

My dose of altitude sickness was mild: headaches, nausea and shortness of breath. Like most men, being a complete wimp and hypochondriac, I was dying... Foolishly, I had assumed that I would be immune to altitude sickness. My head was pounding. My stomach was churning. I felt the chronic need to hyperventilate. Since arriving in Cuzco, I had been drinking lots of coca tea, believed to provide relief from altitude sickness. It was to no avail. We were staying at an upmarket hotel. I had gone to sleep hoping for relief from the symptoms. I woke up in the middle of the night, the symptoms still with me. Jade rang the hotel front desk. They would send up the oxygen. Minutes later, a formally attired butler appeared wheeling a large cylinder of pure oxygen behind him. I was lying there pathetically.

He attached the mask to my face.

'Five minutes,' he said, his voice full of authority and pity at these poor gringos unable to cope with altitude or life's little challenges.

I breathed in the oxygen, feeling the relief with each intake of breath. It was wonderful – lifesaving. I had oxygen once or twice every night. Even Jade, on the occasion that she had the symptoms, availed herself of the oxygen. It was wonderful – His & Hers Oxygen.

The hotel's provision of oxygen ranks as perhaps one of the more bizarre examples of room service that we have ever encountered. It has become almost a benchmark that we judge hotels by: 'Do your rooms have 24/7 access to pure oxygen?' The equivalent with guides is our perennial question: 'Have you ever seen a pangolin?'

## Home comforts

True explorers take accommodation, food and creature comforts with them. Robert Falcon Scott's attempt and heroic failure (failure is frequently heroic) to reach the South Pole is well documented. Scott brought theatrical props and costumes on his trip. The British expedition needed to keep their morale up.

Modern travel does not need to deal with the challenges of true expeditions. It is generally travel to civilization. Eco-travel purports to get off the beaten track. It seeks out new, remote and exotic destinations. This would seem to require the expedition planning faced by the adventurers of the past. In reality, eco-travel too is civilized. An 'eco-tourist' venue in Asia advertised that there was no need to 'rough it out in camps'. The guests could come back to luxury and creature comforts. Each eco-tourist 'attraction' would take only a relatively short time to get to. Guests could sneak in a round of golf at a nearby course.

Peru's Inca Trail traverses the Andes through spectacular mountain landscapes and ruins. The rigours of the modern Inca Trail are seen from the hardships borne by travellers. You carry your small daypack. Porters carry your bags, tents, camping materials and creature comforts. When you reach your camping spot for the night, the porters have already made camp. Sometimes there are hundreds of tents. The travellers arrive at a leisurely pace. Refreshments and beverages greet them. After a relaxing drink in the scenic surroundings, you have a shower. The shower is probably an elevated tank filled with hot water by the porters. You sit down to a three-course dinner. A German group had tables, chairs, starched tablecloths and silver cutlery. Not everybody has this level of ostentatious service on the Inca Trail.

On an English comedy show I once saw on late night television, two immaculately coiffed, empty-headed television reporters interview a couple complaining about their holiday. The travel company advertised that the 'holiday would be just like home'. The man complains that they had a view of the ocean in Portugal; they live miles from the sea in an industrial slum at home. The wife complains that there were no portraits of Barry Manilow; she had to go out and buy a picture of Barry Manilow to put on the walls to make it more like home. Travellers seek to recreate home at their destination, especially in relation to food and accommodation. In the case of eco-travel, with its promise of wilderness and adventure, the requirement for creature comforts of every description is strange. To see a pangolin in a five-star hotel resort compound would be very odd, though in truth, we would probably settle for it. In fact, in all our trekking and travel, we have seen the most amazing array of animals and birds within the lodge compounds or at the entrances to and exits from parks and wildlife reserves. The search for adventure, the exotic and uncertainty, it seems, is shallow and may be entirely unnecessary.

## Home away from home

Your eco-travel adventure will include various types of accommodation. You will travel via major population centres en route to your wilderness destinations.

# CHAPTER 3

There are many towns and cities that seem to function as staging points for eco-travel. In Kenya, Nairobi provides this function. In Tanzania, Arusha is known for two things: the starting point for those who want to climb 'Killi' (Mount Kilimanjaro) and the wildlife safari centre for Tanzania.

In these towns, you stay at a normal hotel. A hotel is an apartment block with 24/7 maid, laundry and take-away food service. The hotel generally, if reputable, provides you with a room, a bed or two and a bathroom. There are restaurants or communal dining rooms. Generally, hotels provide you with a room for your personal use.

In one hotel, one evening, the door opened and in walked a woman. Luckily, I was dressed and wasn't scratching my crotch or picking my nose.

'What are you doing in my room?' she barked. I was a bit surprised to see her.

'I could ask the same thing,' I responded coolly.

The hotel had 'forgotten' that I was in the room. 'It's the computer,' the front desk purred reassuringly. Always check that the hotel guarantees you exclusive occupation of the room.

You will need to select a hotel that fits your taste and budget. Descriptions of hotels are confusing: comfortable hotel, tourist hotel, superior hotel, deluxe hotel. You don't want to stay in an uncomfortable or inferior hotel. I am concerned at the concept of a tourist hotel. It is a tautology of sorts. An entry in a guidebook on Madagascar claims that a hotel has a view of the sea, 'la mer'. A traveller wrote to the author of the guidebook. The hotel looked out on the sea, but at low tide it was an extensive mud flat that the locals used as a public convenience. The traveller mused whether the promised view was of 'la merde'.

Many developing countries have historical hotels. You will frequently be encouraged to stay in them. Jade refers to them as 'hysterical'. There is confusion between decay and significance. The siren call here is the ability to say, 'I have been there.' A good example is the palace hotels, most famously the Lake Palace Hotel in Udaipur in India. The hotel is a grand, ornate royal palace set in the middle of a lake. All transport to and from the hotel is by boat. The traveller is marooned in splendid, luxurious isolation protected from the masses. That is, if there is water in the lake. A friend recently stayed in the Lake Palace Hotel. A drought meant that the lake was completely dry. They had to walk across the mud flats to get to the hotel. Somehow the glamour was gone.

In 1990 in Egypt, we stayed at the Cataract Hotel – the Old Cataract Hotel. The friend who had organized the trip was obsessed by the history of the hotel. It is an imposing structure on the banks of the Nile at Aswan that has seen its share of the rich and famous. It featured in the film of Agatha

Christie's *Death on the Nile*. I was not aware of the hotel's history; hotels are much the same to my uneducated tastes. It transpired that we had been put into the New Cataract Hotel, a modern structure next to the older hotel. Our companion was distraught. She harangued the staff into submission. We were given rooms in the Old Cataract Hotel. The bathroom was the size of our apartment. It had an enormous stone bath big enough for a football team. The rich and famous need a lot of room to perform their ablutions. The hotel had a small amphitheatre by the Nile. It was used for performances in the hotel's past. A set of speakers had been placed where the performers stood. In the afternoon, the hotel staged a 'concert'. They put a record on in these pre-CD days. We sat on the banks of the Nile watching the feluccas – traditional Egyptian wooden boats – in the river. You could see monuments on the islands in the Nile. The banks were dotted with palm trees. We sat watching the sun set to the sound of Leonard Bernstein conducting one of Beethoven's symphonies. The strains floated gloriously above the hubbub of the Nile at the Old Cataract Hotel.

## Your host is...

An alternative to hotels is the bed and breakfast ('B&B'). You stay in someone's house as a boarder. The 'home stay' gives you the ability to live with a local family and 'connect' with the local way of life. You can also interact with your fellow guests. Unfortunately, these are precisely the things you can end up hating. The necessity of putting on a 'happy face' can prove unbearable.

Our experience with B&Bs is not good. In Alaska, we stayed at a B&B in a coastal town. At breakfast, we ate eggs and flapjacks and made polite conversation with other guests. A Wal-Mart manager held forth on how the American housewife would not pay more than a certain amount for fresh fish. A wine merchant explored the merits of real versus artificial corks versus screw tops. It was riveting stuff.

A local couple ran the guesthouse. She was a 'character'. The itinerary mentioned that she would regale us with stories about the 'real' Alaska. We had taken that as a serious warning. She must have found us difficult. We replied in sullen monosyllables. Desperate to establish 'contact', she cornered us and talked about her niece who had visited the 'oooruient'. I haven't heard the countries of East Asia referred to as the Orient for a long time. I fled, trying to suppress my laughter.

Our room had a set of talking scales with a mind of its own. 'You weigh 320 pounds.' 'You have gained 180 pounds since the last time.' 'You have lost 220 pounds since the last time.' It was the best entertainment going.

# CHAPTER 3

## Eco-travel lodges

In eco-travel, there is little choice in accommodation. At your eventual destination, you will be staying in a lodge, tent or worse. The more remote the location, the more basic the accommodation. Remember, the focus is on the wildlife. Remember that you will be spending most of your waking hours searching out the wild animals that are supposed to be there.

When we first started our eco-travels, the accommodation was simple. In the Amazon, the accommodation was generally built from the wood of fallen trees collected from the river. Cutting down trees was against national park rules. Lodge owners were passionate environmentalists and keen not to impact the natural surroundings.

As time has gone on we have become aware that people have tried to make things more comfortable for the visitors, more like home. One lodge had incongruously installed a large satellite dish for CNN and telephones for US visitors. By the time we visited the lodge, the rain and humidity of the rainforest had destroyed the dish. It looked like a giant orchid. It was green from the algae and plants that were slowly engulfing it.

The basic format of an eco-tourist lodge is straightforward. It consists of a number of wooden, stone or mud buildings. Alternatively, tents are used. The lodges generally are located within or just outside the park or reserve that you are visiting. There is a central block consisting of an office, kitchen and dining area. There is a small sitting area festooned with books and photos of wildlife that others have seen but that you will not see. Every lodge in the Amazon has a picture, sometimes very faded, of a jaguar seen just near the camp by a guide or guest. No lodge has ever had a photograph of a pangolin on the wall. You sleep in individual cabins or tents. Staff quarters are at a discreet distance, hidden from view, for the protection of the staff. You may have central shower/toilet amenities if, horror of horror, the lodge does not have 'private facilities'.

Our favourites are the tented camps in Africa. We don't actually like camping per se. But these are no ordinary tents. The tent is pitched on top of a wooden or concrete platform. Inside, there are comfortable beds, wardrobes, tables and chairs. There are 'private facilities'. This is roughing it with a dash of decadence. If you want to fulfil your Hemingway or Livingstone fantasies, then this is the way to do it. When you say you 'camped out', strictly speaking you are telling the truth.

If you want more deprivation then that too can be arranged. In the Peruvian Amazon, you can travel from the cloud forest down to the rainforest itself. What the marketing literature describes as 'primitive accommodation' needs serious consideration. Small tents are pitched on wooden platforms with camp beds. There are 'communal facilities'. Temperatures hover around 38.5°C (100°F) with high humidity. Every type of biting insect is in attendance.

The lure of eco-tourism and the money it brings in sometimes proves irresistible to owners of accommodation. In India, the eco-tourist lodge we had booked turned out to be a hotel. In fact, every hotel within 5 kilometres (3 miles) of the nearby national park famed for its tigers featured 'eco-' in its name. During our stay, the hotel was the venue of the Indian Grease and Oil Executives Conference. There were about 100 executives who were combining their annual jamboree with a spot of eco-tourism. We came across them in the park. We were alone with a guide and had been watching a lone male elephant eating his way through the foliage. The Indian Grease and Oil show arrived. They had been split up into smaller groups, but it made no difference. The noise scared the elephant off. They wanted to know where the elephant was. We pointed in the general direction of where the elephant had disappeared. They couldn't see the elephant. A few got out of the jeep. Jade suggested that they go into the bush to bring the elephant out into the open so we could see it.

The lodge was located on the banks of a mountain stream. The Indian Grease and Oil executives spent a lot of time shouting and skimming stones across the stream. This seemed the way Indians communed with nature. The fact that they scared away all the birds was lost on them. I noticed two of the group by the river. One was on his knees drinking deeply from the river. 'Pure water,' he intoned. 'The water will be being absolutely pure.'

The other nodded sagely. 'It will be giving you good health and long life.'

I did not tell them that just a little way upstream, the lodge had brought their domesticated elephants to bathe. Elephants love water. They had spent about an hour rolling around and bathing in the stream. Oh yes, they had performed, as elephants are wont to do, their bodily functions in the stream.

Sometimes, readers could be forgiven for thinking that they are going to a luxury hotel. The wildlife and natural history are secondary to the romance and luxury. The concept of lodge as the destination has developed:

[Name] lodge is a new luxurious and exclusive wildlife destination in [country]. It is the brainchild of [name of owner]. The lodge consists of 12 suites. Each suite is independently built on a wooden platform on the side of a hill sheltered by ancient trees. Each suite is separate to guarantee privacy. The centrepiece of each suite is a vast romantic bedroom equipped with king-sized beds with exquisite linens. The bed is draped with walk-in mosquito netting. The bedroom has an adjoining sitting room with comfortable sofas for relaxation. The suites open out onto a large balcony and a private plunge pool. You can sit on the balcony by the pool overlooking the vast plains of [name].

The balcony forms a great location for 'sun-downer' drinks, a private dinner or nightcap under the glittering sky. The central dining complex is immaculately decorated. The food at [name of lodge] is the work of [name of famous chef], who is the driving force behind [name of famous restaurant] in [name of place]. The high standard of lodge's varied cuisine is complemented by the extensive wine cellar that features an outstanding collection of wines from around the world. The service is always understated but attentive. There is the spa offering an extensive range of treatments and massages for the guest. [Name of lodge] sets new standards in luxury accommodation.

All lodges have their problems. As we get older, deprivation for the sheer sake of it has become less attractive. But we still try to find simple, small, intimate lodges.

It is impossible to know how full a lodge will be during your stay or whether you will be competing with a large group or with relatives of the owners. We have found that lodges can get very crowded on weekends and during holidays and can be fairly empty at other times. We prefer to have fewer people around so that we can do different, more interesting things than when the guides are very busy with larger groups. But there can also be too few people. In 2001, we stayed in a lodge in Alaska's Kenai Peninsula that normally accommodated about 20 guests. We were the only guests. The camp was run by Bill and Ben who, obviously, came to be known, in private, as the 'Flowerpot Men'. Five people were charged with ensuring our welfare and entertainment. It was a beautiful place and we were lucky enough to see a rare yellow-billed loon and a pair of Arctic loons. But, it was a little too much attention; it was too intimate.

## Lodge life

A tap on the door or drum wakes you early. You stumble out of bed, get dressed and go to breakfast. After breakfast, there are activities: a game drive or a walk. Activities are rationed so you compete to get your choice. Sometimes, the order is reversed. You are woken before dawn, have tea or coffee and head out on your activity. You breakfast when you get back. There is lunch. Then, there is the rest period. Around 3.00pm there is afternoon tea and your second activity. Sometimes, the activity – such as a night drive – stretches into the evening. Then, it is off to bed. Lodges use generators for electricity and they are turned off early. Lights out, literally.

Lodges are different to hotels. Even hardened eco-travellers must be prepared for some degree of privation. Visiting Tanzania, we were advised to take light bulbs and tennis balls. At the lodges, there were no light bulbs; guests were expected to provide them. The poorly paid staff stole the light bulbs to supplement their income with capitalist enterprise. The tennis balls were for the sink. There were no plugs. Half a tennis ball makes a useful universal size plug. You never know what will be missing or unavailable or the conditions that you will find yourself in. You have no choice but to try to deal with the situation as best you can. Over time we have begun to travel with a strange array of useful things. They include goggles, fly netting, head torches, travel towels and various building supplies and equipment.

The electricity supply in most places tends to be eccentric at best. Many a time Jade can be found lying in bed reading with her head torch on. At South Luangwa, the generator for the camp electricity was turned off at 9.00pm – theoretically, anyway. Lights out varied because Gerard, the lodge manager, turned off the generator. He had a VCR secreted in his room and a pile of pirated videos – recent ones, by African standards. Lights out was very late one night. He was watching an exciting film and had insisted on watching it right to the end.

With lodges generally being small, isolated places, there tends to be a lot of trust. The rule seems to be that anyone that is interested in animals and has come this far will not steal, lie or cheat. Passports and money are left behind casually in rooms or tents. In the majority of places there is an honour system for drinks. No bar steward sneaks into your room to check your mini-bar consumption. You simply take what you want and write it down in a book. Choice is often limited, but a beer can be very pleasant after a hot and dusty outing.

Gerard did not believe in charging for laundry: 'I am not going to count knickers and then charge a per knicker amount...'

The location, in the middle of the wilderness, also creates hazards. In Alaska, the safety briefings focused on what to do if a bear wandered into the camp. Two siren blasts meant there was a bear in the camp. You stayed where you were, preferably indoors. When the bear was seen off, there would be an 'all clear' on the siren. In other camps, it was informal.

'Just don't get too close,' John, our guide at Katmai, had said with a smile. As we got very close to bears on more than one occasion, we probably got a little casual about the dangers of bears.

The mosquitoes in Alaska were the things that were really dangerous. They were murderous. The beautiful, romantic sunset on the shores of a mountain lake degenerated into mortal combat with an unseen enemy. Jade put on a facemask made of a fine mesh covering her face and neck: she looked like something out a medieval costume drama. In keeping with the occasion, I put on my mask as well. She had terrified me into getting one.

73

'You will be eaten alive,' she warned darkly.

There we sat enjoying the beautiful sunset. In a final romantic gesture, Jade decided to sleep in her facemask as well.

At one stage we had a room with a wood-burning stove. It was the middle of summer but it was freezing. Our guide kindly made up the fire. Jade, who is better at fires than me, agreed to tend it. I had been excited at the mention of fire. It wasn't the romance; I wanted to dry my wet clothes. I turned my white socks into a blackened charcoal grey in the process.

There was a log on top of the stove. I thought that it was a decoration. Jade, more sagely, had wondered whether it was safe to leave it there; it must be all right as it had been there when we arrived and the guide had left it there after starting the fire. Well, it wasn't. We went out looking for bears, moose and beavers leaving the stove burning. The heat ignited the log and it burst into flames. Fortunately, the room was fitted with a smoke detector to protect the camp and other occupants from city slickers like us. We were lucky not to lose all our belongings.

## Private facilities

Travellers from developed countries are obsessed by their bodily functions. 'Appropriate facilities' focuses heavily on the availability of 'private' and 'Western' lavatories and showers. There is the difference between the Oriental (squatting) and the Occidental (sitting) posture for the performance of bodily functions.

Lodge bathrooms are primitive. Sometimes, they are shared, *quelle horreur!* The very thought can be traumatic. People have taken medication to paralyse their bowels for their entire stay. Septic tanks, drop pit or chemical toilets replace sewerage. The drop-pit toilet is a deep pit into which you evacuate your bodily waste. It is covered with lime or other disinfectants. As the pit fills, it is covered over and another is started. The smell is difficult for those used to rose-smelling bathrooms. Then there are the flies who find the toilets an opportunity of a lifetime. A chemical toilet is a bit like a blender and compost maker. When you flush, it uses chemicals and a series of stirring motions to neutralize your waste. It is like an electric mixer. Frequently, you can't put toilet paper into the toilet; there is a basket next to the toilet for used paper.

In the Peruvian Amazon, the camp had shared facilities: pit toilets and showers about 200 metres (656 feet) from the rest of the camp. At night, if we wanted to go to the toilet we got fully dressed, including boots, left outside so as not to bring mud in. Having dressed, we made our way to the toilet in the dark, using a torch to check for insects and larger creatures. In a previous year, a boa constrictor had taken up residence in one of the toilets. It made me consider the coffee after dinner very carefully.

A New Zealand woman we met had stayed at a tented camp in Africa. The amenity block was a separate tent at the edge of the camp. Sitting on the toilet one day, she felt a gentle push from behind. It was an elephant. The elephant clearly had to go. The woman decided she did not, scampering away in haste.

Lodges often don't have hot water. Jade hates cold showers. Despite the heat of the Amazon, the water in the showers was surprisingly cold. Jade did not exactly enjoy it. She stood on the edge of the shower and splashed cold water over her body, squealing. I cheerfully splashed cold water in her direction. At another lodge, the sun was used to heat the water. There was just enough hot water to have a shower in the late afternoon. On cooler days, the shower was lukewarm. In Africa, the water is heated by fire and transferred into raised holding tanks from where it flows to cleanse you, to the benevolent amusement of the Africans. I remember standing in 38.5°C (100°F) heat with the heated water cascading over me. There was no difference between the heated water and normal water that flowed from the pipes. My favourite shower was in an African lodge: a stainless-steel shower-head stuck on top of a pipe. There was a water pump and the shower was open to the sky. In the late afternoon, I had a shower with the dusk sky above me. As night fell, I saw the brilliant stars against the clear African sky.

The cold showers in the Amazon had a macabre end. It began as three small bites on Jade's back near her shoulder blade. We had been bitten by a variety of invisible but effective insects. Even pure DEET – the active chemical in common insect repellents – doesn't deter rainforest insects. Urban insects are more repellent abiding. We found an Avon product to be the most effective – a skin lotion rather than an insect repellent. The smelly thick gunk prevented insect bites, because it was so thick and slippery that the insects just slid off.

Jade's bites did not get better. As we travelled around Peru and Ecuador, the bite marks became three well-defined holes in her back. She was fine most of the time, but on occasions she experienced sharp stabbing pains in her back. Midway through a sentence, she jerked her torso and gasped. At another lodge, Jade mentioned the bites and holes to Rachel, our guide. I was concerned. Even Jade, always reluctant to see doctors, was concerned. Rachel suggested that we see her doctor in Quito. The doctor recommended by Rachel was in Miami at a conference on tropical medicine. The locum did a passable imitation of a fly, flapping his arms and making buzzing noises. He drew diagrams of mosquitoes biting Jade. Jade was to apply a poultice of some tea. He prescribed alcohol to keep the area sterile.

# CHAPTER 3

Jade followed the regime that he recommended to her. We were going to the Galapagos Islands and she thought that the salt water might also help. Her condition remained unaltered. There was a watery, bloody discharge necessitating the purchase of a large number of T-shirts. Conversations with Jade were liable to be interrupted by an unexpected twitch or jerk and an intake of breath.

On our return to Australia, Jade went to see a doctor. She was getting used to the sudden stabs of pain in her back. The doctor took a swab of the wound. There was no infection. The area was surprisingly low in bacteria. As her condition did not improve, the doctor referred her to a surgeon. The surgeon decided to do an exploratory incision.

Picture the following scene: Jade is lying face down on the surgeon's table. The surgeon has used a local anaesthetic on the wound. The surgeon begins to make an incision. The surgeon gasps. This gasping business is infectious. As Jade is lying face down, the cause of the surgeon's reaction is not immediately obvious.

'You won't believe this,' he says. 'Something just looked at me.' An insect had just thrust its head out of one of the incisions.

Jade had been carrying botfly larvae. Botfly larvae develop in warm-blooded hosts, such as monkeys or pigs. The botfly generally sticks its eggs onto other insects such as mosquitoes. When the mosquito sits on or bites an animal, the botfly eggs are dislodged onto the host and burrow into the flesh. The eggs incubate within the host. When the larvae are mature, the botflies fall out of the host and fly off. A mosquito probably deposited the eggs while Jade was having a shower in the Amazon.

The surgeon cut the near-mature botfly larvae out – all three of them. We still have one in formaldehyde in our house, one is with the surgeon and the other is at Sydney University's School of Tropical Medicine. The surgeon and the university staff were excited and, happily, Jade made a full recovery. Various doctors and our travel agent refer to Jade as the 'bug lady'.

The level of privacy at lodges varies. At one lodge, accommodation was in a single long building with rooms next to each other along a corridor. A low wall not reaching the ceiling divided the rooms. Noise carried clearly, especially at night. In our group, there was a honeymooning couple. It was not entirely a blissful and relaxed start to their life together. If nature called in the middle of the night, there were two choices. You got fully dressed for the expedition to the communal toilet block or you used the potty – the supplied chamber pot. Sleep was inevitably punctuated by tinkling, as of a vibraphone, as guests availed themselves of the second alternative. On our last night, there was a lot of noise. Bodies falling about with agitated, stifled screams. No, it was not the honeymooning couple in the throes of nuptial passion: the resident rat had found his way into a room with two American women. They had reacted in textbook choreographed fashion. Their stumbling and colliding attempts to avoid the rat penetrated the silence of the jungle night.

## Lodge entertainment

Unlike normal hotels, there are no televisions or interactive video games at lodges. Lodge life itself is the principal entertainment. Sometimes the wildlife provides entertainment in unexpected ways.

In Africa, we stayed at an upmarket tented camp. The tents overlooked a river. We had to close the tent flap and tie it down when we weren't inside, as we had been warned about vervet monkeys. Naturally curious, they would enter open tents to look for food. One day, a herd of elephants was crossing the river down from the lodge. Jade and I went to see them, forgetting to close the tent flap. On our return, we found the vervet monkeys inside, having a closer look at their human neighbours.

Vervets are spectacularly beautiful. Small and compact, their dark furred faces are gentle in appearance. Their eyes, like many monkeys, are similar to human beings. These eyes now looked at us, startled. Then, they rushed past in a few elegant bounds and headed for the refuge of the nearby trees. We spent many afternoons reading outside our tent in the company of the vervets who were never far away.

In the Amazon, after lunch, most people headed off for the obligatory siesta. I was sitting in the common area. The first sign of trouble was a small number of ants. The few rapidly grew into a flood. They were army ants. Within minutes a column of them about 30–45 centimetres (12–18 inches) wide was marching through the lodge. Workers and soldiers were on the move. The ants were eating everything within reach. The floors of the lodge were being thoroughly cleansed. Any small living creature was devoured, including some insects and small lizards that were hundred of times the size of the ants. In an awesome display of unity, coordination and collective will, they devoured all in their path. The guides and staff tried desperately to direct the ants away from occupied parts of the lodge. If you weren't directly in their way then you could get close and watch them. Fascinated, I got down on the floor to observe them, strayed too close and got bitten. It wasn't serious but it stung. The army ant column took about two hours to go through the lodge. In the rainforest, most visitors worry about poisonous snakes. In reality, it's the ants and other insects that you have to watch out for.

# CHAPTER 3

In the Okavango Delta in Africa, you stay in 'dry' and 'wet' camps. This has nothing to do with alcohol. 'Wet' camps are located within the delta itself in the myriad of waterways and lagoons. The wet camp we stayed at had its own resident hippopotamus. The hippopotamus liked to graze on the carefully manicured lawns of the lodge. Hippopotamuses are large, shy herbivores and, despite their bulk, are capable of surprising speed in short bursts. They usually emerge at night to graze. In Africa, they are the largest cause of human deaths, the result of a startled hippopotamus making a hasty dash for the safety of the water. The unfortunate human in the way is then trampled as the hippopotamus makes a beeline for the water. The lodge warned all guests about the hippopotamus. He was content as it was safe and the lawn was delicious. Why would he want to move? At night you had to find out if he was about. You needed to make sure that he knew where you were. You took care to move slowly, keeping a safe distance from him and making sure you didn't get between him and his access to the lagoon. The presence of the hippopotamus enlivened the otherwise quiet walks to and from dinner at night. Unfortunately, we have never learnt of any lodge that has a resident pangolin. We would be there in the shortest possible time.

There are few things in life we love more than sitting on the veranda of a lodge watching the natural world unfold around us. Some of our fondest memories are of those times. We remember sitting on the side of a river in Africa. Crocodiles sunned themselves on the bank, impalas came down to drink, little bee-eaters flitted back and forth looking for insects, bateleur eagles circled unsteadily seeking thermals, hippopotamuses wallowed in the shrinking river. In the distance, cape buffaloes or elephants made their way to the river, raising clouds of dust. In India, I watched a pair of giant pied kingfishers fish the stream.

In the Amazon, sitting by the oxbow lake, I watched the giant otters swim past – a whole family of them. I heard their cat-like voices. Far above, I heard the screech of scarlet macaws flying past. In the Amazon, dusk brings special sounds. The light in the forest fades quickly and suddenly it is very dark. At one end of the oxbow lake, I could hear mosquitoes. I heard the 'whooshing' sound of swallows and martins swooping through the half-light into the clouds of insects, taking their fill.

For us, the lodges and the wilderness that they allow us to enter briefly are special. For the people who work and live in these lodges and wildernesses, however, the experience is different. In one lodge in the Amazon, we met a young woman who worked at the lodge. She was a gentle and kind woman of Indian descent. She cleaned the rooms and, at dinner, with great formality, she served meals dressed in an old, frayed white coat.

The coat was to please the notions of our German guide. She worked long hours and, by our standards, she was paid a tiny amount. She worked for three months at a time before going home to her family for a short break.

I remember her saying to Jade: 'Manu is a beautiful place to visit, Señora. It is a sad place when you have to work and stay here.'

## Floating gin palaces

In some eco-travel destinations, you live on a ship or boat. Your conveyance and accommodation are the same. They pose different challenges. One of them is seasickness. In the Antarctic we travelled on a Russian icebreaker, the *Kapitan Khlebnikov*. It had once been used in Northern Russian ports around Murmansk and Vladivostok. The *Khleb*, as it was fondly known, had been adapted for tourist travel to the Antarctic and Arctic. Accommodation for 100 tourists had been added, making the ship resemble a surfboard with a seven-storey apartment block on top. Icebreakers don't have stabilizers to get in the way of ice-breaking operations. The *Kapitan Khlebnikov* rolled a lot.

We sailed from the Falkland Islands to New Zealand, completing a semi-circumnavigation of the Antarctic continent. The seas were not especially rough. Even Drake's Passage, the feared stretch of ocean between the Atlantic and Pacific oceans at the tip of South America, was calm. However, we did have days when the swell was heavy and the *Kapitan Khlebnikov* rolled wildly. In the Southern Ocean, at one stage the ship rolled 45°. Two of us had lingered on the bridge chatting to the Russian officer on watch. We were going downstairs to lunch when the ship began to roll. It was an eerie feeling. It seemed that it would flip over. Finally the ballast began to exert its power, the roll slowed and the ship began to correct itself, swinging rapidly in the other direction.

On the *Kapitan Khlebnikov*, everyday tasks became a challenge even in a slight swell. Leaving our cabin required timing actions to the motion of the ship. As the ship rolled away from us, we opened the door (which opened out) and hurled ourselves through. As the ship rolled back the other way, the steel door slammed shut. It was the only way to enter and leave the cabin without injury. If several people were leaving adjoining cabins at the same time, then they comically fell out of their cabins simultaneously.

We crawled along the floor to get to the bathroom keeping our fingers away from the heavy steel doors to stop them being crushed when the doors closed. A shower required wedging oneself in a corner and turning the water on. As the ship rolled, the motion of the ship directed water towards or away from you. I shaved on calm days.

# CHAPTER 3

Our cabin had two bunks. One was aligned bow-to-stern (mine) and the other was aligned port-to-starboard (Jade's). Jade quickly discovered the joys of her bunk. As the ship rolled, her stomach moved up and down, creating a peculiar feeling. She also slid up and down the bunk, hitting her head on the wall, then sliding back down, then up again. Driven by Darwinian self-preservation, I refused to give up my bunk, where I was hanging on in order to avoid falling out of bed.

Our trip on the *Kapitan Khlebnikov* took about four weeks. At the start of the third week, a strange woman appeared on the bridge. By this stage, most people on board knew each other and the familiar bonds and antipathies were clearly established. None of us had seen this woman before. We were passing two penguins standing on ice floes as the ship travelled through light ice. We had seen several hundred by this stage and they had lost their novelty.

'Oh, my God!' The strange woman was screaming in an American accent. 'It's a penguin!' We all looked at each other puzzled. She had been seasick throughout the trip, having to be sedated and confined to her cabin. It was her first day out. She had several scopolamine patches on her neck, slowly releasing the chemical (a truth serum), to relieve seasickness. Most people only needed one or half of one.

The trip to the Antarctic was Jade's idea. To convince me, Jade brought home a video a friend had taken on her trip. The video showed several minutes of the bow of the ship disappearing into the sea that broke over the entire front deck of the ship. The spray hit the glass front of the bridge. I was petrified. I had never been on a ship. I was seasick watching the video. Jade convinced me that the trip would be fun. I gritted my teeth and went. To my eternal relief, I didn't get seasick. This was an immense surprise given my susceptibility to every other malaise.

The sea gods like to remind you of their power. In Alaska, the boat ride to Round Island took about three hours through relatively sheltered waters. We sailed across the swell and the boat rolled. I was fine initially. I have learnt that a full stomach, fresh air and keeping your eyes glued to the horizon staves off the worst of seasickness. Unfortunately, I had to go to the toilet. In the tiny boat, the lavatory was tiny and claustrophobic. That did it. My stomach heaved; my head pounded. Even this short experience of seasickness was unpleasant.

In the Galapagos Islands, our ship rolled hopelessly. It was low on fuel and riding high in the water. One evening, the sea was choppy and we were rolling a lot. At dinner, we sat with a couple from Boston, Tom and Jo, with whom we had struck up a pleasant relationship. The dining room was not full. A lot of people weren't feeling well. The first course was, predictably, soup. That we survived with the obligatory splashing and spilling. The dining room emptied during the soup course. We were undeterred: a full stomach avoids seasickness. By the main course, only the four of us were left out of the 60 passengers.

Seeing walruses on Round Island in Alaska required us to live on a boat. The boat was small. There were only four of us: the owner, an American woman and the two of us. We were on the boat for two nights. The idea was to visit Round Island to see the walruses and the bird life. It was the end of the world, literally. Alaskan weather is unpredictable. It was misty and raining one moment, Aegean sunshine the next. We gained an insight into the lives of fishermen. They fish for salmon during the summer runs. We learnt the importance of self-reliance in this isolated place. To get water, our boat anchored in a small cove where there was a fresh-water stream. The owner made several trips in a zodiac with two containers to fill up the boat's water tank. We had to help. I wondered how he did it on his own.

Refuelling meant sailing for two hours to a tender, run by a couple who had their child with them. They bought salmon from the fishing boats and supplied them with fuel and foodstuffs. We bought fuel there and chatted for a while. They seemed hungry for human contact. He didn't have any fresh fish, having already frozen what he had bought. If we came back later he would have fresh salmon for us. We sailed back that evening, a round trip of three hours, to collect our dinner.

Apart from a few fishing boats, three rangers on Round Island and the tender, there was no one else in an area the size of New York. It was beautiful in its isolation and wild splendour. At night, we used to tie up at a protected anchorage in the lee of one of the small islands. Generally, we were the only boat there. There is a protocol about these things. You don't anchor if somebody else is already there. One night, a second boat arrived and tied up near us. The owner of our boat was outraged. He was no longer alone. He wanted to sail to a more 'private' anchorage. The definitions of 'crowded' and 'private' were different in the gulf of Alaska.

## Gastronomic delights

Travellers have to eat. Sylvia, a woman of Greek extraction, has cut my hair for about 15 years. She has two sons, Charlie and Yanni. The family was planning a trip to Greece. Charlie, upon being told of the trip, looked worried. Eventually, he spoke to Sylvia. 'Is there, like, food there?' he asked.

Food is a form of display. Once, only the wealthy ate at more than a subsistence level. The rich were fat. Now that food is cheaper, thinness is the new luxury. The rich no longer pursue this obvious and accessible pleasure

CHAPTER 3

that is readily available to poorer people. The thin aesthetic means the rich
eat less and get thinner. The poor eat more and get fatter. Middle-class
moralists berate the poor for excess and lack of self-control.

Travel involves cultural misunderstandings around food. The locals have
expectations of how and what rich foreigners eat. You, being rich, will want
to eat a lot. In many traditional cultures there is a reverence for excess. 'We
shall eat until we vomit.' 'We shall eat until we cannot stand.' The amount
of food you are served is fit for a king – in amount. You couldn't possibly eat
their 'simple fare'. Films and the experience of previous guests shape local
knowledge of the eating habits of foreigners. Hamburgers, meat and chips –
'freedom fries' – figure prominently.

Geography and availability shape most local cuisine (that is a polite way
of saying that people eat whatever they can lay their hands on): wild game
such as sea-turtle meat, snakes, rats, monkeys, snails, insects or domestic
animals such as horses, cats, dogs. Some consider the flesh of the pangolin
a delicacy.

The wealthy in these cultures associate exotic fare with sophistication.
In many oriental cultures, there is also the aphrodisiac quality of rare and
endangered species for 'men whose flags are drooping'. You can have a
meal of whole roast civet cats, porcupine steamed with ginger or roasted
cat or dog meat washed down by shots of liquor flavoured with bear's paws,
tiger's penis, silkworm, snake, crow or goats' testicles. This places limits
on experimentation and sampling local cuisine.

There are different survival strategies. The Japanese are not interested in
sampling local dishes. In the Antarctic, the Japanese group ate separately.
Their guide, a pleasant, patient woman perpetually apologizing for her group,
had an endless supply of rice and seaweed. I try to eat what the locals do,
cautiously. Local food is fresher and better cooked than the local version of
foreign food. In Egypt, on the boat sailing down the Nile, I convinced the waiter
and cook that I really wanted Egyptian dishes. From then on I was served two
meals: an Egyptian one and the Western meal served to everyone else.

Eco-travel offers a range of interesting culinary choices. Jade has sampled
most of animal kingdom: crocodile, ostrich, kudu, zebra, impala, gemsbok
and springbok.

'It's like chicken,' she said, chomping crocodile tail. 'A bit dry but gamey,'
she remarked, biting into kudu. She is a cunning logician. 'It's dead already.
How will not eating it help?' She draws the line at endangered species. And
no, she hasn't tried a pangolin. She wouldn't... At least I hope not.

Eco-travel creates practical limitations on gastronomy. The trip on the
*Kapitan Khlebnikov* lasted four weeks. The ship carried food for 80 passengers and an equal number of crew stored in large refrigerated compartments.

# 'NO PLACE LIKE HOME': TRAVEL, FOOD AND ACCOMMODATION

Early in the trip, Bob, the Antarctic historian, picked up a radish from a bowl on the table and munched it with relish. We could hear the crunch of the fresh radish.

'Have them now. They won't last past the first week.'

His bearded jaws worked up and down. By the end, fresh vegetables had given way to canned ones. The menus were dictated by longer-lasting food stocks on board.

Sometimes the limitations are self-inflicted. On the trip to Round Island, the refrigerator on board did not work. There was no working galley. Oh yes, and the owner couldn't cook. The owner also could not count. For one meal, there was a single steak. With Solomonic seriousness, the steak was divided into four and eaten gravely. It was reminiscent of ancient explorers whose supplies had run low. The fresh salmon gifted us by the tender proved a lifesaver and even survived the owner's cooking efforts.

Returning from Round Island, we were stuck at Dillingham airport, having missed our flight because of a delay out of Round Island due to bad weather. There was a Chinese restaurant at the airport. The food was dreadful. It was a gooey, salty, MSG-saturated mess straight from a can. But we wolfed it down. It was the only thing approaching food we had since breakfast days before.

In eco-tourist lodges your eating choices are limited. Back in civilized surroundings after your spell in the wild, you have a greater choice. A peculiarity of hotel food is the 'buffet'. Its origins are in a 'smorgasbord' – a Scandinavian buffet of cold foods containing herring and, well, more herring. The roots of the word are said to be *smor* (butter), *gas* (goose) *bord* (table) – butter goose table. In Singapore, the Prime Minister berated his thrifty citizens about their buffet behaviour. Apparently, Singaporeans are rather intoxicated by the concept of fixed-price buffets. Their appalling conduct was creating a national and possibly an international scandal and contributing to obesity problems among the population.

One hotel had a lunch buffet that stretched for about 6 metres (20 feet). It was full of 'delicacies' and 'specialities' including many local dishes. I tried to parsimoniously sample a selection. The mixture of tastes and flavours was overwhelming. By the end, I had little or no idea of what I had eaten. A little later, my stomach joined the protest against buffets.

One night, we decided to go to a pricey restaurant to sample 'truly authentic' Moroccan cuisine. I selected the 'speciality': lamb with couscous. Our meals arrived. My lamb seemed to be a complete animal. There was enough couscous to create a reasonably sized beach. The meal was on a plate about 1 metre (3 feet) in diameter. The food rose about 0.5 metres (1.6 feet) from the plate. Jade wisely had chosen a more modestly sized fish tagine. The food smelt good and tasted better. I hoed in with gusto. My mother had convinced me that food left on the plate contributes to starvation in the world. History records that Maximus the Thracian ate 40–50 pounds of meat and drank an amphora of wine at a single meal. I rivalled Maximus's achievements that night. The waiter, returning to collect plates, looked at mine with disbelief. I had eaten everything. Guests rarely scaled this height of achievement. He looked at me, he looked at the plate. He took the plate and walked off shaking his head.

Eating out while travelling is not easy. At lodges in wildlife areas, you cannot leave the camp, as then *you* would be on the menu. Most food provided by lodges is simple and remarkably pleasant, particularly since they are very limited in what they can provide. Also the fact that you are hot or cold, tired and very hungry after being out on treks and early morning drives contributes to eating whatever is provided with relish.

When it comes to places to eat in a strange city, the guidebooks are an accumulation of dated facts, factual errors and reviewer biases. At the restaurant, you have to negotiate the formalities and deal with menus in foreign languages. In South Africa, you are served by 'waitrons', a peculiar gender-neutral compression of 'waiter and person'. In Africa, we ate several times at a restaurant where the resident cat would visit us. She was a scrawny little thing. Jade has had cats most of her life. We now share our lives with Alice, a black cat, or, to be more accurate, she manipulates and rules us. This cat had three little kittens. We secretly fed her and her brood. The restaurant would have failed a health inspection but it gave us a sense of belonging and being home.

On any journey, there is a point when you feel homesick. The privations of the journey get to you. In Cuzco, our homesickness was not helped by altitude sickness. On our second visit to Cuzco, Jade and I saw an Italian restaurant with traditional red-and-white checked tablecloths. Returning to Cuzco from Machu Picchu, we decided to eat there as an antidote to our homesickness. We went looking for the Italian. It wasn't there. Now, the centre of Cuzco is not a big place. We searched for our Italian with its red-and-white checked tablecloths, walking up and down every street. It had disappeared. Still we searched. There were no obvious signs of a recently closed restaurant. Where had it gone? To this day, we cannot explain it. Maybe we simply imagined it – a collective hallucination influenced by the altitude sickness.

## Local cuisine

At Kapawi Lodge in the Ecuadorian Amazon, the activity for the day was fishing for piranha. We would travel by motorized dugout canoe for one hour.

A raft would be inflated when we got to the oxbow lake, then we would fish from the raft and eat the piranhas we caught. The white flesh of piranhas is a local delicacy. We set off. The guides had forgotten to bring the pump to inflate the raft. We couldn't go back to get it as the river level had fallen and would not rise again until later in the day. We decided to go to where Uncle Walter lived instead.

Uncle Walter was an older Indian man who worked at Kapawi. He and his family lived upstream from the camp, an hour away in a motorized canoe. Uncle Walter frequently poled his way in a tiny canoe between his home and the lodge. He had a sun-darkened face, was wiry and strong, and said little. There was an enormous dignity about him. Uncle Walter and his family lived in a collection of thatched huts. He greeted us warmly. We headed to a small lake nearby. The piranha fishing at the lake was not a success. Even Ramiro, our Indian guide, didn't catch anything. We had failed to hunt and gather. Uncle Walter invited us to lunch – an act of great kindness and generosity.

We settled down on the dirt floor while he fetched a variety of foods. I remember the agouti – a small rodent, considered a great delicacy to be shared with special guests. We were being honoured. The six foreigners tasted the roasted agouti tentatively. The piece of agouti meat was passed around and you tore a bit off and ate it with your fingers. I sat on the dirt floor chewing the rich and strongly flavoured meat. The generosity and hospitality of this man was amazing. We barely knew him. He barely knew us. Yet, he was willing to share his food with us without reservation. After lunch, we said goodbye and thanked Uncle Walter and his family; several generations were present. I shook his hand and tried to express my gratitude for the great honour that he had bestowed upon us.

On the bank of the river, there was a little girl, one of Uncle Walter's grandchildren. She was pretty and shy with a smile on her face. She had not had much contact with foreigners. Her curiosity and desire to communicate with us was clear. She carried a round fishing net. She threw it into the river in a quick flick and then hauled it in with a twisting motion. She caught some fish. In fact, she had caught quite a few fish. She carried them in the hem of her dress and smiled at me. I talked to her in English. She smiled back before disappearing down the bank, reappearing a few minutes later. She had caught more fish. When she showed me the fish, I clapped my hands and she smiled. Her mother took the fish and put it in a small container in water. They would roast, smoke or dry them later.

I remember that day at Uncle Walter's, his hospitality, his generosity and his granddaughter, who would be a grown woman today. It was a moment of connection that transcended the differences between our worlds. Uncle Walter and she had wanted to share their world with strangers.

# CHAPTER 3

The privations that travel imposes on us are modest. Zaire in 1991
was desperately poor. It was the reign of Mobutu Sese Soko. Backed by
foreign governments as a bastion of anti-communism, Mobutu plundered
the country's immense mineral and natural wealth. (At least, he plundered
what the Belgians had not already taken from the Congo.) The murderous
genocide and civil wars were still ahead. In hindsight, 1991 was a golden
age in the Congo. The poverty of Zaire was palpable. The gaunt and tired
faces of the people spoke of the struggle to get food. If you stopped anywhere, beggars and street vendors came up to you. The land and soil was
rich but there was a large population and primitive infrastructure. There
was a pervasive sense of decay, as if years of neglect and failure had
eaten away the will of the people.

We were there for the gorillas. We stayed at the Paradise Club on the
shores of Lake Kivu. It was an old house built by a Belgian colonialist to
escape the summer heat. Lake Kivu was once the Switzerland of Congo.
There were four Americans and the two of us. (This was where our friendship
with Cindy and Dennis from Boston began. We have now met on three
continents – America, Africa and Australia – and are trying to see if we can
meet up on all of the remaining ones.) After our treks, we talked about the
extraordinary experience of seeing the gorillas. The world outside rarely
intruded into our conversations.

We had returned from visiting a family of gorillas and were waiting at
the side of the road for the car to pick us up. It had been an exhilarating
hour. Cindy produced some red liquorice, sharing it with us, the guides
and the rangers who had accompanied us. The red liquorice fascinated
the Congolese. They had no idea what it was. They accepted it shyly.

At breakfast, I asked if there was 'fromage' (French was the easiest
way to communicate). The waiter would see if he could find some for me
the following day. They only bought the minimal amount necessary for the
guests. There was nothing to spare. The way he repeated the word, 'fromage', spoke of longing and suffering that comes from a deep deprivation.
I realized the crassness and unnecessary nature of my request. I really did
not need cheese at breakfast. I looked at the long and haggard faces of
the Congolese at the Paradise Club. They were tall and skinny with very little
flesh on their bones. They lived on the edge of subsistence.

On our last night at Lake Kivu, it was Cindy's birthday. Jade ordered
a bottle of red wine. We had mainly been drinking the local beer. The wine
was terrible – a left-over bottle in the cellar somewhere. The bottle of wine
cost US$20 – several times the monthly income of the people working in the
Paradise Club. I remember standing on the balcony of the club in the twilight,
looking out at Lake Kivu. We could see the flickering lamps of the fragile

dugouts in the water that served as homes for fishermen. They lived on these boats and tried to feed their families from fishing. It was primarily subsistence economy. Money had no meaning here. I remember thinking of the beauty of the place. I now remember the beauty along with the terrible poverty and suffering of those people.

# CHAPTER 4
## 'Walk On The Wild Side':
## Wildlife Viewing

*... 'You throw your hat to the snake,' our German guide advised. 'It uses up some of its venom in biting the hat, which smells of you. When it bites you, there is less venom. You might survive.' The assembled tourists looked uneasy...*

# CHAPTER 4

## The beaver dam

In the end, it is all about the animals. You have suffered the long journey. You have put up with the (mostly) imagined deprivations of the journey, accommodation and food. Now, it's down to the business end of eco-travel. You have come in the hope that you will see a pangolin. In any case, you will see 'things', even if the elusive pangolin proves true to form.

We are in Alaska, 150 kilometres (93 miles) from Anchorage. The lodge is an old fishing camp, now used for recreational salmon fishermen and eco-tourists. Three guest huts hold 10 guests. Every day floatplanes bring day trippers who go out to see bears, come back for lunch and then fly back to Anchorage. Our guide, Ken, is studying Zoology. This is a summer job. He is relieved that we are not fishermen.

The wildlife viewing is from small boats powered by outboard motors. Each morning and afternoon, we head out into the lakes, rivers and streams, stopping when we see something. Often, we anchor at a vantage point and wait. It is hit and miss. A group of day trippers did not see any bears. They were 'guaranteed' bears. We are unsure of how anyone can 'guarantee' anything to do with wildlife. Wild creatures do not perform on cue.

Today we head out to a beaver dam. It is 6 metres (20 feet) long, a solid construction of tree branches and compacted mud as hard as concrete. At another lodge, the owners dynamited a beaver dam to restore the river flow. Within a few days, the beavers had rebuilt the dam bigger and stronger than before. The owners conceded defeat.

Beavers, as most people know, are large aquatic rodents about 1 metre (3 feet) in length, with distinctive protruding teeth and a wide flat scaly tail. They live in small shallow streams that they dam to make beaver ponds, and as a result, they need a lot of woody vegetation for food and construction of their dams. Beaver activity is evident by the clear notches on branches made by their front teeth. They are active around the clock, and, where humans are about, they are active at night to avoid disturbance. In winter they are active under the ice that covers the lakes and waterways.

The plan is to go to the beaver dam around dusk. The days are long, with daylight till 10.00pm. After dinner we put on our warmest clothing and head out in the direction of the beaver dam. Alaskan summers are colder than winter in Sydney, our home.

On the way, we stop at the floating bog. From the boat, it looks like a lawn at the water edge. Ken races the boat towards the solid green surface. At the last moment, he turns the boat parallel to the edge. The wake from the boat makes the green surface move. Ripples shift across it as if it were fluid. The green surface is a mass of living vegetable matter floating on the surface of the lake. It is about 30 centimetres (12 inches) thick. On the underside, long roots float in the water. The bog is solid enough to walk on. It feels like a trampoline. In the thinner areas the water comes up through to the surface.

We anchor the boat near the beaver dam and wait. We have never seen beavers in the wild. An hour passes. The light fades. A mist floats above the water. It is freezing cold. There are no signs of the beavers.

We are about to abandon the vigil, when Jade sees a movement in the water. Then we hear the splash. There are two beavers in the water, swimming about and foraging for food. One of them has obviously spotted our boat and given the warning signal – a loud slap of the tail on the surface of the water (in the quiet of the Alaskan wilderness, the noise is very distinctive). There is a succession of these warning splashes. Then, they are gone. We assume that they have probably returned to their den via one of several underwater entrances. Kits – the beaver's young – may be waiting for them there.

We wait in almost total darkness. Ken says we must go back. We motor back to the lodge. The cold of the Alaskan evening penetrates our clothes. The river is glassy. A low mist hovers over the water. Other than us there is no one. We have seen beavers!

Towards the end of our stay, we surprised two more beavers in a different part of the river near a main channel. We saw them clearly this time.

'It is strange,' Ken mused. 'I have never seen beavers near the main river. It is unusual to see them there.'

At the same lodge, I remember standing thigh-deep in water wearing fishing waders – in the middle of a salmon-spawning stream. The water was pinkish red with the fish in their spawning colours, the salmon and their eggs clearly visible in the water. We could see them pairing off to spawn, while the edges of the stream were lined with dead or dying salmon. Half-eaten fish lay on the banks where the bears had left them. Signs of bears were everywhere. The scene was primordial.

Ken had liked us and our passionate interest in wildlife. He was excited that we were willing to do different things and willing to wait for something to happen, for something to appear. He was pleased that we were not too disappointed when we saw nothing except the amazingly beautiful scenery. He had taken us to the salmon-spawning stream as a special treat. We were privileged to see it.

## Luck of the draw

Eco-tourism is about seeing wild animals in their natural habitats. A sighting is never guaranteed. It is the paradox at the heart of eco-travel. The Coliseum, the Tower of London or the Great Wall of China are not likely to disappear when you reach your destination. Your chance of seeing things will depend on where you are going and what you are hoping to see. If you travel to the savannah, woodlands and riverine forests of Africa, you will see an incredible array of herbivores: wildebeest, zebras, cape buffaloes, giraffes and elephants. Tourists come to see the top predators: lions, leopards and cheetahs. These are the hallmark species. In Africa, it is the big cats; in South America, the jaguar; in India, the tiger.

Jade and I have been fortunate to see many of these species. They were all chance events. No amount of planning and effort guarantees a sighting. Ensuring you get the kind of sighting where you can take good photos, such as the ones in the wildlife picture books or documentaries, is impossible.

Leopards, for example, are notoriously difficult to see. In 1991, however, on our first trip to Africa, we kept seeing them. Our favourite memory is of a young leopard sleeping in a sausage tree in Samburu in the heat of the late afternoon. She was fairly oblivious to us, having seen tourists before. We became rather blasé about leopards. On a subsequent trip we only had a brief glimpse of one in Namibia and another in Zambia. We stayed at a place in South Luangwa famed for its leopards. Our stay coincided with the full moon. The light makes it harder for them to hunt and they tend to lie low. But they were around. We arrived late at our lodge. Our guide got lost. The afternoon game drive was about to go out. Tired and dehydrated, we stayed behind. On the drive, the guides saw a female close to camp: she was in oestrus, looking for a mate, vocalizing her availability, a low sound like a saw cutting through wood. We were cross at having missed her. At dawn and dusk every day, we tried the places where the leopard was sometimes seen. We never found her.

On the last day of our visit, we went to a wooded area near the edge of the Luangwa River, which was full of tall ebony and mopane trees. It was a favourite haunt of the leopard. We waited in our jeep. The dappled afternoon light in the ebony grove was mystical. Baboons played in the trees. It was a beautiful, peaceful couple of hours. No tell-tale alarm calls came from the baboons or the puku (a small antelope endemic to the park) to announce the presence of a predator. In the morning, as we were leaving, the camp manager asked us to follow him. On the edge of the camp, there was a clear set of paw prints in the soft earth. It was the female leopard. She had walked by the camp, very close to our hut, sometime during the night, patrolling her territory.

In India, we were keen to see tigers and we were lucky enough to see three. In Nepal, we missed a tiger crossing a river by minutes. The female tiger's fresh pugmarks were visible on the riverbank. We heard the barking alarm call of langur monkeys and chittal (spotted deer) a short distance away. In Ranthambore, we tracked a big male tiger by his pugmarks. The BBC crew had briefly seen the tiger moments before. We never saw it.

At Kanha Park in central India, however, a Dutch couple, Harms and Susanna, seemed to literally fall over tigers. On the afternoon that we were due to arrive, they saw a big male close up. It walked straight past them. The guide joked that the tiger had been attracted by Susanna's bright red top. (It was not true. We tried that trick.) On another day, we went off with different guides. They saw another tiger. We did not. The disappointment must have shown.

'We are leaving all the tigers for you,' Harms said, as they departed the next morning. We never saw a tiger in Kanha. In fact, we have never seen a male tiger in the wild.

One guide told us that a friend had recently seen a jaguar after guiding in the Amazon for 10 years. One researcher told us that he was tracking a jaguar that had been radio-collared. The signal indicated that the jaguar was a few feet away. He could not see it. It was invisible in the dense rainforest – perfectly camouflaged. In the end, it is all luck. Frequently, you see signs that a jaguar or other great predator has been there. You rejoice in the knowledge that these creatures continue to exist. You hope that one day your efforts and patience may be rewarded with a brief glimpse of these majestic animals.

Tourists to Africa want to see all the key species before lunch on their one-day trip to a wildlife reserve. Unrealistic expectations create immense pressures on guides. They are offered large tips. Some succumb and end up hounding animals, and putting them under great stress as a consequence. Some lodges are organized around these pressures. Upmarket South African lodges radio-collar or track major predators to guarantee guests a photo opportunity – this is 'wildlife on demand'.

Despite the disappointment of failing to see some species, we have become more sanguine about the uncertainties of wildlife viewing. (Jade is chortling in the background as I write. She finds it hard to believe that I can cope with the disappointment of not seeing some animal or bird that I have meticulously researched over years. I have just learnt to put a braver face on it.)

We would love to see a jaguar – we would be liars if we said that we didn't. We would love to see polar bears and wolves. But we would also like to see less well-known species: caracals, fennec foxes, meerkats, shoe-billed storks, hyacinth macaws, giant anteaters, bush dogs, porcupines, snowy owls, wolverines. We are grateful for what we see in their natural habitat.Of course, we are still searching for pangolins. Maybe our patience and persistence will be rewarded one day. It is, I know, just the luck of the draw.

# CHAPTER 4

## Game viewing: then and now

The practical aspects of viewing wildlife have changed a lot over the years. A Zimbabwean friend recalled a relative's trip to Rwanda in the 1970s when Dian Fossey was building her reputation through her study of and efforts to save the mountain gorillas. He was visiting friends near the national park where gorillas could be found, and one weekend, they decided to try to catch a glimpse of them. Finding a guide, they set off, and after half a day or so, they came upon signs – gorilla dung and broken bamboo saplings. The guide looked cursorily at these markers. The gorillas had been there a long time ago, and it was now too late to get to them and back before dark. The group turned back. The relative did see the gorillas on a later trip – the silverback, some females and juveniles, although they all disappeared quickly into the forest.

These days your trip is arranged months in advance. You need a permit to visit the gorillas. When we went in 1991, there was a maximum of 32 permits costing US$100 each. You could turn up at the office and get a permit. Today, permits are harder to get and they cost US$250. If you haven't pre-arranged your permit then your only hope is that someone doesn't show up. You are allocated a guide, armed guards and porters who, for a fee, will carry your backpacks. The armed guards are there to protect you from the remnants of militias operating in the jungle. In 2000, Western tourists were taken hostage while trekking to see the gorillas in Uganda. The tourists had stumbled across the wrong kind of 'guerrillas'.

The gorilla groups you visit are habituated to humans. Each family is visited daily to ensure that they remain used to us. Eight people are allowed to spend one hour with the gorillas. A sighting is guaranteed. Trackers monitor the accessible groups closely and the gorillas are not surprised by the daily appearance of their strange descendants. The managed encounter does not detract from the experience. For every individual who makes the journey, the emotion of the encounter is real. Given the routine, the magic bears testament to the power of these wonderful, gentle creatures.

## Drives in the park

Much game viewing is done from a car. If we are woken up when it is still dark and our whole bodies are numb from cold, then I take it as a sign of serious wildlife viewing. Jade stands, barely awake, cursing me. Then we pile into the off-road vehicle and move off. The car is open – all the better to see the wildlife. As a result, the open, moving vehicle is cold, while the ride on the corrugated tracks is bone crunching and uncomfortable.

# 'WALK ON THE WILD SIDE': WILDLIFE VIEWING

If you take a cheaper option, then your transport doubles as your game-viewing platform. The soft top of the van retracts, allowing you to stand and view game. Everyone jockeys for position to get a closer look at some exotic beast. There is commotion and jostling as camera lens and angles are explored. A painful fellow traveller takes photos first with a still camera, the lens of which he has already stuck in your face, and then with a video camera.

The cheaper options don't go out at dawn either. It is not a concession to the social and holiday requirements of travellers. You have breakfast and then head off. Travelling between camps is camouflaged as a game drive. You drive around looking for wildlife. When you find something you stop. The guide points out the animal and tells you something about the species and its behaviour. When you have seen enough or taken enough photos, the driving resumes. This goes on for about four hours depending on the day, the opportunities and the enthusiasm of the guests and guides.

The location of your lodge is important. The deeper inside the park you are the better – that is the Das and Jade position. That way, you can get into the park before other people and their vehicles disturb the animals. Day visitors rarely tend to venture deep into the park. Like all theories about wildlife viewing, this can be wrong as well. Sometimes an animal will only decide to move and be spotted after a number of vehicles have passed by and it has decided that it really needs to find a quieter spot.

If you are outside, then you need to get into the park. In India, each morning a large queue of cars forms at the park entrances. Guides get permits from the office. Parks do not open until 8.00am, allowing camp officials to perform their morning ablutions and have breakfast. By the time you are in the park, the best viewing opportunities have passed.

In many Indian parks, the routes are numbered and allocated to ensure that traffic is spread out. In Ranthambore, there are four routes. Two of the paths have a lot of water – lakes and streams. In summer, tigers do not stray far from the water. The path allocated is important. In Ranthambore, one of the routes was closed due to roadwork. We got to drive it only once. It was spectacularly beautiful and had very good wildlife.

So, do you see what you came to see? The herbivores present no problems. A colleague took his autistic son to a wildlife reserve. A characteristic of autism is a certain literal view of events. The child reported that he had seen, 'One leopard, a pride of lions, a herd of elephants and buck, buck, buck, buck and buck [antelope-like impalas and gazelles].'

You may see some of the sought-after predators. If you are luckier still then you may see predators hunt or at a kill. If you are really lucky then you will see some rarer creatures, like the pangolin.

The spectacular range and number of birds enthral the enthusiastic bird

# CHAPTER 4

fancier. Over time, we have become avid bird watchers, or 'twitchers'. Salim, our guide at Ranthambore, had taken us on a spectacular drive near some lakes. We had just seen a jungle cat – a wild relation to the domesticated tabby. They are a different species, rarely seen in the forest. Salim's and our excitement at this sighting puzzled our fellow travellers who were unmoved at seeing the feral equivalent of their local moggy.

We were sitting in the car at the lake. The other guests were after tigers. Frankly, so were we. The others were getting restless. Suddenly we heard a low whistling call. It was the stork-billed kingfisher – an extraordinary looking bird. It is about 24 centimetres (9.5 inches) from beak to tail. Its distinctive feature is a very elongated bill – hence the name.

'He is calling to us,' Salim smiled.

Jade got a brief glimpse of the bird at the edge of the lake. It gave its call again and flew away. The others by now considered Salim and us seriously deranged.

As we left the park, I chatted to Salim. Most visitors were not interested if he showed them rare birds. They had come for tigers. Once he knew of our interest in birds, Salim went out of his way to point out different species. He stopped the car, pointing at the stony ground.

'Look carefully,' he said. We could see nothing, but then, there was movement and the beautiful ashy-crowned finch lark appeared, camouflaged almost to the point of invisibility.

In some places, night drives are available. You leave in the late afternoon, finding a spot by water to watch sunset and have drinks. Then, you drive back, arriving in the evening in time for dinner. The cars are usually equipped with a powerful searchlight to spot animals. At night, you see less, but what you see is different. In Africa, we have seen genet cats, civet cats, bush-babies, honey badgers, owls, nightjars and elephant shrews. At one camp, there was a competition each night to see how many shrews we could see. Some nights there would be 30 or more. It kept you focused on searching and sometimes, we saw lions or leopards.

We came across hippopotamuses one night. Once a year, the sausage tree fruits, and to hippopotamuses the fruits are a delicacy. We saw one mother teaching her young calf all about them.

On that same night drive, we saw a porcupine with her baby. She was black and white and truly magnificent. Her quills were half erect resembling the weirdest hairdo imaginable. African porcupines are large, nocturnal animals that are rarely seen. We watched the porcupine and her young in the car's searchlight. A cautious mother, after only a few brief minutes she shepherded her offspring away into the bush. We were very excited. It was a fabulous sight.

In one place, we had been walking in the late afternoon. A car was to pick us up at the end of the walk and take us on a night drive. During the walk, we caught sight of a giant eagle owl. Some fork-tailed drongos, a common small, noisy insect-eating bird, had given the alarm, scared by the presence of the owl. The giant eagle owl grows to around 1 metre (3 feet) in length and is pale grey in colour. It has distinctive, extended feathers on either side of its head that look like quills stuck behind their ears. The characteristic look of owls is the flat facial disk and large eyes. They have extraordinary night vision and very sensitive hearing – 10 times that of humans. The owl's wings are specially designed along the front edge to reduce air disturbance and noise in flight. Owl feathers are also soft and fluffy to reduce sound. They are efficient night killers that prey on smaller birds and rodents.

During the night drive, we drove through an abandoned airstrip. On top of the radio mast, we saw the giant eagle owl again. The guide turned the spotlight slowly on it. You could see the majestic bird clearly. He snapped his head around to look at us. Owls' eyes are fixed in their sockets because they are elongated rather than round. To compensate, they can turn their heads to an angle of 270°. He turned his head almost totally around to look at us, his huge yellow eyes fixed on us, fierce and focused. In the glare of the light, we could see the large grasping feet, claws glinting. They were 15 centimetres (6 inches) long, curved around the radio mast. We could sense the sharp, razor edges and tensile strength. Then with no sound, the owl flew off. We got one last glimpse of those claws. For an instant, we felt the fear of a victim as the owl soundlessly hurtled through the forest. Its legs and claws would extend in the last moments of attack. Those claws would wrap their vice-like grip around you. You would breathe your last.

How do the wild animals react to you? Animals are used to cars. The smell of oil and diesel exhaust does not smell like enemy, predator or prey. Given that you are sitting in an open car with nothing separating you physically from the animals, it is a strange feeling. Once, we came across a large male elephant. He was busy eating, which is what elephants do most of the day – they have inefficient digestive systems and need a lot of food to get sufficient nutrition. We parked some distance away. You are required to keep your distance from the animals. Animals are not subject to the same restriction. The elephant, 3 metres (10 feet) high and weighing several tons, ambled towards us. He ended up right next to the car. We could touch him. He thrust his trunk into the car to smell us. It is a strange feeling to have a wild elephant's trunk in your face. Curiosity satisfied; he wandered off. He had continued munching throughout.

In one park, a resident male leopard has learnt to incorporate cars in hunting. The noise and smell of cars makes it difficult for antelope, its normal prey, to identify the threat of the leopard. The cars provide cover for stalking as it tries to manoeuvre closer to the prey. It is an interesting aspect of evolution at work.

We spent most of one night drive amidst a large herd of buffaloes. On the way back we came across a hyena. A large and efficient predator with huge, powerful jaws, the hyena has a sloping back, strong shoulders and neck muscles. Known primarily as a scavenger, it is an efficient hunter in its own right. Close up, it is a vision of ruthless killing strength.

We stopped the car. There was Gerard, another guide and us. Hyenas are generally shy. This one did not retreat but stood there sniffing the air. He was interested in something. He approached the car, tentatively at first, then more confidently, coming right up to it. I could have leant out and patted him like the large dog he resembled at that moment. He was smelling the tyres: they were coated in buffalo dung. The hyena had smelled the dung and was having trouble reconciling the bovine odour with the creature before him. Eventually, he lost interest and wandered off.

'Lucky, he didn't decide to take a bite out of the tyres,' Gerard commented wryly. If he had we would have had to spend the night out in the bush.

## Walks on the wild side

You can sometimes see wildlife on foot. For us, the ability to see animals close up on a walk is special. It gives an intimacy and immediacy to the encounter that you don't get from cars. You may see an unused hyena den or insects such as dung beetles at work, or ant-lions constructing traps. You might see the marks of a puff adder that has travelled through the bush the night before. You track animals using their signs. The earliest explorers and naturalists would have seen animals this way. There is a languid pace and a feeling of being within nature. You can't get as close to animals as the smell of humans tends to frighten most off. On foot, the eco-tourist is vulnerable. An accidental encounter with a large predator or mammal cannot be taken lightly.

'We are looking for herbivores smaller than us.' With these wise words, one guide strode out ahead of us.

In Canada, our guide made it clear that our aim was not to encounter grizzly bears. We were looking for the signs of bears: a day bed they made, a shallow construction where they rest during the day, or the rubbing trees that they had marked with their scent.

The guide strode into the bush shouting a loud greeting, 'Hey, Bear!' It was to let any bears know that eco-tourists were about.

One of the walkers was British: 'Polite people, these Canadians. They even say hello to bears.'

# 'WALK ON THE WILD SIDE': WILDLIFE VIEWING

Guides always accompany you. In Africa, we generally had an armed escort – a park ranger armed with a World War Two Lee Enfield .303 rifle. In Zaire, the guide had what seemed to be an air rifle. If there was any danger he would fire into the air to scare the animal away. The major danger was elephants. I was sceptical. I wondered whether there was a Plan B if Plan A did not work.

Some of what we have experienced on our walking trips remains with us. In Africa, we came across a Nile monitor – a large lizard that generally lives around rivers. It is well adapted to living both on land and in water, being an excellent swimmer. Nile monitors prey on insects, rodents and birds, especially birds' eggs. It had heard us coming and hid in a hole in the riverbank. Its tail was partially exposed. We were peering over the edge of the bank looking at the monitor's tail. Suddenly, he backed out of the hole and dashed past us to a branch that was lodged in the side of the river. Feeling secure, he turned and looked at us. Cameras clicked. The monitor posed barely 3 metres (10 feet) away, then dropped into the river with a faint splash and swam away.

In some riverine forest, I sensed something watching us. It was a big adult striped hyena, only about 10 metres (33 feet) away. About 1.2 metres (4 feet) in height at the shoulder, he was looking intently at us. His mouth was open and prominent large teeth were visible. He was panting in the heat. There was a line of foamy white spittle around his mouth. We could see the power in the shoulders and jaws. We sensed the ease with which the jaws could crush bones. (Hyena faeces are generally white from the calcium of the bones that they eat.) The whole encounter took only a minute or two. The hyena moved away in its characteristic, elegant loping gait.

In the Okavango Delta, our daily routine was a boat ride to an island where we would walk about. We frequently came across groups of three or four male elephants. They swam between the islands following food sources. The sheer size of elephants only becomes apparent when you are on the ground. African elephants are 4 metres (13 feet) at the shoulder. Frequently, we were within 10 metres (33 feet) of them. We stayed downwind to prevent them from smelling us. The elephants walked quite close past us, pictures of serenity. One male stopped at a large marula tree. He pressed his head against the tree and wrapped his trunk around the tree. Pushing his huge body against the tree he shook it. He kept shaking. The marula fruit was being shaken off the tree. The elephant stopped. With great dexterity and care, he walked around the tree picking up the fallen fruit.

On one walk in the delta we came upon two cheetahs. Cheetahs live on some of the islands but are rarely seen. Its blistering pace, around 100 kilometres (62 miles) per hour, is famous. The motion is balletic in its grace and beauty. We were walking through tall grass. Our guide heard its low, mewing, cat-like noise before we did. Ahead on a low branch were two of the cats. They had been sitting there scanning their surroundings for signs of prey. In seconds they had disappeared into the long grass.

In Nepal, at Bardia, the camp staff suggested that we take a day hike within the park. Raj Kumar was our guide. He did not carry a gun; all he had was a large knife. He also had our lunch in a backpack. We were walking in a prime tiger, rhinoceros and elephant habitat. Oh yes, and the area also had highly poisonous cobras and king cobras. Bardia is in the Terai, which was once a forested area of great beauty, rich with a wide variety of wildlife. Land clearing for agriculture has largely destroyed the original landscape and only national parks, such as Bardia and Chitwan, are now left. There are monkeys (grey langurs) and numerous species of antelope and deer (chittal, barking deer, hog-nosed deer and swamp deer). There are elephants, tigers and sloth bears; there are Indian rhinoceroses with skin resembling armour plating; there are smaller animals, such as mongooses, and over 400 species of birds and reptiles.

It was a beautiful late winter day with soft light. Raj Kumar's plan was for us to head for one of the streams, look around for footprints and then follow them to see where they led. At the stream, we picked up the trail of a rhinoceros and followed it. After about 40 minutes we came across a steaming pile of dung. The rhinoceros was very close! We were on the edge of a patch of elephant grass, which was rising above head height. We moved forward.

Suddenly, Raj Kumar motioned for us to stop. We heard the snort. It was the rhinoceros and it was very, very close. We inched forward. We heard another snort. We saw the steam of the rhinoceros's breath. It was next to us in the tall grass. We could smell it.

Rhinoceroses are timid creatures with acute hearing and smell but poor eyesight. They also panic easily. We were a few metres away from it. If it became frightened and charged in an attempt to get away then we had a problem. A charge by a short-sighted animal weighing over 1 ton at 50 kilometres (31 miles) per hour does not bear thinking about if you happen to be in its way. The steam from the rhinoceros's breath was visible above the grass in the cold morning air. The snorting moved away. The rhinoceros was wandering off.

Raj Kumar looked at us. He motioned with his head. Did we want to go into the tall grass? Jade and I looked at each other. I smiled ruefully, shaking my head. We never did actually see the rhinoceros.

If it had been a pangolin then there would have been no stopping us. But then pangolins are unlikely to pose much danger to humans.

## Walking in the rainforest

In the rainforest of the Amazon, the biodiversity is staggering. In a small area, there are hundreds of species of trees, plants, birds, reptiles, amphibians and mammals, and new species unknown to Westerners are being discovered on a fairly regular basis.

The conditions, however, are inhospitable. The jungle dictates specific dress codes. Guides wear rubber boots. Fancy Velcro-ed, Gore-Tex-lined, waterproof boots don't last. I had a pair of old leather walking boots. Bees-wax made them waterproof. Jade made fun of them. I was sad when they eventually expired. She places her faith in expensive, ultra-high-tech boots.

You wear a hat to protect against things falling out of trees onto your head: spiders, frogs, snakes.

'You might be chased by a bushmaster [a large, aggressive, very poisonous snake].' If it happens, throw your hat to the snake,' our German guide advised. 'It uses up some of its venom in biting the hat which smells of you. When it bites you, there is less venom. You might survive.'

The assembled tourists looked uneasy. It is unlikely that you will encounter a bushmaster. It is unlikely to attack unless you step on it. We all wore our caps just in case.

Activities include walks or boat trips. There are levels of activity: easy, moderate and hard. 'Easy' means you don't leave the lodge. 'Hard' means torture. You trek in unexplored, wild areas wading through waist-high water hoping that you don't disappear into the mud. 'Moderate' is more civilized, but not easy. You hike natural trails used by forest animals or cut by guides or Indians over the years.

On our first excursion at one lodge, we boated down the river to where a trail started. The river level was lower than Ramiro, our Indian guide, expected. The boat could not reach the steep bank. Ramiro decided that we would get off on the mud flat and walk to the forest edge. The boat ran up onto the mud easily. It was a warning sign. We clambered off and began to walk gingerly towards the bank. The mud was very soft. Our legs quickly went in to our calves and beyond. An older, short Japanese woman was in danger of slip-ping entirely into the mud, at least, in her mind she was. The water and mud was above the top of our rubber boots. Within a few steps our feet were very wet. The boat was long gone. We waded clumsily to the bank in wet socks and flooded boots. Ramiro had skipped quickly across the mud in his bare feet. He waited on the edge of the river to help us up the bank.

On another occasion we were making our way to a grove of dead palm trees, a nesting site for macaws. We had to cross a marsh with about 1 metre (3 feet) of water in it. Ramiro, who had gone on ahead, wandered back casually.

# CHAPTER 4

There was a huge beehive along the way. He had accidentally disturbed the bees and they were swarming. We would have to run past them to the other side of the swamp, from where the boat was picking us up later. We put on our raincoats for protection, then we ran for it. The path wound its way over logs placed across the swamp as an ingenious kind of bridge system. The logs were round and covered with algae and plant material. They were slippery. There were no hand-rails. I have no practical experience of tightrope walking. Jade has 'balance', having studied dance. She cursed under her breath and then strode across the swamp. It was about 200 metres (650 feet). I ran across practising 'rational emotive therapy' – what was the worst thing that could happen? Even the terrified Japanese woman made it across.

The Indian guides are short with long straight dark hair and cherubic faces. In the rainforest, they are your eyes and ears. The forest is dark and relatively quiet. Little light penetrates the forest canopy and reaches the floor. One day, it began to rain. We could hear and see the rain coming down heavily. On the forest floor, there was only the occasional drop of water. Only after the rain had continued for a while did the water make it down to the forest floor. Huge sabre and kapok trees rise hundreds of feet into the air on all sides. Strangler figs rise in twisted shapes on trees that will eventually be crushed by the parasite. Epiphytes sprout from tree branches at strange angles. Vines and lianas hang from tree branches. The green of the forest is broken by the colour of an occasional flowering tree. Shafts of sunlight create striated patterns in the forest. On the forest floor, amongst the decayed branches and trunks of fallen trees, there are mosses, ferns and luxuriant fungi slowly unlocking the nutrients and energy from within the dead wood. You may see a colourful poison arrow frog. Indians use toxic secretions from the frog to tip their arrows. You see ants and spiders. Occasionally, you see large millipedes or centipedes.

The guides constantly look for wildlife. They listen to the forest sounds and follow them. Their sharp eyes pick up movement of branches and trees indicating a monkey or bird. The chance of seeing large animals or reptiles is low. You see signs where they have been. They pick up the sounds of humans walking in the forest long before you are close enough to see them.

You see many birds. The most spectacular are the macaws – parrots on steroids. You see scarlet macaws, blue and yellow macaws and red and green macaws, along with various parrots and parakeets. You see flocks of macaws streak past. You hear the squawking birds. You see them perched high in the canopy – a male and female pair. Macaws mate for life and frequently live for 50 years. They sit grooming each other, hanging at impossible angles from the tree. To look into a macaw's intelligent and curious eyes is wonderful. Hunted to near extinction for their gloriously colourful feathers, this is one of the last places on earth you can see them in the wild.

You hear the chachalacas and oropendulas in tree branches. There are impossibly shaped toucans with oversized beaks, and their distinctive cries. You spot their dipping flight as they search the forest for food. On the rivers and lakes you see hoatzins, with blue faces and what look like disordered hairpieces. These primitive birds feed on leaves that a large gullet full of bacteria and micro-organisms help to digest. The olfactory effects of fermentation in their gullets give them the native name, 'stink bird'. Young hoatzins have three claws on the middle wing joints. When frightened, they jump into the water. When the threat has passed, they use the claws to drag themselves up the riverbank to their nests.

Black skimmers are startlingly beautiful birds with black bodies, white necks and red-coloured beaks. They look like they don't have eyes. Their bills are uniquely adapted to be horizontally flat with their lower mandible longer than their upper mandible. They fly low over the water with their bill just skimming the surface. They eat any small fish that their beaks bump into. We saw a flock of black skimmers fishing a part of the river. Their elegant shapes scythed through the air, flying low over the water. In the soft light, their reflection on the still water was perfect as they flew backwards and forwards looking for fish.

In the jungle, we heard a hummingbird. We heard it but never saw it. It was like the buzzing of an electric shaver. It was very loud, right next to us in a bush. We could hear the furious beating of its wings as it hovered, sipping nectar from a plant.

One afternoon, we went for a canoe ride with Ramiro. We came around a bend in the river. On an overhanging tree, there was a troop of dusky titis, small monkeys about 30 centimetres (12 inches) high. They were dark brown with wizened worried expressions. They had been surprised. There was much squealing as the troop called to each other. Then, with a few jumps, they disappeared into the forest. We could hear them briefly before the jungle swallowed up the sounds.

Near our camp, there was a clay lick where we could see macaws and parrots. The birds use the clay to process toxins in fruits they eat. Scientists do not understand the process. Macaws are cautious and reluctant to come down to the ground. They are wary of the predators that frequently wait at the clay lick. They arrive in large flocks, wheeling around. The sky becomes a kaleidoscope of colour. Satisfied there is no obvious danger, they land. On the ground, they walk in a characteristic staggering, interrogative walk. On a sunny afternoon, the light catches their feathers, illuminating the forest in incandescent colours.

Manu Lodge, which we visited, is built on Cocha Juarez, an oxbow lake that is home to a family of giant otters. In Spanish, the otter is *lobo de rio* – wolf of the river. They are large, up to 1.8 metres (6 feet), voracious and superb hunters. Giant otters have been hunted to the edge of extinction for their pelts. Between 1946 and 1971, prior to a hunting ban, 24,000 pelts were exported from Peru alone. No more than a few thousand survive. In Manu there are probably no more than 60 remaining.

At Manu, we saw the otter family on several occasions. The otters hunt communally for fish. In between fishing expeditions, they spend time on the lakeshore amongst fallen trees. One day, we followed them on a hunt. There were six: two adults and four juveniles, probably the previous year's litter. They swam with their heads out of the water. Then they dived, using their whiskers to feel for movements of fish in the water. Once they detected a fish, they gave chase. The disturbance of the water gave you an inkling of the hunt underneath. Sometimes, a head came up with empty jaws. Then, an otter would emerge with a fish. It would eat the fish in the water near the bank. It would rip the fish apart with its strong jaws. You could hear the otter ripping the fish apart, mewling its pleasure. You heard the begging sounds from other family members for a share of the fish.

We witnessed an extraordinary scene. An adult otter emerged from the water with a fish it had caught. It did not eat it but held up the fish to the younger otters. It then dived with the fish between its jaws. The younger ones dived after the otter that was carrying the fish. The adult was teaching the youngsters to hunt. Later we saw them resting on some fallen trees. The young were playing, chasing each other on and off the branches.

In the rainforest, we frequently came across a colony of leaf-cutter ants – the gardeners of the rainforest. There were thousands of them. Each carried a piece of leaf, some larger than they were. We knelt amongst them. If we were in the way they calmly walked around us, focused on their mission. The leaf-cutter ants do not eat the leaves, but store them in a deep underground chamber in their nest. As the leaves ferment, a fungus grows. The leaf-cutters eat the fungus. A Swedish family with young children had stayed at the lodge we were staying in. On a walk, they had come upon leaf-cutter ants. A child had spotted them.

'Look, look,' she said excitedly, 'The leaves are dancing.'

## Boating along

Another alternative is to view wildlife from boats. In the Okavango Delta, you use a *mokoro*, a dugout canoe that holds three to four people – usually you and a guide. The guide sits in the back and steers. The boat moves slowly through the water among the reed beds. It is a great way to see wildlife – especially the prolific bird life of the area. We sometimes saw hippopotamuses and crocodiles. Fully laden, the water comes up to within a few centimetres of the lip of the canoe. You are literally sitting in the water. The channels are not deep and the current is slight. I asked about the channels.

'They are hippo paths,' the guide said. All the channels are made by hippopotamuses travelling through the swamp.

'What happens if a hippo comes along?' I asked.

'You jump into the water, out of the way,' the guide replied.

In Alaska, wildlife viewing was from boats. The tides were sometimes 10 metres (33 feet). At low tide, we waded across mud flats and shallow water to get to the boat. One day, we noticed movement in the water around our feet – there were flounders everywhere. On the mud flats, clams buried themselves as they heard our approach, while in the water, we saw sea otters floating in rafts, harbour porpoises and harbour seals. On rocky islands, there were puffins and other seabirds, while on land, there were brown bears.

The Alaskan Katmai Peninsula is rich in bird life. We saw a peregrine falcon sitting impassively, looking for prey, though in the main, we saw bald eagles. Our guide John took us to see one of their nests – there were two chicks in there. As we watched, a parent flew in, holding a salmon in its talons – a pink streak clearly visible in the afternoon light. The bald eagle dropped the salmon into the nest and landed nearby. The excited chicks attacked the dead fish ravenously. It was a clear and sunlit day: we could see all the way across the Shelikof Strait to Kodiak Island itself. The fireweed was in bloom; the purple added spectacular colour to the scene.

In Nepal, we boated down the Karnali River for a chance to see severely endangered Gangetic dolphins. Indian river dolphins are similar to those in the Amazon. They both live in fresh water and are almost totally blind, relying purely on echo-location to navigate the murky rivers and hunt fish. In Nepal and India, the river dolphins are under threat from overfishing, human habitation and hunting. The damming of rivers also threatens the species.

If dolphins are about, then you see them when they come up for air, but you need to scan the water carefully. The dolphin's head just breaks the surface of the water and you see its breathing hole. You hear it take a breath before it dives back under the water. Sometimes, it rises further out of the water or swims briefly at the surface. If you are lucky then you see the complete shape. The uneven head and long narrow snout, adapted to fishing in rivers, may be visible. We saw them twice on the Karnali.

There was a village near the bend in the river where there was a funeral in progress. We sat quietly in the boat waiting for the dolphins to appear. In the background a funeral pyre was burning. The dead person's relatives were sitting on the riverbank as the priest conducted the funeral. The black smoke from the funeral fire rose into the sky.

## Alternative conveyances

Sometimes you can go beyond the normal drives, boat trips or walks that are part and parcel of seeing animals in the wild. Elephants are used in some places for wildlife viewing.

In Nepal, we generally used a young female elephant, Raj Kali. The route into the park crossed a mountain stream. At the stream, Raj Kali inevitably stopped. She had a drink making loud slurping sounds as she used her trunk to siphon vast quantities of water into her mouth. Then she would squat slightly to urinate. We suddenly tilted at an odd angle and could hear a sound like a garden hose. Sometimes she did a Number Two. There was a sound behind us like coconuts hitting the ground or water. Elephant faeces are like dry tufts of compacted plant and grass matter. Fully prepared, Raj Kali, under the exhortations of the mahout, was ready to meander into the park.

One day the mahout got down in the middle of the park – nature was calling. We stayed with Raj Kali. As soon as the mahout got off, she immediately attacked a tree and tried to knock it down. Elephants like nothing better than to use their strength to push down trees. It was interesting being on the back of an elephant as it exuberantly tried to push down the tree. The mahout returned. It took a sharp blow to her head from the *trisul* to dissuade Raj Kali from continuing.

We never encountered a tiger on Raj Kali. This was probably a good thing. We learnt that Raj Kali was petrified of tigers, although adult elephants are not under threat from them. Her reaction was to either shake uncontrollably or to run away. The thought of sitting on an elephant as it shook like a large bowl of jelly or careered out of control through the bush was not pleasant.

We saw a lot of Indian rhinoceroses from the elephants – a male on one occasion and, on another, two young rhinoceroses grazing. On a morning trip, we saw a female rhinoceros with a very young calf. One of the mahouts picked up the trail of a rhinoceros. The mahouts wheeled the elephants through the thick forest. We tried to avoid decapitation by overhanging branches as Raj Kali made her way through the trees. The elephants separated to make it easier. Finally we saw the rhinoceros and her calf. The young calf was obviously frightened. The mother was anxious at the approach of the elephants. Rhinoceroses are fiercely protective mothers. The rhinoceros and calf were in view for only a few minutes. The calf had been suckling. You could see traces of milk on its face. The mother turned and led her calf deeper into the forest.

Domesticated elephants made me very sad. I have seen wild elephants very close and looked into their eyes. There is a certain exuberance and spirit in these animals. When I looked into Raj Kali's eyes and she looked back at me, I saw only sadness and resignation. In those big dark sombre eyes, I saw what seemed to me then and still does now, the sorrow of servitude and imprisonment. She was well treated and fed, but she was not free.

## Darwin's footsteps

We spent two weeks in the Galapagos Islands, linked forever to Darwin's study of finches that shaped his theory of evolution. The wildlife experience there is different again.

The islands take their names from the Spanish for 'saddle-like tortoises'. The islands are both famous and infamous for tortoises. Sailors decimated the island's population. Easy to catch, they were taken onto the ships and placed in the hold on their backs, then used as a ready-made supply of fresh meat as required. Tortoises are now protected, but near extinction. We saw the giant tortoises at the Charles Darwin Research Station on the island of Santa Cruz. They hold 11 remaining sub-species of the giant tortoise; three of the other sub-species are now extinct.

'Lonesome George' is the last of the line of giant tortoises from the island of Pinta. Efforts to find another of his species have failed. He spends his days tearing leaves and chewing them contemplatively. Giant tortoises live for over 100 years. Lonesome George has lived for most of the 20th century. When he dies, his line of giants will be extinct.

The wildlife has no fear of humans. You must keep a certain distance from wild creatures, but it is fine if they choose to come closer. The great attraction of the Galapagos is the sea lions. You can swim with them. You can also see and swim with penguins. At one of the islands, you can even see white-tipped reef sharks and stingrays in the water.

Marine iguanas, the only sea-going lizard, sit on the black volcanic rocks, perfectly camouflaged. You don't notice them until they move. Then you see masses of dark spiky bodies, huddling together motionless, waiting for the sun to warm them. If you are close, then you see their half-closed eyes and expressionless faces. By mid-morning, the sun has heated them to a point where they begin to stir. One by one they move forward, determined and purposeful. At the water's edge, they hesitate. Then, they dive slowly into the water and swim out to sea, their heads bobbing in the water as they swim through breakers and waves. They head out to their favourite feeding spots, shallow submerged reefs where seaweed grows. They dive underwater. The water is cold. The marine iguanas' bodies cool rapidly. You can see them swim back through the rough white water. They grab hold of a rock with their sharp claws. It doesn't hold. They try again and again. Finally, they get a strong enough grip. They drag themselves ashore slowly amidst the churning waves. At dusk, large groups of them pile together to maintain body warmth.

There are brown pelicans, flightless cormorants, silver-winged gulls, black lava gulls and herons. There are red-billed tropic birds, frigate birds, waved albatrosses and boobies. There are hawks and owls. There are the penguins that once followed the cold-water currents north and stayed. Frigate birds soar and glide at sea or near the coast. They generally attack other seabirds, forcing them to drop their catch or even disgorge their food. Superbly adapted for flight, with hollow bones and supreme agility in the air, frigate birds are the pirates of the Galapagos. During the breeding season, male frigate birds inflate their red throat sacs in display to attract female frigate birds. Every time a female flies past, the males throw their heads back displaying the size of their air-filled scarlet 'gular' sacs.

The island of Espanola is home to the rare waved albatross, a smaller species with a wingspan of 2.5 metres (8 feet). It is a beautiful bird – the beak is deep yellow, the head is sulphur. We saw nesting pairs minding eggs. We saw them greet and groom each other with the characteristic scissoring of their beaks, like a mock sword fight performed to renew lifelong bonds. There are blue-footed, red-footed and masked boobies, famous for their displays – the 'dance'. The dance of blue-footed boobies begins just before landing, when they raise their bright blue feet to display them clearly. On the ground the dance proper begins with its complex movements. The bird bows and nods; it deliberately struts and mimes the movement of placing nesting material as if building a nest. It lifts each foot in turn – the webbing is fully spread to display the blue feet. At the end, the bird points to the sky, its wings outspread. The male makes a whistling sound. The female honks. It is impossible not to stand there fascinated.

One morning the boat pulled up at Floreana Island. It was not quite light, but I was up on deck. The only other person there with me was a New York veterinary surgeon with a taste for bright-coloured sun creams spread lavishly on her very pale skin. Flocks of swallowed-tailed gulls flew around the boat, their pink feet and large red-rimmed eyes – an adaptation for night vision – visible. The dawn glow gave the whole scene a gentle serenity.

It was then that I saw it – a bird whose feathers were the brightest pink I'd ever seen. It was a flamingo. Later that morning, on a lagoon, we saw a whole flock of them. In the prehistoric past, the flamingos had travelled from the mainland of South America to these islands.

## Ends of the Earth

In 1994, travel to the polar region was relatively novel. There was a sense of pioneering adventure. We travelled on the *Kapitan Khlebnikov*, a Russian icebreaker, doing a still fairly infrequent trip, a semi-circumnavigation of Antarctica. The environment dictates a very different form of wildlife viewing. Most activities involved getting onto land or ice, usually by a zodiac (a small rubber dinghy). Once on land we walked around, generally amongst the wildlife. The icebreaker also carried helicopters to access the interior or spots inaccessible to the ship or zodiac.

On one helicopter flight we were heading to the Dry Valleys, near the Ross Ice Shelf. The valleys are exposed to strong winds that keep the area relatively free of snow. On either side of the valley there are huge hanging glaciers. The helicopter took off, flying low over sea ice and then inland along the valley itself. There were six passengers. One of the passengers, a woman in her 80s, was sitting at the back of the helicopter next to the door. I was sitting further forward. Shortly after take-off I felt a cold breeze in the cabin and turned around. The door was unlatched and swinging open. It was banging against the side of the helicopter. The deafening noise and helmets meant that we couldn't hear it. I could see the sea ice below. The helicopter was bouncing around in the poor conditions. The woman took decisive action. Unbuckling her seat belt, she reached out, grabbed the door from a crouching position and relatched it. She resumed her seat, put on her seatbelt and gave me a toothy grin. The other passengers were unaware of what had happened.

The Dry Valleys had turned into White Valleys. A blizzard had swept through and covered them in snow. Some were disappointed at not seeing the Dry Valleys in their normal condition. Others were excited at seeing the Dry Valleys in such an unusual state.

The temperature was frequently below zero. The coldest, with wind chill, was about −15°C. The ship was wedged into the ice to sit out the blizzard. On the sheltered side of the ship, the Russian crew and some travellers played a game of soccer on the ice.

We acclimatized. We felt the cold less. An air temperature of just above 0°C was positively balmy. I remember strolling out on deck in a T-shirt. There was an announcement about wildlife in view. I didn't have shoes or socks on. I wasn't wearing any gloves. I was about to rush out on deck. It was about −1°C. The steel decks and railing were frozen and icy. If I touched the steel,

I would have stuck to it, ripping off my skin when trying to remove my limbs. Jade reminded me of my state of dress; I pulled on my shoes and gloves before venturing out.

Inside the ship, the temperature was sub-tropical. Preparation for a landing was time-consuming. We put on layer after layer of clothing. We put on underclothes; we put on thermal underclothes, normal warm clothes, some woollen clothes. Finally we put on thick parkas. We pulled on several pairs of socks starting with a thermal sock and our rubber boots or walking boots. Then we put on several gloves and a warm hat making sure our ears were covered. We were now ready to go out. Dressing and undressing filled in the days. With practice, we got better, quicker.

Travel clothing includes noisy quick-drying synthetic fibres. You can hear the wearer's every move. There are trousers with zips halfway up your thigh to allow ready conversion to shorts and jackets with lots of pockets with nothing in them. There are the ubiquitous daypacks, back-packs and water bottles. In the Antarctic, humans are so out of place anyway; the clothes didn't make much difference. There was no way to blend in with the locals.

The ship provided us with bright red parkas that stood out against the whites, greys and blacks of the landscape. The guides could keep tabs on us. What the penguins and seals made of the red creatures that had arrived amongst them, we don't know. Our red parkas had many pockets. On Enderby Island, in the Sub-Antarctic Islands near New Zealand, we wanted to see the crepuscular yellow-eyed penguins. The day had been very wet. We were contemplating whether or not to go ashore again at dusk to wait for penguins. We decided to go back. Jade had her camera. Before leaving the ship she put two extra rolls of film into one of her parka pockets. At dusk, the yellow-eyed penguins appeared.

Jade was taking photos of the penguins and ran out of film. She rummaged around in her parka for a spare roll but couldn't find it. We shrugged our shoulders and sat close together on the beach taking in the moment. A few days later, Jade found the spare rolls of film – both of them. There were so many pockets that she had missed the one with the film in it.

On Enderby Island, the beach is crowded with Hooker's sea lions. The bulls are large and have a tendency to be aggressive, which we discovered when we got off the zodiac. The trick was to stand your ground and make loud noises. The male sea lions would waddle off quickly when confronted. We watched a zodiac with the Japanese group arrive on the beach. They got off in shallow water and waded ashore. The greeting party of sea lions was there. An unhappy-looking Japanese woman hesitated when confronted by one of them. She started to back off. Seeing this, the sea lion bounced across the shallow water towards her yelping excitedly. The woman tried to turn and run. She fell into the water along with all her expensive camera gear. The last we saw of her, she was being ferried back to the ship.

A 'wet landing' meant that you got off the zodiac into, hopefully, shallow water. A 'dry landing' meant you got off on rocks or a dry spot. Wet landings meant rubber boots; dry landings meant trekking boots. Occasionally, a dry landing turned into a wet landing when the zodiac had to use a different landing point. To get into the zodiac you walked down a narrow gangway on the side of the ship. The zodiac driver manoeuvred the craft, wedging it under power against the side of the ship. You hopped on during the brief instant when everything was aligned. This all required a fine sense of timing. There was no margin of error. On the zodiac you sat down quickly on the edge and slid towards the front. If you survived without being pitched headfirst into either the zodiac or the water then you had done well. Getting back on board required the same thing in reverse.

The *Kapitan Khlebnikov* was moored off one of the Sub-Antarctic Islands. There was a heavy swell, 3 metres (10 feet). The zodiac ahead was trying to dock. The first person got onto the gangway. It was a close call. The zodiac driver brought the craft close as the ship rocked down towards it. The passenger jumped onto the gangway helped by two Russian sailors and scooted up it. The zodiac made a second pass to disembark the next passenger – a research scientist from New Zealand. She tried to get back on the ship as it rolled sharply towards the zodiac. The gangway dipped into the water. The Russian crew and the woman were in the water up to their necks, and their life jackets opened, triggered automatically by their immersion. They were absolutely soaked. We were now definitely worried. There was much radio chatter between the zodiac drivers and the bridge. The ship swung around into the swell making it easier to get back on.

On another voyage, they tried to launch zodiacs from a moving ship. The first zodiac tipped over, dropping the driver in the water. The water was cold – about 0.5°C. They tried to launch another zodiac to rescue the first driver. It too tipped over, landing the second zodiac driver in the water. In this water temperature, they had maybe 10 minutes to get to the two men. The cold would trigger hypothermia, and as their core body temperature fell, vital functions would turn off and they would die. A third zodiac was launched successfully. It fished out the two zodiac drivers. Fortunately, the ship had several baths, two of which were filled with hot water to warm up the drivers. They were fine and suffered no permanent injury.

In the Antarctic's brief summer, there is 24 hour sunlight. Jade spent night after night trying to photograph the sun slipping momentarily below the horizon and reappearing. There were arguments over whether it was a sunrise or sunset. The almost permanent light meant that wildlife viewing was possible at all hours. The expedition leader was keen to 'seize the moment'. We spent hours on deck watching fantastic shapes of ice appear, including huge icebergs. On the ice itself, there were crabeater, weddell and ross seals. Penguins would appear close to the coast. In the open sea, we saw minke whales, humpback whales and orcas. Sea birds were always about: petrels, fulmars and seagulls. Two huge wandering albatrosses flew near the ship on their restless globe-encircling travel. It was mesmerizing.

We had been told that there was no chance of seeing emperor penguins – the largest penguin species. They stand about 1.5 metres (5 feet) high and are the hardiest of birds, breeding in the Antarctic winter. Documentaries show groups of ice- and snow-covered adults and chicks huddled close together in blizzards to stay warm. Little is known about the summer range of the emperors. Malcolm McFarlane, a member of the New Zealand Antarctic Programme, had managed our expectations about seeing any.

Late one evening there was an excited announcement that an emperor penguin had been spotted on the ice. The ship stopped. Passengers poured onto the deck. Cameras clicked and video cameras whirred. During the evening and night, emperors were repeatedly spotted on the ice in small groups of seven or eight. By the end of the night we had seen over 50 birds. At one point, the ship manoeuvred right next to an ice floe on which the penguins were resting. Most of the penguins decided that this was too close and dropped onto their stomachs and paddling away across the ice at speed. One individual wandered over for a closer look at the ship. His sulphur yellow and orange bib was superb. The dark black head and silvery body was clearly visible. He trumpeted excitedly at the ship. Over the next few days, we saw several hundred emperor penguins. We must have passed through part of their summer range.

'This is so unusual,' mused Malcolm having spent the evening and night with us on deck. I sometimes think we should ask Malcolm to take us in search of our elusive pangolin. He would probably stumble across hundreds of them.

We stopped at Cape Adare to see a colony of around 250,000 adelie penguins. Adelies are small, black and silver in colour with smallish eyes and look like a cartoon of a penguin. It was a glorious sunlit day under blue skies. Cape Adare is a vast plain ringed with volcanic cliffs. There were freshwater melt ponds along with the ever-present smell of penguin guano. It was the end of the nesting season and thousands of chicks were moulting. Their down was a light grey. They stood around uncomfortably, waiting for their parents to return from fishing trips. The young chicks chased any returning adult and pleaded for food. The penguins found their own chick and regurgitated a mix of krill and squid into their open mouths.

At the gravel beach, adults gathered at the edge of water watching intently. Then they would dive in almost simultaneously and swim quickly through the water. They clustered together, wary of the presence of predators – leopard seals – near the colony.

In amongst the penguins you saw fat brown skuas. The skuas seek out the weaker chicks and kill them ruthlessly, literally pecking them to death. They make a hole in the body and extract most of the flesh and organs through the hole.

In places the snow was bloodstained and the discarded carcasses of young penguins lay here and there on the ground. Other penguins wore small, bloody puncture wounds on their otherwise perfect skins.

We visited Macquarie Island to be greeted by thousands of king penguins. Slightly smaller than the emperors, kings are extremely curious and engaging birds, with the comical gait typical of large penguins, and they could be described as the extroverts of the penguin family. Surrounding the ship, they trumpeted and splashed with excitement all around us. In the zodiacs, we were encircled by the curious birds and we had to make our way through large groups of them. On the beach they followed passengers. A woman wearing a very colourful Gore-Tex jacket caught the attention of a small group of kings, who followed her, waddling behind. Curiosity got the better of one of them. He bent his head, extended his neck and gave the woman a short, sharp peck with his beak.

There was also a large colony of royal penguins. The royals are much smaller than the emperors and kings, with a distinctive array of yellow feathers on their heads, lending them the appearance of punk rockers.

Among the king and royal penguins there were several large elephant seals – large grey brown barrels of blubber. They were moulting – elephant seals shed their skin annually. They must find it annoying and uncomfortable; they lay around snorting and scratching on top of each other. Jade was on the ground taking a photo of one of the bigger adults. His prominent nose was evident. A large king penguin walked into the scene and strode past the elephant seal, paused for a second to look and then, quickly and surreptitiously, leant across and gave the seal a violent peck on its nose, before moving on. The elephant seal had no chance to react.

On Campbell Island, we climbed the green peat-bog hills to see nesting sites of the royal albatross. The royals are a species of large albatross that are closely related to the wandering albatross. We found a nest and sat in tussock grass for several hours to be near to them. When the breeding season is over, the birds leave Campbell Island and take to the great Southern Ocean. The sub-adults spend years at sea. They eventually return to the island to mate.

# CHAPTER 4

As the winds picked up, the albatrosses took off from the cliffs. Several flew close to us. We heard the hissing sound of the air flowing over their wings first, then we saw the birds flying past, riding the wind on their huge 3-metre (10-foot) wingspan. At the edge of the cliffs, several light mantled sooty albatrosses flew by. They are perhaps the most spectacular of all the albatrosses, with grey heads and silver bodies. We heard the cat-like sounds of them calling to each other. Over the sea we saw two – a male and female – flying together, riding the air currents in perfect synchronization.

We got to see numerous whales, but one sighting remains very special. At 30 metres (100 feet) long and 160 tons, the blue whale is perhaps the largest animal ever to have inhabited the Earth. I think that I may just have glimpsed one. Would I trade a sighting of a blue whale for one of a pangolin? Now there's a tricky question…

Sunday 30th January 1994: we were sailing across the Amundsen Sea. Most people had gone down to dinner. A couple of us were still on the bridge chatting to Sacha, the officer of the watch. We all saw it almost simultaneously – a huge spout from a whale, a *very* large whale. Sacha turned the ship in the direction of the spout. By the time we got closer, the whale had sounded and dived. When they dive, whales leave an impression of their flukes on the water. The fluke prints in the water were enormous. We chatted excitedly to the guides and naturalists. Could it really be a blue whale? Hunted to the edge of extinction, little is known about them and their behaviour. Scientists theorize that blue whales use thermoclines (layers of water in the deep ocean of differing temperature and salinity) to communicate with each other. It was exciting to know that they continue to exist, leading their solitary, nomadic lives in the great expanses of ocean.

The Ross Ice Shelf is an astonishing ice sheet floating on the water. The approximate size of France, it extends hundreds of miles into the sea.

We woke up to find the ship next to the shelf. It was a magnificent clear sunny day with calm and mirror-smooth seas. The shelf rose up 30 metres (100 feet), its white cliffs stretching as far as you could see. We were ferried by helicopters onto its surface. It was a magical experience standing there, experiencing the stillness and incomprehensible enormity – a vast unbroken expanse of white extending to the horizon. On the edge of the shelf, we spotted a large pod of orcas. They were cruising around the edge of the ice hunting for seals or penguins. We spotted several penguins on a small ice floe – they had seen the orcas and were terrified. Swimming around the ice repeatedly, the orcas used their huge bodies to create bow waves in an attempt to unsettle the floe and force the penguins into the water.

The Great Whale Show happened later in the voyage at McMurdo Sound. We had visited the US and New Zealand Antarctic bases and were sailing away from the base when we spotted several pods of orcas. There were more than a hundred whales: males with their huge dorsal fins protruding 2 metres (6.5 feet) out of the water and smaller females with calves alongside them. They were right next to the ship. Some were spy hopping, raising their heads vertically out of the water to get a better view of the water surface or ice edge. They were also trying to get a better view of us. The Great Whale Show lasted over an hour. The naturalists and crew had obviously never seen anything like it either. The ship was manoeuvred as close as safely possible to the whales and ice edge. The stern deck of the *Kapitan Khlebnikov* was crowded with passengers, naturalists and almost all of the crew. Eventually the whales began to disperse. The ship resumed its journey. The sunlight penetrated gaps between the clouds that had moved in. Shafts of light fell onto the silvery ice. Between the ice floes and open leads we could see minke whales swimming and diving beneath the ice to feed. In the distance we could see the Trans-Antarctic Mountains.

## Hiding and waiting

Sometimes, you can just sit and wait and let the animals come to you. In Manu, there was a raised platform in a kapok tree about 40 metres (130 feet) above the forest floor in line with the forest canopy. It was a small square of wood, probably 3 square metres (10 square feet). It was a misty, damp morning. There were six guests, two guides and four people from the camp to do the hoisting up to the platform. The guides and camp workers worked out our weights. We would be hoisted up from heaviest to lightest.

(These days I understand there is actually a set of stairs. 'It was harder in my day,' I rail.) Anyway, I put on my harness. Then the four men pulled on the rope. The rope went tight and gradually I rose through the canopy layers. At the top a guide, El Gato, secured my restraint to a safety rope and pulled me towards the platform. He helped me clamber on to the platform. The platform had no railings. Jade gradually appeared from below the tree and strode onto the platform. I am uncomfortable with heights. I had parked myself firmly in the middle of the platform. Jade is extremely comfortable with heights. She walked unhurriedly to the edge and looked down

'Just what I have always wanted,' she said. 'A tree house.'

We saw lots of birds in the trees close by and flying past. People have had close encounters with monkeys: emperor tamarins and howler monkeys. We were not that lucky, but it was a great perspective of the rainforest. To get down you clambered into a fork in the tree where El Gato unhooked your safety rope and hooked you instead to the harness. Then you stepped off into thin air. El Gato had to push me out. You saw every layer of the forest as you descended slowly to the floor.

In Namibia's Etosha Pan, the campsites have artificial waterholes. Wildlife comes down to the waterholes, especially during the dry season. The waterholes are lit at night when visitors gather with food and drinks to keep an evening vigil for animals. We saw zebras, giraffe and elephants. A pair of lionesses came down for a drink. A family of mongooses lived near the waterhole and inevitably appeared at dawn and dusk. They played and quarrelled in the endearing way that mongooses have.

In India, we met with the Director of the Corbett National Park at his office. He took us to a hide that had been recently constructed nearby. It was a beautiful spot overlooking a stream. While we were there we heard the sounds of elephants. They were in thick jungle on the other side of the stream, about 100 metres (330 feet) from where we were. We could hear branches breaking and the rumbling sound of elephants communicating with each other. We stayed for an hour but they did not appear. The Director was quite content. He was as happy listening to the sounds of the animals in the forest as he would have been to see the creatures themselves.

In the Aberdare Mountains in Africa there are two famous lodges: Treetops and the Ark (which is located in a park overlooking a waterhole). Most people spend a night at one of these venues. You can stay on the open deck throughout the night watching for wildlife. The park authorities scatter mineral salts on the ground near the waterhole in order to create an artificial salt lick that attracts the animals. We spent one night at Treetops. It was an interesting novelty. We spent much of the night watching. We saw elephants and a lone rhinoceros. In the early morning a herd of buffaloes come down to drink. Lions and hyenas also came down.

The elephants arrived at dusk. The smell and sight of the water excited them. They trumpeted loudly and ran towards the waterhole. There was a family of ducks there. One of the young elephants decided he did not want to share the waterhole with the ducks. He charged at them, flaring his ears and flapping his trunk. They took little notice. The ducks just waddled out of the way. When a white rhinoceros appeared, the elephant tried the same with him. The large rhinoceros was having none of it – he put his head down and charged. The elephant beat a hasty retreat.

## Tiger show

Visitors are eager and anxious to see wildlife in their short and crowded holidays. I remember young American men at a lodge in the Masai Mara:

'I want a cheetah today. I want to see it hunt. I haven't got any video of that. It would be really coooool!'

The unrealistic demands place enormous pressure on guides and parks. There is a delicate balance between seeing animals and letting them live naturally. The worst effects are hounding animals to provide tourists with a good and close view. Wild animals may be fed, encouraging them to approach humans aggressively in search of food. If food is available then it can lead to loss of hunting habits, reliance on unnatural food sources and over-breeding resulting in subtle changes in the natural balance between species.

In Samburu, a car spotted a leopard. Once one car makes a sighting of a top predator, other cars make a beeline for the area. The cashing-in is literal. The guide's tips depend on success in finding sought after species for the visitors. Twenty vehicles pursued the leopard. It took refuge in a thorny thicket. There was a traffic jam. We barely glimpsed the animal. Jade spent much of the time photographing the amazing crush of cars around us.

The cruellest form of wildlife exploitation is the 'Tiger Show' devised by Kanha National Park, in India, to make it easier for visitors to see tigers. In the morning, the rangers set out on elephants to track a tiger. If they find one they use elephants to contain it in a small area. Then, the 'Show' commences. Rangers conduct elephant-back visits to the tiger for an extra fee. The activity is justified in that tigers are difficult to see in the wild and it ensures that visitors see one.

The tiger is usually a female. Bigger male tigers are likely to charge and attack the elephants. The tiger has usually made a kill – a spotted deer or other herbivore, and is therefore easier to contain, as she will be reluctant to abandon her hard-won prey. The rangers hem the tiger in all day. Tigers generally require a lot of water, especially when they have just killed, and they deny it the opportunity to drink. For one Tiger Show, a beautiful, young tigress was held for three days. It was an act of excruciating cruelty, all in the name of eco-tourism and conservation.

In the Masai Mara in Africa, naturalists have noticed the changing behaviour of cheetahs. Cheetahs rely on their great speed for hunting small antelopes such as Thompson's gazelle. The animal has little in the way of power, so is unable to defend a kill from larger predators such as lions and hyenas. Under natural conditions, cheetahs lose a certain portion of their kills to other more powerful hunters, but eco-tourism has shifted this balance. Eco-tourists are keen to see cheetahs, especially to see them hunting – like on *The Discovery Channel*. Tourists make it difficult for cheetahs to hunt. They need to get very close to their prey and cars make this difficult, as the herbivores are more wary. Lions and hyenas use cars at a cheetah kill as a marker to locate the kill and drive the cheetahs away from their prey. As a result,

CHAPTER 4

cheetahs now find it difficult to hunt normally during the cooler early morning and dusk hours. They hunt during the middle of the day when the tourists are back in their lodges resting by the pool. The larger predators are also less active during the middle of the day. Hunting during this period of the day is both stressful and difficult. A vital constraint on the cheetah's ability to sustain its speed is the capacity to lose heat – hunting at this time of day limits the burst of speed a cheetah can sustain. Cheetahs are less successful in the hunt and place greater stress on their bodies, and they are now severely endangered in most parts of Africa.

## Watching and waiting

For the addicted eco-traveller, watching wildlife is a game of chess. There is the uncertainty of the quest, the excitement of spotting a wild creature in its natural habitat. It is a game you play against yourself, against others in your group, against the guides and, in the end, against chance itself. It is intoxicating.

In Manu, on a boat trip, a brown shape retreated quickly into the forest upon hearing the sound of the motor. I carefully memorized the specific part of the river. On the return trip, in that part of river, I scanned the river and its surrounds. In the water were two capybaras – the world's largest rodent.

'Capybara! Capybara!' I shouted. The animals swam towards the shore and stood at the water's edge. In the sunlight, the water shimmered on their fur. Everyone was taking photos, but I had spotted them first.

Canada's Johnstone Strait is a famous place for seeing orcas. Large pods often join together in 'super' pods of hundreds of whales. They feed on salmon. They do not dive deeply to feed, making them relatively easy to see. Unfortunately, we weren't lucky enough to see the large pods there. The trips are on motorboats. When one craft sights a pod, the other boats steer in that direction. The radio chatter was not promising. The orcas were in a different part of the Strait. The prospects of a barren day loomed large. Everybody was a little disappointed and the lookout was less enthusiastic.

I scanned the waters looking for a sign – it was a forlorn hope. But then I saw what looked like a dorsal fin. I wasn't sure, but another one appeared: definitely, an orca. It was a small itinerant pod – a male, a female and two juveniles. We radioed the position of the pod. Another boat from Vancouver Island joined us. A guide identified the male by the unique colour and shape of its dorsal fin. It was definitely an itinerant group. We spent an hour with them. They circled a rock ledge where a number of harbour seals were hauled up. The harbour seals had spotted them and took the wise decision to stay out of the water.

There are different strategies in wildlife viewing. Gerard, our guide in Africa, believed in sitting and waiting. If you found something, you stayed with it and waited to see what happened. At Moremi Reserve, Theba believed in moving. We were hoping to see wild dogs there. The dogs have distinctive brown and black stripes giving them their common name – painted dogs. The camp cook who was with us spotted them: a family of wild dogs resting under a tree. We pulled up and watched, wondering whether to wait. Superb hunters, wild dogs generally look for prey during the day. It would be great to see them in action. Theba decided that we should keep moving and check on them later. When we came back, they were gone. They had slipped away and we had missed our chance.

Sometimes, you see wildlife in the most odd places. In India, great hornbills are an attraction. Great pied hornbills are huge, 1.25 metres (4 feet) in length, with characteristic long curved beaks. In flight, their wings make a loud droning sound, like a helicopter taking off. It is an incredible, unforgettable noise. Near a river, we heard the tell-tale wing beat and looked up to see one flying past. Another day, near the entrance to the park, a guide came running up to us.

'Come quick,' he shouted. Just outside the entrance in a large fig tree sat eight of the birds. They love figs and the tree was fruiting. Too full and tired to fly, they had roosted in the tree overnight.

There is a game of hide-and-seek between you, the viewer, and the animal. In Kanha, we heard the alarm call of a langur monkey. The calls were about 15 metres (50 feet) from us. The forest was thick and we could not see anything. The alarm calls continued. There had to be a tiger or leopard. We waited. Other cars pulled up seeing us parked there. We were in a jeep with three young Norwegian women. The guide and I insisted that we wait. We waited. The other cars soon gave up. Undeterred, we hung on for another hour. In the end, we drove on. An hour later, we drove back along the sandy track to the same spot. There was no sign of activity. The guide looked carefully at the ground. On the sandy soil there were the clear, fresh tracks of a large leopard. The prints lay on top of the jeep tracks. The leopard had waited us out. Once we had left, he had walked down the track undisturbed and disappeared into the forest. The guide, Patel, and I looked at each other full of admiration at the crafty feline. The Norwegians were mystified.

## Eco-tourist species

There are many different species of eco-tourists. There are people for whom animals and natural history are irrelevant. For these travellers what matters is that they see the major animals on 'the list' so that they can say they have seen them. In Africa, we travelled for 10 days with an American veterinary surgeon. He couldn't tell the difference between a warthog and an antelope.

We got used to the sound of a drawling voice tinged with a back-country American accent: 'What is that we're looking at?'

At the end of the trip, he sat down with Benjamin, our driver and guide. He opened his East African travel book.

'Have we seen an eee-laaand?' he asked.

Benjamin replied in the negative.

'Why not? Why didn't we see an eee-laaand?'

In the Antarctic, the Japanese group was mystifying. While other passengers fell quickly under the spell of the beauty and wildness of Antarctica, the Japanese looked permanently displeased. There was no animation or excitement. They only became animated when they discovered that the glacial ice was many thousands of years old. They took some back to the ship to drink with Scotch. It had therapeutic properties. Had they really travelled to the Antarctic to drink Scotch with thousand-year-old ice?

Then there are the other travellers who come to see all the creatures that share the remaining tracts of wilderness on the planet. They are genuinely interested and delighted to see all types of wildlife, not just the signature species. They are knowledgeable, patient and take an interest in everything that there is to see and experience. They revel in the knowledge that they are privileged visitors to unique and wonderful worlds.

## Wild memories

The attraction of the wild goes beyond simple explanations. It is visceral. In the wild places and among the wild creatures we seek, there is serenity and peace. For us, each encounter is special – they remain an essential part of our lives. The moments we hold close are these connections with wild animals, exhilarating and powerful experiences that make our lives worthwhile.

In the Galapagos Islands, we were in a boat.

'*Tortuga! Tortuga!*' the boatman shouted. In the water was a mating pair of sea turtles. The male was above and behind the female whose head was barely above the water. The male slipped off the female and slid into the water. In a few seconds the turtles disappeared into the sea. On the shore we walked along a line of dark volcanic rocks. The sun gradually set behind the dark clouds. Bright red sally lightfoot crabs scurried across the rocks. A brown pelican settled down for the night, head tucked into the body, silhouetted against the setting sun.

# 'WALK ON THE WILD SIDE': WILDLIFE VIEWING

Off Batholome Island, we snorkelled. There were blue triggerfish and colourful reef fish. A bright orange octopus swam into deeper water. We swam towards the sea lions. In a single sinuous motion they effortlessly changed direction and moved away. Then they turned and began to swim towards us, twisting away at the last moment with astonishing speed. The enchantment and rapture of sea lions is impossible to describe.

In the Amazon, one afternoon, we travelled to a salt lick. At dawn and dusk forest animals gather to extract mineral clays. A family of red howler monkeys was at the salt lick. Red howlers are large monkeys that inhabit the canopy. Their cry is astonishing – a loud roar that reverberates through the treetops, carrying kilometres through the forest, marking their territories. The Japanese woman described it as 'the sound of a tsunami'.

As we approached, they were retreating into the nearby trees, to settle in for the night. Some were sitting quietly on the branches of a tree about 10 metres (33 feet) above us. Trying to get a better view, I forgot to look where I was putting my foot. I felt my leg slip. Putting your leg into a hole in the Amazon is not wise. Snakes, such as the famed brown bushmaster, like to hide in them. I withdrew my leg hurriedly. The monkeys simultaneously turned to look at the excitement. A young howler cocked its head to scrutinize the clumsy human below.

As we walked back we heard something moving through the trees. It was a troupe of squirrel monkeys. They are striking in appearance with black snouts, black upper heads and white fields around their eyes. They have very large ears giving them a comic appearance. There were hundreds of them: adults, young, infants on their mother's backs. The monkeys were all around, passing less than 1 metre (3 feet) from us, and they showed no fear whatsoever. The young monkeys often stopped to take a good look at us – strange monkeys dressed in khaki trekking clothes and colourful raincoats. It took them almost an hour to pass. We watched, captivated by their presence and proximity.

Towards the end of the voyage on the *Kapitan Khlebnikov*, we approached the Balleny Islands, a tiny spot of land off the coast of Antarctica. We were near Sturge Island (latitude 67'34.79 south; longitude 164'52.43 east). There was a tiny spit of an islet near the shore. We were to attempt a landing. We might just be the first human beings to ever set foot on this point of the planet. It would be some compensation for missing out on Peter I Island. At Peter I, our group was the last scheduled to be ferried to the island for the dubious honour of being one of few people on Earth to land on this speck of barren ice and rock. The weather had closed in while the helicopter operations were proceeding, and only one or two groups made it across. On the Balleny Islands, we were not going to be denied.

CHAPTER 4

The islet was about 100 metres (330 feet) long and about 40 metres (130 feet) wide – an inhospitable rocky outcrop with a small steep rocky beach. Jade and I were among the first to scramble ashore. A number of weddell seals at one end of the island did not look pleased at the arrival of potential colonizers.

In India, we were driving through a forest. A pair of lapwings, a type of plover, flew near the path. Suddenly, a crested serpent eagle flew past (the name comes from its large crest that can be erected as a ruff.) The eagle had taken one of the lapwings in flight. The eagle flew to a nearby branch. We could see both it and the crushed, bloody body of the lapwing. The eagle looked at us. With a casual flap of its huge wings, it flew deeper into the forest, the dead lapwing held firmly in its talons.

In Etosha, at a waterhole, we watched lions at a kill. Vultures waited at a distance for the lions to finish. A flock of red-billed queleas wheeled around the waterhole looking to land and drink. Queleas are tiny finches about 12 centimetres (5 inches) long that congregate in large flocks of thousands of birds. A sudden movement caught my eye, a brownish streak moving at a very high speed. It was a lanner falcon. Falcons are the fighter jets of birds of prey. The peregrine falcon is famed for it ability to reach astonishing speeds in flight, while the lanner is a medium-sized falcon, about 30 centimetres (12 inches) in length, which flies rapidly with a characteristic fast angled dive when chasing prey. The lanner dived from great height into the flock of queleas. It turned and twisted, chasing the desperately wheeling queleas. A clawed foot extended in flight, grabbing one of them. It streaked away disappearing into the woods. This was the transition between life and death for the lapwing and the quelea.

We have come to enjoy the sight of signature species and lesser animals. In the marshes and flood plains of the Okavango Delta, there are red lechwe – an unusually shaped antelope whose hindquarters are higher than the shoulders. Red lechwe feed in shallow water on semi-aquatic grasses. The shape of their bodies allows them to move at pace through water. One of the grand sights in the delta is a herd of red lechwe galloping through the shallow water and reed beds. The sitatunga is similar to the red lechwe. The sitatunga's hooves are long – around 18 centimetres (7 inches) – and can be spread out wide. This is for the semi-aquatic environment of shallow streams and reed beds in which it lives. The sitatunga is shy and secretive. It is a capable swimmer and when disturbed or alarmed, runs into the water and submerges itself with only its nostrils above water.

On an afternoon boat trip in the delta, we were near a large reed bank. We all heard the noise.

'Stand up, stand up!' The guide's voice was excited. You could see a sitatunga in the reed beds. It was moving away from us rapidly. The reed bed was wide, allowing us to see the sitatunga for a few minutes before it disappeared from view.

Klipspringers are short, stubby antelopes covered in coarse spiky hair. They inhabit mountains and rocky habitats. They can move sure-footedly and quickly over this terrain. They are the only antelope that walk on the tips of their hooves. In Namibia, we surprised a pair of klipspringers. They took off up a rocky hill with uneven rocks and boulders. In a few bounds they reached the top of the hill, perhaps 100 metres (330 feet) above the road. At the top, one klipspringer stopped and turned to look in our direction. Its distinctive body was silhouetted against the dusk sky in the dying sunlight for a brief instant before it disappeared over the crest.

The honey badger is a small weasel with a powerful body and short legs. The legs and underparts are black. The top of the head, neck and back is silver grey. Honey badgers are fearless and have been known to attack much larger animals. There are stories of honey badgers killing wildebeests and waterbucks many times their size. In the case of large antelopes, honey badgers tear off the scrotum, ensuring that it bleeds to death. Most animals understandably give honey badgers a wide berth. In Etosha, near a waterhole, we saw one near the trail. It quickly retreated into the bush.

We waited at the waterhole, watching for leopards that were known to frequent the area. By this time the sun was setting, and at Etosha you had to be out of the park or in your camp by sunset. Suddenly, near the waterhole, we saw a honey badger – almost certainly the same individual we had seen earlier. In the fading light the distinctive colours were clearly visible. The honey badger looked up and sniffed the air. We were downwind. He sauntered away with a distinctive swaggering walk.

Bat-eared foxes are small jackal-like carnivores, standing about 30 centimetres (12 inches) at the shoulder. The body is silver grey in appearance, the ears are huge – around 15 centimetres (6 inches long). It hunts termites and other insects. In Zimbabwe, there was a bat-eared fox den, which housed two adults and a litter of three or four young. On a sunlit morning, we watched the family, the young playing around the den. We also saw the foxes hunting, the whole family spread out, cocking their heads and aligning their huge ears towards the ground. They listened intently for sounds of insects or termites. If they heard a sound, they moved their heads and ears to locate the source, then used their strong claws to dig out the insect and eat it. Several other groups drove past us without stopping or showing any interest in the bat-eared foxes.

In Alaska, we saw sea and river otters. The sea otters have the appearance of old men. We saw them along the seashore floating alone or in large rafts.

Occasionally they dive for clams. They rise to the surface and eat their clam floating on their backs.

The playful and curious river otters, on the other hand, are entirely different. They hunt fish but spend a lot of time out of the water. In Katmai, our guide, John, took us to a family of river otters that lived around the bay. We watched them fish and eat their catch. Curious about us, they stuck their heads out of the water to take a look at us in the boat. We heard them calling to each other, their sleek, dark bodies contrasting with the green seaweed. Some of them hauled themselves up onto the shore to groom each other or play.

One day in South Luangwa, Gerard took us to a lagoon. It was the dry season and the water level in the lake was low. The lake was crowded with thousands of birds: egrets, herons, kingfishers, storks, ibises, hammerkops, fish eagles and pelicans. They had come to the lake for a feast. The fish were concentrated in the shrinking ponds, making it easy for the birds to catch them.

The birds systematically fished out the drying ponds. The pelicans lined up at one end of the lake in a single line. Then they paddled across the lake dipping their heads into the water in perfect coordination. The heads emerged with bills full of fish scooped out of the water. They were herding shoals of fish in a demonstration of cooperation. Other birds picked off the fish that escaped the pelicans.

Near us, a saddle-billed stork stalked its prey. This is an unmistakable bird with a huge bill coloured in a series of red and black bands with a yellow saddle at its base. It is 1.5 metres (5 feet) in height. It stepped through the water and repeatedly caught fish in the shallows. A pair of crowned cranes landed. Their bodies were grey, with a red bib that hung on their neck. Their heads were a striking combination of black and white with a crown of golden feathers. They were only a few metres from us. With a honking cry, they flew off. We sat there the whole morning watching this amazing spectacle. A few days later, the lake was completely empty. The Great Bird Show was over for that year.

In Katmai in Alaska, one afternoon, we saw 10 or more grizzly bears – a mother, an old sow, and this year's cub close to the boat, several females and a few young males. The females with cubs frequently stood up on their hind legs and looked around to make sure that they were safe. At one point a large male ambled out of the woods. The females with cubs smelt him. They took off at great pace – fully grown males frequently kill young cubs.

We dropped off two of our party on a rock ledge near a stream. They wanted to fish for salmon. John dropped us back at the lodge and went back to pick them up. We later learnt that shortly after we dropped them off, a female bear with a young cub, probably last year's, turned up. The ledge wasn't that big and the bear was only 20 metres (66 feet) away from them. The female was teaching the cub to fish. They watched the young bear being given lessons by its mother.

The greatest of all spectacles you can see in the wild is watching a large predator hunt or kill. We saw a group of lions hunt at South Luangwa. Having waited with the pride all afternoon, we followed when they stirred and wandered off at dusk. There was moonlight, but there were clouds that might provide the opportunity to hunt. The prey was a herd of puku, a small antelope endemic to the park.

The lionesses arranged themselves. A young cub was instructed by its mother with a low growl to stay behind right next to the car. Gerard turned off the spotlight so as not to influence the hunt. The moon went behind a cloud. We heard the sounds of the hunt: a rush of bodies and galloping hoofs. Then, it was quiet. Gerard turned the spotlight on. The lions were some distance away. They had not made a kill. The process continued for a while but the lions did not make a kill that night.

We did see a kill in the Serengeti. There had been a thunderstorm, a time when lions frequently make kills, because the noise, rain and wind make it hard for herbivores to detect them. The lions had killed a blue wildebeest. A big male lion was nearby, his stomach distended from gorging. Lionesses with full stomachs were also resting. The male staggered a few feet and then collapsed. He turned over onto his side and fell asleep.

Lions prefer buffalo, zebra or large antelope. In Etosha, they hunt giraffes, the only herbivore in the park large enough to feed a pride. Lions had taken a giraffe at a waterhole. Giraffes are at their most vulnerable when drinking. In the morning, the lions were finishing off the carcass. Once the lions were done, the black-backed jackals moved in, and then the vultures. The ferocity and speed with which the carcass was stripped bare was startling. The sun was up and it was getting hot. The pride, its hunger sated for the moment, was looking for a place in the shade to rest. One of the cubs followed the pride. In its jaws it carried a foot and some bones of the dead giraffe. The cub was taking along a snack or a trophy.

In Botswana we also saw a kill – a kudu (a large striped antelope). There was an old lioness at the kill. She had been part of the pride once. At her age and with her worn teeth, she was probably not able to bring down large game any more and scavenged food from kills that her original pride made. As she rested, I noticed a gash across her head. She had probably got too close to the other lions at the kill, and taken a swipe from one of the others. We saw the old lioness later at dusk near the river. She was there with another lioness, possibly a daughter. We watched the pair of them walking away slowly into the bush in the fading light.

# CHAPTER 4

Sometimes it is the size of the spectacle that is exhilarating. On Round Island in Alaska we walked along a steep and slippery trail that led up a cliff. We followed a single narrow plank of wood that had been laid down to avoid damage to the soil. At the end of the trail, a vertical cliff stretched before us for 4 kilometres (2.5 miles). The cliffs were covered in hundreds of thousands of nesting birds: puffins, thick-billed murres and kittiwakes. The air was dark with them. Every crevice and ledge was full. Small chicks eagerly awaited the return of parents with food.

In South Luangwa, we saw a cloud of dust about 2 kilometres (1.2 miles) from the camp. A herd of buffaloes had come down to drink in the river. At dusk, on our way back from a drive, we headed in their direction. We found them all right. More accurately, they found us. There were over 1,000 of them. They surrounded us; there was nothing to do but wait. We waited for three hours. The buffaloes were still all around, making it dangerous to try to push through. If the herd panicked and stampeded then the jeep would afford no protection against the stampeding buffaloes. Each adult weighed in excess of a ton. We used our guide's night-vision glasses to watch them more closely. Eventually, the herd thinned and we edged our way clear without incident. The sheer mass of the herd was beyond comprehension.

In Etosha, at each camp in the warden's office there was a sighting book. Visitors and rangers recorded major wildlife sightings. The book alerted us to a spotted hyena den. Hyenas are despised as scavengers, but we love their distinctive long 'whooo-up' contact calls at night as they spread out for the hunt. Highly social creatures, they live in large clans of up to 80 animals. These clans are matriarchal and tightly organized. Clan members greet others by sniffing them and behaving animatedly in order to re-establish clan ties. Spotted hyenas are accomplished hunters. The majority of their food comes from kills made by the clan. Hyenas use their speed and stamina. Cooperative behaviour contributes to their hunting success. They use hunting strategies including decoys and attacking from different sides. In the Namib Desert, hyenas herd their prey onto soft sand where their padded feet give better footing and a significant advantage.

The den was close to the trail. There were a few animals about including a number of young cubs. One curious cub came right up to the car. We spent an hour with the hyenas, watching them and taking photos before moving on. A few days later we returned to the den. There was something wrong. As we approached, we noticed a hyena on the trail. It seemed distressed and did not move away when we approached. We noticed another car nearby. A South African man explained that he thought the hyena's back legs were crushed, that a car had probably run over them. He asked us to go back to the camp and get the ranger. He would wait.

We drove back to the camp. The ranger wasn't there. When he arrived we explained what had happened. He did not look pleased. He would have to destroy the animal, there was no choice. We drove back with him to the den. The hyena was not in sight: she had dragged herself to the den to get her cub. It might have been the very young cub that had come up to our car the previous visit. She was trying to move the cub to another den for its safety – hyena mothers frequently change dens to safeguard their young from predators. The crippled female had followed her maternal instincts to protect her young, despite her obvious pain and difficulty. The ranger took his rifle and headed off in the direction the hyena had taken. I couldn't watch this. We drove off back to the camp.

On the earlier visit, Jade had taken a photo of the hyena cub, a close up of its face. It is looking directly into the lens. For many years, the incident was painful to me. I did not talk about it. Jade loved the photo. It is only recently that she printed and hung it. Looking at the picture still causes me pain.

The ranger probably destroyed the female and the cub. If he did not kill the cub, then the cub would have died. Hyenas do not nurse or bring up young other than their own and the cub was far too young to survive on its own. I cannot forgive the human beings whose carelessness destroyed the lives of these wild animals. I cannot forget the stupid actions of some visitors that interfered with these animals right to live and die naturally.

# CHAPTER 5

## 'The Bridge Club, Lens Envy And Other Traumas': Travel Companions, Travel Conversations

*...We are in Alaska – Jade, me, an American ER surgeon with a Mexican moustache, a German man, our guide. The ER surgeon has three cameras and even more lenses...*

# CHAPTER 5

# The Bridge Club

Eco-travel, to some extent, is about getting away from people and escaping to nature. Ironically, you can only do it with people. You meet all kinds of them in eco-travel.

We laid eyes on the Bridge Club for the first time on the bus taking us to Cuzco airport for the charter flight to Manu. They were six anxious, older American women. They always took holidays together. This year they had decided to do 'something different'. It was not quite what they had expected. Outdoor shared pit toilets and lack of hot water and laundry were unexpected privations on an expensive vacation. 'Bugs' (ants, spiders and other biting insects) were a frightening part of this exotic experience. They were painful and rude to the staff. They complained about the primitive conditions. They complained about their suffering.

'It's like camp!' Not having experienced 'camp', we could not corroborate the statement.

At night they sat writing in their diaries, thumbing through the lodge's library and making notes. They seemed a little old to be doing homework. After dinner they cleared the table for bridge. The evening inevitably ended with a final complaint – the lack of electricity.

Activities at Manu include walks, boat trips and going to wildlife-viewing hides. The other guests enjoyed the natural beauty and wildlife of the rain-forest. The Bridge Club did not grasp that viewing wildlife requires effort, patience and silence. Their behaviour annoyed other guests. Not that it made any difference – they were on vacation.

The Bridge Club decided to tape some birdcalls with a tape recorder. The guide got them close to some macaws and toucans so that they could record them. The ladies were excited. They would play the calls for us. This was 'one-upwomanship'. They regarded us – especially me – as eco-tourist snobs, who looked down on them. They were entirely correct. On the tape, there were muffled noises. All you could hear was the Bridge Club: their screaming and shouting had drowned any sounds from the birds.

'You can't hear the birds,' one of them complained. Jade and I exchanged amused, knowing looks. They were completely oblivious to the amount of noise they had made.

On one walk, we came across a tortoise. The rule is that you never crowd an animal and never use flash photography. The six women surrounded it. With great 'oohs' and 'aahs' they photographed it many times, flashes going off repeatedly. The guide asked the women to maintain their distance and not to use the flash. It was to no avail. The women had short attention spans. Only having taken their photos did they move on.

At breakfast on the last day at Manu, we heard the chatter of a group of capuchin monkeys. Excited, the Bridge Club grabbed their cameras. They wanted photographs. The camp staff, in expectation of bigger tips, began throwing bananas at the wild monkeys. The Bridge Club squealed excitedly like adolescent schoolgirls. Jade and I were horrified.

On the same trip, we met Saki, a Japanese woman in her 60s. From the very start, she attached herself to Jade, at times physically. Unusually, she was travelling independently. She had visited many eco-tourist destinations, but was terrified of most of the staples of eco-travel – mud, insects, spiders, scorpions. That said, she never said no to any activity: she would screw up her face in fear, then she would do it. Her curiosity about the natural world was immense.

She sat with Rachel, our guide, asking detailed questions, while she made notes about poison arrow frogs: the colours – electric blue, brown and red, whatever Rachel had told her about the frog's biology and the local Indian myths about them. Now she needed a picture of the frog. Jade volunteered me. The best I could manage was a bad, angular, geometric version of one.

Saki scrutinised my drawing.

'It is very good,' she said, lying.

## Conformity, social engineering or selfishness

The title of the *Lonely Planet* series of guidebooks evokes the solitude and escape of travel. *Crowded Planet* would be a better title. Travel in our crowded world takes several formats. There is group travel or 'conformity'. You sign up, pay up, turn up. The operator puts together the programme. If enough people pay up, then the tour proceeds. You hand over responsibility for everything: itinerary, transport, accommodation and activities. It is like a school excursion. You become a conformist or the group troublemaker.

Eco-tourism can entail group travel: 'Highlights of East African Game Parks' or 'Birding in the Zambezi Valley'. There are unfortunately no 'In Search of the Pangolin' tours. If there were, we would join it quick-smart, despite our aversion to group travel.

Travel with friends is 'social engineering'. In theory this has the benefit of group travel, without the downside of being stuck with people whose tastes, manners and expectations are incompatible with your own. But your experience of people is confined to social contexts. They provide limited guidance to compatibility as a travel companion. One person takes responsibility for the caravanserai – the 'martyrdom complex' sufferer. When we travel, I am the 'planner'. Occasionally things go wrong.

131

'What a screw up..! You should have listened to someone who knew better... Won't you ever learn?'

'Would you have done better..? You organize it next time then.'

We have learnt to work our way through these difficult moments, but they have the potential to create a little friction between friends.

Jade blames me for not being accommodating of other people. It has something to do with being an only child. I think of myself as independent. I preface comments with 'Being an only child,' providing background and context for my behaviours. When planning this book, we talked about including a chapter on the people aspects of travel. Jade's comment was that it would be a short chapter. I do prefer the company of animals. Whatever the reasons, we both prefer independent travel.

Even if you travel independently, you end up being grouped together with other people. Accommodation and transport arrangements are shared. At best, you share campfires and meals but have your own guide and undertake your own activities. At worst, it is the dreaded conformity of group travel. There is no escape from your fellow humans.

## Walking clichés

The people you meet are often walking clichés, in their dress, behaviours or attitudes, in that they look and act exactly as you would expect them to. Eco-tourists need to get a quick fix on their companions. From there all else follows: the way you interact; whom you sit with at dinner; whom you want to go out with on drives. You want to be with others who are also searching for pangolins. Believe it or not, we have found the odd one who is as passionate about them as we are.

Dress clichés abound. Large individuals consider the oversized T-shirt, Lycra shorts and obligatory bum-bag (or fanny pack) to be the epitome of classic holiday couture. Another fashion statement is the wearing of socks with sports sandals, beloved of Germans and Scandinavians. Many travellers have an innate belief that the local dress code will suit them. If you look at political leaders at various summits where they shed their dark suits for national costumes, you quickly see that native attire looks best on local people.

Eco-travel has its special clichés. Men are keen to demonstrate the advantages of a multi-pocketed jacket. There is a specific use for each of the many pockets, only they have forgotten them. A Swiss Army knife is the obligatory accessory. Then there is safari wear and individuals wearing full khaki regalia (you have to imagine the pith helmet). There are cameras, long lenses and binoculars hanging around necks. There are water bottles dangling from waists. People are dressed this way at the airport check-in, some days away from their destination. They are going on safari. They just haven't actually started yet.

Billy Connolly, the Scottish comedian, did a television programme on the Arctic regions shot in Nunavut, Canada. The plot lines are thin: Billy alone in a tent in the frozen Arctic environment amongst dangerous polar bears; Billy dancing naked on the ice...

Billy goes to meet his Inuit guide, to ensure that he is kitted out for the conditions. He has the latest cold-weather gear sold in London. The Inuit man looks at Connolly's clothes with contempt.

'We will have to get you some cold-weather clothes'. This consists of traditional sealskin garments and animal-skin boots.

Connolly holds out his expensive expedition clothing and asks in his thick Scottish accent, 'This stuff's not much good then, eh?'

There are always people from particular countries who reinforce national stereotypes. They wouldn't be stereotypes otherwise would they? Americans are loud, delighting in screaming at each other, blissfully ignorant of a world outside the 'US of A'. They are discomfited that the rest of world is foreign. They do have a wonderful politeness: 'Have a nice day now,' 'Why, thank you,' 'Mighty obliged,' 'That nice young man has been ever so helpful.' There is a naïve, childlike sense of wonder, coupled with the confidence and constant need to express it.

Intrepid travellers all seem to come from the same countries. The joke is that at the end of the world, you always find an Australian, a Kiwi or a German. Conversations with German travellers inevitably turn to cost: 'No, it was cheaper there.' German inflexibility is a legendary stereotype, as is their desire for accuracy.

In a series of extraordinary documentaries, Robin Anderson and Bob Connolly, two Australian filmmakers, recorded life in Papua New Guinea[17]. A German traveller visits the site where a white missionary was killed.

'So, he was killed here?' the German man asks the guide.

'Yes.'

'Here, exactly here?' He points at the ground.

'Yes.'

'Exactly here? Are you absolutely certain?'

The guide nods.

The German looks around unconvinced.

German eco-tourists are insistent and fastidious in their concern about detail: 'It cannot be a scarlet-rumped trogon. My book says they do not occur here at this time.' Nobody has told them that animals rarely read the books describing their behaviour.

# CHAPTER 5

We frequently meet British travellers in eco-tourist destinations. A significant number are birders. Eyes glued to binoculars, they muse whether it was a greater or lesser racket-tailed drongo that flew past. They make good travel companions. They are knowledgeable and enjoy the wilderness experience. The niceties of the English class system carry through into their travels. The upper-class English couple with a sense of *noblesse oblige* talk about the natives or their ancestor, Clive of India. They have a wondrous stoicism when things go astray. The accents are delightful – something like speaking with two ping-pong balls in one's mouth, while trying not to swallow either.

Major cultural characteristics of the Japanese are the formation of large groups and the ability to hold two opposite and contradictory ideas simultaneously. In the Antarctic, a guide tried to engage a Japanese party on the subject of whaling. The Japanese and Norwegians continue to hunt whales for 'research purposes'. The research seems to take the unusual form of eating whale meat. During the trip we saw many whales and everyone delighted in their presence. A total ban on whaling and the creation of a whale sanctuary in the Southern Ocean is proposed. The Japanese are vocal opponents. There was muttering about 'cultural differences'. The major interest of the Japanese, stereotypically, is photography. The individual must be portrayed with the historical monument or animal in the background. Salim, our guide in Ranthambore, had to ensure that the Japanese could be in the photo with the tiger if they saw one.

In Alaska we took a cruise on the Prince William Sound. There were some Taiwanese. We were dressed in warm clothing and Gore-Tex jackets. The Taiwanese men were dressed in casual sports clothing. The women were dressed for a dinner party. One had a fur coat. The men wore casual slip-on loafers. The women had high-heeled shoes. We had on our muddy walking boots. Everything they had seemed to be a famous fashion label. We approached a surreal blue glacier. Pieces had broken off and were floating around the boat. Sea otters were hauled up on the ice. The Taiwanese came out on deck. Given their dress and the temperature – 10°C (50°F) – their absence from the deck until now was understandable. They pushed us out of the way. They were posing for photos with the glacier in the background. The men produced expensive digital and video cameras. There was an orgy of photo taking. The major problem was getting the people and the glacier into the same shot. The rest of the trip was spent below deck watching replays of the photos and videos on their tiny camera screens.

Occasionally you meet people who do not understand the impact on the wildlife of your just being there. One example was a man on our ship in Antarctica. The rules regarding animals are clear: do not get any closer than

5 metres (16.5 feet) away; do not cause distress to wildlife; do not use flash photography. The animals are wild. The Antarctic is a harsh place. We were there during the brief Antarctic summer – the breeding season. We must do nothing to affect the natural life of these creatures. The man broke all the rules. The guides spoke to him on many occasions. He just didn't get it. One evening we landed on an island. In the gentoo penguin colony, there were many chicks on their pebbly nests. The chicks were late. It was almost the end of the summer. They needed to fledge quickly to have any chance of survival. I was near a group of penguin chicks. The man pushed past me and got very close to them. I spoke to him, politely pointing out the rules. He ignored me. He began taking pictures, his flash firing repeatedly. I spoke to him more strongly. The flash went off again and again. A few of the chicks were starting to get distressed. They were trying to move away from the nest. I had enough. I aimed a kick at his backside. It missed him but caught his tripod. The camera slipped. He grabbed it and strode off giggling. The guides remonstrated with him about his behaviour again.

## Lens envy

The mother of all travel interest groups is photography. We are in Alaska – Jade, myself, an American ER surgeon with a Mexican moustache, a German man and our guide. All, apart from myself, have a camera. The ER surgeon has three cameras and even more lenses. There is a grizzly bear nearby.

The surgeon and the German are comparing lenses. There is much quiet discussion about the merits of different cameras. Nikon and Canon feature a lot, as do zoom lenses, doublers, image stabilizers, type of film. The bear is almost irrelevant.

Jade is the only one taking photos. She is a purist – automatic cameras are not for real photographers – shooting on her manual Nikon using a 300mm zoom lens. The bear is so close that the zoom is irrelevant, unless you want a close up of the bear's eye. The bear is so close that the surgeon finds it impossible to focus with his massive 500mm zoom lens.

The guide is behind taking photos of us with the bear about 3 metres (10 feet) away. We joke about the publicity value – close encounters with a grizzly. The surgeon and the German are still comparing camera equipment, looking through each other's cameras.

'How big is your lens?' one asks the other.

Travellers take photos to record their travels. Photographers travel to take photos. There are many traumas and phobias among travel photographers: 'My lens is bigger than your lens.' This is the world of lens envy.

# CHAPTER 5

## Proof

Travel photographs are the ultimate proof that you were there. The ER surgeon's wife was diabetic. She was very ill and had limited mobility. The surgeon carried her to the base of a waterfall. He waded out into the fast-flowing, icy water. He was going to take a photo of his wife under the waterfall. The surgeon was thigh-deep in the water and the current rocked the camera tripod.

'I have this thing about waterfalls,' he explained. The real reason was his wife: he wanted her to be able to do things. The photo of her at the waterfall was proof that she could still handle a bit of adventure.

In Tanzania, there is a gate to the Serengeti Park made out of animal bones. There is no fence as such – it is symbolic. An American vet and his wife wanted a video of themselves walking though the gates. He asked me to record this event on his camera. He had never seen me handle a camera. In 1991, video cameras were primitive. I couldn't see anything through the small black-and-white viewfinder. I pointed it in the direction of the vet and his wife.

'Ready?' I nodded. I had no idea what I was doing. I had to press a button and pan to follow their movement. A red light would appear on the screen indicating that it was recording. I pressed but nothing happened. It was too late. I pretended to film. 'Thanks!' (This was before you could do instantaneous playbacks.) The vet carefully removed the tape and labelled it carefully: 'Entering Serengeti Reserve'.

On a later trip to Africa, we met a man from California travelling with his aunt, who had been to Africa before. During her first trip she was preoccupied with taking video footage. She had seen Africa through the small black-and-white viewfinder of her video camera. She had proof of her visit, but she had not really seen it at all. She had returned to see Africa normally.

While we were there, a golden-tailed woodpecker appeared at the lodge as we were relaxing one afternoon. It had streaks of red on its head, setting off the brown on its breast and belly. It flew to a nearby tree, exploring the wood for insects. It cocked its head to one side and listened. Then it attacked the bark with its beak. There was a persistent tapping sound as it hunted insects below the bark. It is very difficult to take photographs of woodpeckers. They move constantly and are always a long way up a tree. This one was just in front of us. It was very exciting. Jade took a number of close-ups. When we developed the film from that African trip, the woodpecker was missing. Had we actually seen the woodpecker? In the case of a pangolin, a photo would be essential. No one would otherwise believe that we had actually seen one.

## Me too

Most objects and places encountered while travelling are familiar from photographs seen before we travel. Some travellers even want to recreate the photo that inspired their journey.

A friend visited Angkor Wat in Cambodia. At dawn they were taken to the main temple. The classic photograph of Angkor Wat depicts the temple at dawn and its perfect reflection on the still waters of the lake that faces the building. The visitors have the opportunity to take the very same shot.

Hardened photographers adjusted their expensive, complex equipment. Others fiddle with less impressive kit, feeling the twinges of lens envy. Suddenly, the temple lit up with coloured lights: red, yellow and then red again. The lights alternated. José Carreras, the famous opera singer, was holding a concert at Angkor Wat. This was the rehearsal of the light show. The waiting crowd was bemused and distressed at the strange colours of Angkor Wat as they tried to take their 'ideal' photo of the temple.

An image taken by Tom Mangelsen, a wildlife photographer, shows three polar bears at Churchill in Canada. They are waiting for winter ice to form on Hudson Bay. When the sea freezes, the bears head out to hunt and live their solitary existence. In the interim they congregate on the edge of the bay. The three bears are together: one lies on his back, head propped on a mound of snow like a pillow, the other two lie beside him. They resemble college students in front of the television, having a drink, relaxing. The photo – Bad Boys of the Arctic – is used to promote tourism. The picture shapes tourists' expectations. The inability to see bears playing in this manner disappoints visitors.

Jade and I compared notes after our trip to see the mountain gorillas. I had been fascinated by the detail of their bodies and faces. Their fingers and toes were similar to those of humans. The gestures and movements were human. The behaviour of a young gorilla was that of a human child. Jade had been preoccupied with taking photos in difficult conditions. She had not noticed the details to the same extent.

## Hunting

Photography is also a form of consumption: we must 'take only pictures, leave behind nothing other than footprints.' To an extent, photography is also sanitized hunting: the camera has replaced the gun.

Jade was taking a picture of an impala (a small gazelle) as it ran. Her manual Nikon made a loud click and the gazelle fell as if shot. She had shot it. The gazelle had bounded into a hollow, disappearing from our vision. It reappeared shortly. Everyone laughed in relief.

You can even hunt plants. In Alaska, we noticed moss and lichen growing on the rocks around a lake. Jade thought that they might make interesting photographs. In the afternoon we cruised the shoreline looking for the 'perfect' moss and lichen. At each promising site, Jade would look through her lens. She would try a few angles. We looked at a lot of rocks. Eventually, she found the right one. The lichen was white and red on a dark, weathered background. The dusk light was perfect. The colours glowed ethereally, fragile yet solid. Jade took a number of shots with different settings. It had been quite a hunt to get this image.

## Combat

Jade's 300mm lens, when fully extended, is very long. People frequently comment on it: 'My, you have a long lens.'

Photography is a form of fetishism: this manifests itself in different ways. In Canada we came across a group led by a well-known photographer. They were retired, elderly Americans learning how to take wildlife shots. They were rich, judging by the brand new camera equipment on display. The owners were working out the fine details of wildlife photography,

'Where is the button I press on this thing?' All talk was about the cameras and photographs, F-stops, film speed, light meters. No one talked about the grizzly bears nearby. No one talked about the beautiful birdlife.

At Alaska's Brooks Falls, there is a viewing platform that overlooks a waterfall. Many photos of bears catching salmon in their mouths are taken from here. There is an extraordinary image of a bear poised with his mouth open and the fish jumping through the air, heading straight for his open jaws. Space on the platform at Brooks Falls is limited and people are rotated through for short stays. This is 'combat photography'. People push and shove each other in a desperate struggle to get photos. These are not professional wildlife photographers: they are dentists, accountants, lawyers and machinists taking holiday snaps. A podgy Englishman pushed me out of the way to set up his camera tripod at what, he considered, the best vantage point.

Seeing that I was displeased, he grumbled, 'But you don't take photos.'

Some people will go to any lengths to get a shot. In the Antarctic we got caught in a blizzard. The ship parked against an ice sheet and the crew and guides went to check the ice thickness. Marking out a safe area, they let the gangways down and we went out onto the ice. The ship acted as a wind-break: on one side, the blizzard blew cold and white, on the other, it was cold but calm. We were warned not to go beyond the marked area. A Japanese passenger had not understood the instruction or chose to ignore it. She approached the area where the ship had broken through the ice. She wanted to take a photo of the ship anchored in the ice. The uneven and soft ice gave way. She sank in up to her waist. She was slipping under. One of the guides saw her and ran to help. At great personal risk, he pulled her out. And all because of the need to get a photograph.

## The ideal picture

Tom Walker records the wildlife of Alaska. One of his best-known photographs is of a nesting red-throated loon. The loon is all soft grey-browns. The muted red throat and the clear red eye are visible. The grass stems in the background are gold. The bird is sitting on the nest with its head slightly raised. The perfect reflection of the loon is on the still surface of the pond. It is a study in serenity and beauty.

Tom Walker described the conditions under which the photo was created.[18] He waited for days in terrible weather, a fierce wind blowing across the tundra. Infrequent sunny days brought out mosquitoes. He succumbed to a flu-like illness. The photo was taken at around 2.00am, as the wind died down briefly and the Arctic sun shone. The loon was sleeping. Disturbed by a nearby Arctic fox, it raised its head to look. The photo was taken that instant. Moments later, the magical scene disappeared. Walker talks about wildlife photographers 'fantasizing endlessly imagining the perfect picture'. Photographs allow the idealized image of an event or place to be possessed.

## Frozen moments

Jade's photos are frozen moments in our lives. The beauty of a fleeting moment caught on film reminds us of where we have been and the sights that we have seen. It is like a trigger that unlocks the sights, smells and sounds of the occasion that have been locked away in memory.

There is a photo of reeds in the still water in the Okavango Delta in Botswana. You cannot tell where the reeds end and the reflection begins. The greens and blues are tranquil and calm. There is a Japanese feel to the image.

A lioness and her sister hunt in Botswana's Moremi Reserve. She is golden in the sunlight. Her head turns away from the camera. The muscles in her shoulders are taut. She is focused on some impalas. The power and athleticism of the lioness is tangible.

# CHAPTER 5

An Indian rhinoceros, metallic blue, looks at us in a quizzical, short-sighted manner. Stems of grass are visible at the edge of his mouth. The tufted, hairy ears tilt forward as he strains to hear.

A tigress lies down in the long grass. Yellow stems of grass angle across the photo. When that was taken, we had heard the alarm calls of monkeys. We followed them backward and forward. The tigress doubled back, almost eluding us, but then we came across her in a clearing. She sat down on the ground, lying with her head on her outstretched front paws – a study in languid grace.

A sea lion climbed onto a rock and went to sleep. Our photo of him is a close-up of his folded front flippers resting on his stomach. The relaxed repose of the animal permeates the grey-black image.

Sally lightfoot crabs scurry across volcanic rocks. Dark clouds are gathering in the sky. The late afternoon sunlight falls in shafts at strange angles and colours. The crabs are the brightest reds. In the pre-storm light the basalt glows obsidian black. The contrast between the rocks and the red crabs is startling. Jade only had time to take one photo before the crabs were gone. The image glows with an incandescent combination of tones from this moment.

There is the photo of the hyena cub, a study in brown. The hyena looks directly at you. The ears are large, every hair is visible. The left side of the face is in shadow. The eyes look at you curiously.

A group of walruses all look in the same direction in a mysterious alignment of heads and tusks. It was on Second Beach on Round Island. We had perched on the cliff overlooking the beach for several hours. There were 200 walruses hauled up. Some would go off to fish for clams. Walruses returning from fishing trips hauled up on the rocky beach. Suddenly there was a noise, a falling pebble. All the walrus heads snapped around in the direction of the noise. The perfect alignment of walrus heads and tusks is frozen in the photograph.

The grizzly bear was a few feet from us. The photo only shows its front legs. The fur there is wet. The dark brown of the bear's leg contrasts with the yellow-grey colour of the riverbed. His power and size is palpable. The bear's claws are like solid steel: they glint in the sunlight.

Photographs are elegiac in nature. Each photo speaks of transience, the frozen moment speaks to the mortality of things. In eco-travel, the nostalgia and sense of loss is deeper. The camera captures landscapes and creatures that are disappearing. Untold areas of the natural world have disappeared or are under threat. Many species have been made extinct or are endangered. The photograph records the fragile magical world and is testament to its disappearance.

## Making friends

Travel, it is said, offers the opportunity to meet local people. This is rarely the case in eco-travel. Eco-tourist fare is priced out of reach of the local population and sold to the affluent eco-tourist from the developed world.

In the Galapagos Islands we met an Ecuadorian man. He was visiting the famous islands for the first time.

'It is very, very expensive for us to travel to the Galapagos Islands,' he lamented.

In Tanzania's Ngorongoro Crater, I chatted to the guide.

'Where are you from?' I asked (the staple question of travel conversation).

He wanted to visit Australia. He had only travelled as far as Arusha, a few hours drive from the crater. I explained the time needed to travel to Australia. I saw his lack of comprehension of the distance. I did not talk to him about the cost. It would have been several lifetimes' earnings.

Not wanting to insult or shame him, I said, 'I am sure that you will travel there one day.'

In eco-travel, you mingle with your fellow eco-traveller. The only locals you see and meet, if you are lucky, are the guides and camp staff. The lack of interaction also reflects the traveller's requirements. The stock phrases in a travel guidebook speak to the major concerns of the traveller:

Hello
How are you?
Goodbye
See you soon
Good, Very good
Bad, Very bad
Please
Excuse me
Thank you, Thank you very much
What is your name?
My name is . . .
Can you tell me the way to . . . ?
How far is it to . . . ?
Where is the toilet?
Can I have the bill please?
How much is it?
Too much
Lower your price
Go away

There are the numbers 0–10, invaluable in shopping and bargaining, and various food and drink items.

In a guidebook targeting a different demographic the following phrases appeared:

I love you
I do not want to have a baby

Tourist–local interactions do not cover discussion about the cultural significance of colonial rule or the theory of relativity. Nor do they provide travellers like me with the local-language equivalent for the phrase: 'Take me to a pangolin!'

I grew up in Calcutta in India. In the late 1960s the Beatles embraced the Maharesi; India became fashionable. When I was around 10 years old, I got to know a group of Americans who lived nearby. They were college students in their early 20s. (My mother tells me that as a child I was outgoing and made friends easily – something must have happened since then.) We called them 'hippies' though we had no idea what the term meant. They came seeking an understanding of Indian culture. What they really sought was an answer to the disillusionment and boredom of their lives. They studied with a holy man. (We fell about laughing. He was a quack that everybody knew.) They studied obscure Indian writers that we had never heard of. There were cultural differences. They had no furniture. We speculated whether they were poor. The women wore revealing clothing that was several sizes too small, leading to gossip. A young American woman wanted to dress in a sari. My mother helped her buy one and wear it. Indian women were dressing in Western clothes, while Americans were wearing saris.

It was easier to fit in with the foreigners' conception of India. It was too difficult and time-consuming to try to correct them. They searched for 'authentic' Indian culture. It made them happy, this sense of being Indian. Then one day, they were gone. The reality of studies, careers, family and home had won out.

Most interactions that travellers have with local people are based on falsehoods. In the case of the eco-traveller, there is a refreshing honesty: 'I am only interested in your forests, your wild animals and bird life.'

An American in our group in Africa organized a visit to the local Masai village. We paid our guide who paid the villagers after deducting his commission. The visit was going to be 'natural'. The village was a collection of mud and earth huts. A fence of prickly bushes surrounded the huts to prevent predators attacking the villagers or their cattle at night. We stood around awkwardly. The Masai villager, acting as a guide, took us to his hut. Would we like to go inside? It seemed impolite to refuse. The hut was simple. It had one long narrow circular passage spiralling into a central living area. There was a fire burning in the centre. The air was thick with smoke. It was claustrophobic. We couldn't get out fast enough. Outside we took deep breaths trying to get rid of the fetid smell. The American emerged a few minutes later grumbling that there wasn't enough light inside for photos.

In Ecuador, we visited the local Achuar community. Our guide Rachel briefed us carefully. We should not stare at anybody, especially the Chief's many wives. We should not refuse any hospitality. We would be offered maize beer, an accompaniment to the process of meeting guests. Under no circumstances were we to refuse an offer of beer. In Werner Herzog's film *Fitzcarraldo*, the eponymous hero meets the local Indian tribe. The Indian men sit around stirring a fermenting drink. They take turns to spit into the bowl. This drink is offered to Fitzcarraldo. In order to build trust with the Indian villagers, he drinks it. I hoped the maize beer was not made by a similar method.

The Chief met us alone in a large thatched roof hut with open sides. We all sat on the ground. There were remnants of a fire in the middle of the hut. The Chief began talking to Ramiro, our Achuar guide. There was a careful protocol. The Chief said something long. Ramiro waited for the Chief to finish. Then he would say something short. He then waited for the Chief to say something. The onus of conversation lay with the Chief. This went on for a long time. This was apparently the structure of conversations. The maize beer was served in a communal bowl. The Chief took a long, deep drink. He then passed it to Ramiro, who took a long drink. The bowl was refilled from a large earthen jar and passed to Rachel. It was passed to the visitors. There was Saki, a Greek man, his Ecuadorian wife, Jade and myself. I took a sip. It was a cross between a weak beer and curdled milk. The drinking went on for a while.

Rachel told us that Ramiro had said the Chief had greeted us. The Chief was happy to see us. We indicated that we were happy to see him. The Chief said that he was happy we had come. We indicated that we were happy to have come. The conversation was reaching startling depths. He was sorry he couldn't speak to us in English.

Rachel expressed this as: 'He would like to hang out with you guys.'

I tried hard to imagine the Chief and me hanging out together. Would we like to ask him something?

There was silence. I asked whether he liked foreigners from far away visiting his world. There was a long translation. I had asked a complicated question. I was worried.

Rachel told us that Ramiro said the Chief had said, 'Yes'.

Then our visit was over. It was the reverse of the greeting phase. Ramiro did more of the talking. The Chief did the responding. Then we got up and made our way back to the boat.

As we were walking back, Rachel said it had been a very good meeting.

'God, that beer was strong, I shouldn't have drunk so much,' she burped.

I have no idea what the whole thing was about. I have no idea what Ramiro and the Chief talked about. They may have talked about the village and people they knew. Maybe they were commenting on the visitors: 'You have no idea how stupid that one is'; 'That one is really strange'; 'He is really fat.' Maybe they discussed the Chief's visit to New York. Who knows – he may have been there. Maybe they talked about how the tribe and guides could make more money from tourists. The Chief may have complained about having to get into tribal fashions and play-act for tourists. Ramiro may have complained that it was hard to put up with the gringos. They could have been working out how they could get more aid funding. It was a total mystery to me.

## Guiding about

In eco-travel, you get to know your guide well. Guides need history, geography, linguistics, political skills, psychology, interpersonal skills and knowledge of group dynamics. Good eco-tourist guides also need to know biology, geology and natural science. They need great eyes to spot wildlife.

We are on the Galapagos Islands. Our guide, Bettinia, is drawing shapes in the sand.

'What does this look like?'

Only Jade and I are looking at the squiggly line in the sand.

'Can anyone tell me what this is?'

I don't have a clue. It is a drawing of the South American continent and the Galapagos Islands. Bettinia illustrates the fault line under the Galapagos Islands. She talks about the volcanic activity and how it shapes the islands and affects the wildlife. She is good.

Later in the trip, the boat is berthed at Puerto Ayora on Santa Cruz Island. I see Bettinia in one of the ship's zodiacs. There is a little girl with her – her daughter. The pair have spent an hour or two together between trips. Bettinia works on the boats all year. She gets a break of a week every 2–3 months, depending on the season. All the guides work freelance and are hired separately for each cruise. It is important to be reliable and available. The work pays well, mainly as a result of tips from foreign tourists. Bettinia had worked this routine for a long time. There was little other work. She saw her daughter when she could.

We sent them a book on the unique wildlife of Australia to thank her. She wrote back saying that she found the animals fascinating and unlike anything she had seen. Her world was also like nothing that we had seen.

The life of a wildlife guide is hard. Guides must, like Bettinia, be away from their families for extended periods. Rachel, our guide at Kapawi in Ecuador, got a break of one week every two months. Her boyfriend was a guide at another lodge. It was hard for them to be together. Why do they do it? It can't be the pay. Tips, usually in desirable foreign currency, are a major attraction. Disproportionate rewards mean that people with training and skills are attracted to guiding in developing countries. In the Galapagos Islands we met a woman who was a schoolteacher but had become a tourist guide to earn more money.

In Africa the 'guides' are from local tribes. They double as drivers. They have some English, and their knowledge of the wilderness comes from living in the bush. In countries where employment opportunities are minimal, guiding offers the prospects of a reasonable life, though a hard one. Acting as a guide to foreigners allows local people to parlay skills in a foreign language and a basic knowledge of history, geography and nature into a lucrative profession. Young guides flirt unashamedly with single Western women, the thinking being that a relationship may provide them a passport.

Some wildlife guides are scientists; some hold Masters or higher degrees in Biology or Zoology. There are limited career options in their chosen fields. They may like fieldwork and the wilderness. They can combine the lifestyle with making a living. Tracy, our guide in Canada, was a herpetologist with a Masters in Biology. She had become disillusioned by academic research. She liked working in the wilderness. She could not conceive of any other life.

The guiding cultures in each destination are different. In Africa, many of our guides have been black Africans. Jade always talks about 'African eyes', referring to their exceptional ability to spot wildlife. In Botswana, Theba, our guide there, suddenly stopped the car and pointed to a low branch on a tree.

'Barred owl,' he said in his matter-of-fact voice. The owl was camouflaged in the tree. We speculated whether he knew that the owl roosted there. It didn't matter. We would not have spotted the owl without Theba.

Theba was a taciturn man. His fellow guide at the lodge, Segal, was more talkative. He used to box (once almost representing Botswana in the Olympics) and was also a fan of action fiction such as *Rambo: First Blood*. Despite our different tastes in literature, we got on well. Black guides are cautious in expressing opinions. If you spend enough time with them then you establish a bond. Segal was pleased that we were spending two weeks in Botswana.

'People spend a day and say they have seen Botswana,' he sneered. He had visited other parks in Africa. He gave us his views of several places that we want to visit. We had a common dislike of hunting and the idea of killing for pleasure.

In Tanzania, our driver/guide was Mohammed, a Muslim, who spoke excellent English. He found my Indian heritage interesting: he had grown up around the Indian trading communities in east Africa, and now lived near Arusha, the centre of safari activity in northern Tanzania. He had a large family, with six or seven children, but was away from home a lot. He said that he did not mind. The money was good. What else could he do? He was luckier than most.

At the end of the trip, he went off shopping for something for his children. He returned with a big bunch of bananas. Fruit was expensive: his family would be pleased with the special treat. Mohammed smoked. His coughing and breathing betrayed early signs of emphysema. An American insisted on explaining the health issues of smoking to Mohammed. He had good intentions. He was going to send 'literature' on nicotine patches that would help quit smoking. Smoking was one of the few luxuries Mohammed could afford. He could not read or write.

In the Serengeti, Mohammed tried really hard to find cheetahs. The closest we came was near a flock of Thompson's gazelle, a popular prey of cheetahs. The flock suddenly took off. A cheetah had begun an attack. Our presence caused the cheetah to stop. We never saw it. Mohammed said we had been 'unlucky'. I had said not to worry – we had seen a lot: lions at a kill, a large pride with a lot of young cubs, but he was disappointed in not being able to show us cheetahs.

Jimmy, one of the guides at South Luangwa, was also from Tanzania. He was a large, gentle and calm man. He had waited, without complaint, almost all day for us at Mfuwe airport when our flight was late. On game drives, you could see him looking for signs of wildlife. He would see if the vultures were soaring or coming down, perhaps at a kill. He would cruise past familiar haunts of many species. His eyes scanned the soft sandy soil looking for tracks. His eyes were cloudy, the early signs of cataracts or another disease that would affect his sight. Would he get treatment? Medical facilities in Zambia were poor and expensive.

In the Okavango Delta our guide was Prince. His uncle featured in the lodge's marketing. The uncle ran the *mokoro* safari, taking a small group out for a few days camping in the delta. One day, Prince demonstrated the Bushmen's click language. I tried to imitate him. I could not click and speak at the same time. Prince found this very funny. His real name was not Prince: the lodge had given it to him. He did not care for his new name. His uncle did not much care for his given name – Mr Eagle – either.

We have had white guides in Africa. Some were students on working-holiday jobs. Others were people looking for a change in life. In South

Luangwa, we came across 'The Cousins': good South African stock, very white, blonde and arrogant. The son was a guide at the park. He went out with one of the African drivers or spotters to help him find and identify wildlife. He was studying in England and this was a holiday job. His parents got special rates, and had brought two younger daughters with them. Going out on a game drive with The Cousins was like being an intruder at a family outing. The parents were superior. They thought of themselves as very knowledgeable about wildlife.

There were lots of in-jokes. 'The game was better in [insert name of park]'. They were critical of black Africans: 'they don't think like we think.'

Gerard was a white Zambian, born and bred there. He had worked in the copper industry. He had acted as a representative for English companies in Zambia. He loved the bush and had been coming to South Luangwa for over 30 years. He had wound down his business interests and now managed the camp to indulge his love of the outdoors. Gerard was a wonderful guide. We were the only guests at the camp and could pretty much do anything we wanted. He told us about the history of the place, its various owners and the country's political difficulties. Gerard got us interested in birds. We had enjoyed the bright colours, the bewildering variety. The organization of the bird world was extremely confusing. But, around Gerard, it was impossible not to be interested in birds and their behaviours: he had a genuine joy and fascination for them. There was the 'go-away' bird, the grey lourie, whose call sounds like you are being dismissed from its presence. There was the 'dead-battery' bird, whose cry gradually faded away. Gerard laughed his way through nature documentaries, pointing out that the birdcalls and birds did not correspond.

John was our guide in Alaska. He lived on Kodiak Island working the summer 'season' at the lodge on Katmai coast. His love of the magical Katmai coast was infectious. The walls of the lodge were covered in his exquisite photographs of the region's bears. One shot showed a large grizzly turning over a rock on the coastline. It was a shot of its head and showed the concentration involved in seeking out a clam or other morsel. The bear's delicacy of movement was captured in the photo. The light caught the droplets of water on the coat glistening magically.

John had a deep affinity for the place. One day, in the distance he spotted an old friend – an old male bear called 'Blondie'. Blondie looked intently in our direction. You suspected that he recognized John. The bear had come down to a stream to see if the salmon run had started. He snorkelled, putting his head underwater. The salmon run had not started yet. Blondie ambled away.

John talked about a scar on Blondie rear leg, from a fight with a rival bear. One of Blondie's ears had a bit missing from it, as a result of another fight. John was clearly pleased to see him. He wished his friend a good season and a good winter. It was not anthropomorphic or sentimental. If you spent time with John you saw the last great wilderness of Alaska and its grizzly bears through his eyes.

We have had difficulties with guides. Sometimes, they are caused by a clash of personalities or a mismatch of expectations. Our German guide in Manu had lived in South America for a long time. She had lived with Indian tribes, the Machigenga people. She chewed a lot of local coca leaves, a mild narcotic. She had gone 'bush'. We found her rigidity and attitudes to wildlife viewing difficult and her treatment of other guides and staff at the lodge appalling. I am sure she found us opinionated and difficult. She was used to more compliant guests. A clash of personalities is awkward as you are stuck in the same place until the end of your stay.

One day we travelled to an oxbow lake noted for its otters. There was a platform that held 2–3 people at a time. We climbed up when it was our turn. When we climbed down again, everybody had wandered off. They reappeared an hour later. They had seen some woolly monkeys. The monkeys had put on an extraordinary demonstration for the visitors. The guide claimed that she had come back for us. We mustn't have heard her, she insisted. We weren't convinced that she came back to get us. It was her revenge, and it was a pity. We would really have liked to see the woolly monkeys.

In India, you must have a guide to enter a national park. You are allocated one at the park entrance. In rural India, jobs are scarce. Near national parks, the choice is subsistence agriculture, working at tourist camps or guiding. The system of allocating guides is designed to spread the work around. It is also about 'baksheesh'. The guides kick back a share of their US$ tips to the park officials. Most guides were abysmal. You take a chance with the allocation system or make alternative arrangements.

Lodges are supposed to have professional guides on staff. At Kanha, the main guide was an enthusiast but not a naturalist. He knew about the park. He also knew where the wildlife tended to be. The other camp staff included a group of giggling English schoolgirls. They were from proper families and the right schools and were well versed in the lifestyles of the rich. They helped with the guiding. They had no knowledge of wildlife. They were unpaid. The lodge covered their board. We had landed in a 'finishing school' for English girls. We insisted that the camp get us a proper guide.

In India, we frequently hired guides ourselves. In Kanha we had a guide called Shalil. At Ranthambore we had Salim. They had both worked with BBC natural-history film crews and were immensely knowledgeable. With them an entirely new world became visible. Shalil and Salim talked about the lack of equipment. They did not have any binoculars. What they had was old and damaged. They relied entirely on gifts from friends or visitors for their most basic requirements, even blankets and clothes. They talked about the pressure placed on them by visitors to see tigers. That was all that the visitors generally came to see. The guides could earn good tips if they could show them a tiger.

In Corbett, we met Shiva, a Bengali like me, which made communication easy. He originally worked in a government department, where he had met a man trying to save the gharial from extinction. This man was an inspirational character and, through him, Shiva became involved in wildlife. The gharial is a large fish-eating crocodile found mainly in the Chambal, Mahanadi, Brahmaputra and Ganges Rivers in India, and is named after the male's distinctive large pot-shaped nostril (*ghara* means pot). They were hunted to near extinction for their skins, which were used to make bags, shoes and belts. The Indian Government stopped hunting and set up a captive-breeding programme to restore the species to sustainable levels in the wild. The gharials are still severely endangered from destruction of their habitats and competition from humans for fish stocks.

Shiva worked on captive-breeding programmes. This involved observing where the female gharials laid their eggs. They would harvest the eggs, incubate them and allow them to hatch. The baby gharials were reared in captivity until they were larger, increasing their chance of survival, then released into the wild. Harvesting the eggs involved long hours of patient observation in hot and inhospitable conditions. The eggs had to be removed while the gharial was not nearby to avoid the risk of attack. One time, bandits held up Shiva and his boss and took everything of value. Shiva and his boss pleaded to be allowed to keep the binoculars essential to their work, but to no avail. It took months to replace them.

Through these guides we learnt the politics and difficulties of wildlife conservation in India: poor pay, misuse of funds provided for conservation, corruption within the parks systems and rampant poaching. It was a hard and unrewarding life for the Indian wildlife guides. Shalil, Salim and Shiva did it out of their love of these last remaining pieces of the great Indian forests.

## Political correctness

The traveller is usually not interested in knowing about the poverty, inequality, injustice and lack of democracy in the country they visit. Tales of woe would reduce the enjoyment of their holiday. For the locals, sharing their political views is dangerous. It may result in arrest, detention or, worse, punishment. If you spend a short amount of time with a guide, you usually do not get into any political discussion. However, the longer you spend together and they begin to understand who you are a little better, the more likely it is that political issues will come up. Comparisons between your country and theirs are made, particularly between education, health and social services. Conversations about the pangolin fall into the category of obtuse but not subversive and can be held at any time and with anyone.

In Zambia, one lodge resembled a rest-and-recreation venue for UN and NGO staff. There was a Moroccan UN aid worker with his family. His wife was Panamanian and their common language was French. A Dutch woman, a private tutor to the aid worker's children, found everything about Africa 'fascinating'. We wondered if she knew any other English descriptive words. She came from Utrecht, which explained why she found Africa fascinating. She was working from a low base. The aid workers had the airs and graces of expatriates or colonials. The talk was of the 'problems' and 'issues': deforestation, overpopulation, HIV/AIDS, government mismanagement. There were also two Irish UN aid workers stationed in Malawi. There was a zealous intensity about them. They talked about the plight of women forced to travel for several hours a day to get water. They were genuine in their desire to help, but couldn't see any quick or easy solution. They saw the inexorable cycle of decay, poverty, hopelessness and dependence. You could see traces of fatigue in their eyes as they talked. They were in their mid-20s.

People descended from original colonists believe that it was they who were wronged when the country gained independence. Following independence, things have 'slipped'. White people with colonial pasts run African lodges. Many have no way back to a mother country from which their ancestors arrived. They cling to the past. The African staff is definitely not in charge. Decolonization and independence is leading/will lead/has led to ruin. 'They can't run things.' 'They can't manage money.' Black African staff members do the work in the lodges and provide essential continuity. Without them the lodges would not function.

The middle-aged white Zimbabwean woman transferring us to the airport was dressed in a colourful floral dress. She had on a lot of costume jewellery. It was a minor miracle that so many rhinestones could fit onto her spectacles. She gave us a history of Zimbabwe.

'You don't mind if I call it Rhodesia? I still think of it that way. Europeans discovered and settled the land.' Seeing our surprised looks, she corrected herself: 'I am giving you the history of white Rhodesia.'

At Hwange, we asked one of the white guides about the number of staff at the camp.

'Four,' he said. 'And some blacks.'

The Anglophile whites present a European front for the overwhelmingly white visitors. They control the lodges, especially the finances and customer relations. An English couple managed a camp in Botswana. He missed bangers, mash, mushy peas, roast vegetables and other delicacies.

'The turkey here is frozen,' he moaned.

In Botswana we met the owners of the lodge. It was a family business. They owned three lodges in Botswana and Zambia, a tour wholesaler and an air-charter business moving people and supplies between the lodges. They were originally farmers in South Africa. They wanted to build a holiday home in the Okavango Delta. A tented hunting camp came up for sale. They bought it 'for a song'. Hunting had been banned and the old concessions were worth very little. They developed the property with help from friends in South Africa, who were familiar with game lodges. Their timing was perfect. They sold their farm, concentrating on eco-tourism. They were constantly adding new properties. Tourists wanted new 'truer' wilderness experiences. Expansion depended on political considerations.

They were coy about their relationship with black Africans: that end of the story we learnt from the guides. Black Africans were vital in getting concessions and licenses. Many black staff had been with the same lodge for many years, reflecting loyalty and also lack of opportunity. The black guides felt powerless to change their situation. There was a lack of money, fear of a lack of management skills. Would tourists come? White interests controlled travel wholesalers. There was a lack of mercantilism and entrepreneurial skills.

In South America, operators lease the lodge site from indigenous people and build the facilities. The Indian tribes help build and operate the lodge. At the end of the lease, the lodge reverts to Indian ownership. They receive a modest annual licence fee on the basis that the operator must make a major investment. The rainforest is harsh. Lodge facilities rarely last beyond the term of the lease. There is a constant need for reinvestment. The operators shrewdly do not invest beyond the term of the lease. The Indians get a lodge that is in poor condition or they renew the lease.

In Alaska, the local Inuit people have greater ownership of eco-tourist businesses, because of the region's oil wealth. We were on a bush plane. Our pilot was Inuit. He and another Inuit passenger were chatting about investments made by the Inuit tribes. One had invested in a casino in an Indian reservation in the 'lower 48s', mainland USA. The tribe had lost the entire investment.

In some places, local people are definitely in charge. In Zaire it took us a while to work out what was different. There were no old people. The oldest people were in their late 30s or early 40s. They were gaunt, skeletal. The roads and infrastructure was decayed. This was the Zaire of Mobutu Sese Seko Kuku Ngbendu Wa Za Banga, the 'All-Powerful Warrior who Goes from

Conquest to Conquest, Leaving Fire in his Wake'. We knew little about Zaire, now the Democratic Republic of Congo. We knew that Mohammed Ali had won an epic fight against George Foreman there, but this did not provide the basis for understanding the country. Mobutu gained power in a military coup. The USA supported Mobutu as a staunch anti-Communist. In Cold War days, this was important. He held power through violence, administered by his private army, and largesse handed out to favoured sycophants. Laurent Kabila, who overthrew Mobutu, boasted that all you needed to mount a revolution in Zaire was US$10,000 and a satellite telephone.[19]

Zaire is rich in natural resources. It received billions in US aid, which went to finance plunder and keep Mobutu in power. Since independence, there has been a steady decline in the country and its people. We were witnesses to the reduction in life expectancy and the ruin of the country's meagre infrastructure. Mobutu's reign ended with his death in exile. A fratricidal civil war was unleashed. Since 1998 an estimated 4 million people have died, 90% of them civilians, in fighting between irregular militias. Laurent Kabila's budget ran into millions, financed by neighbouring countries and foreign firms to whom he sold mineral-exploitation rights. Kabila funded his revolution by a system of ingenious pre-sales.[20]

In 1991, one alternative destination to see gorillas was Rwanda. We had been forced to Zaire because of civil disturbances in Rwanda. In 1994 the civil war between the Tutsis and Hutus began in Rwanda. In one of the greatest genocides of the 20th century, 800,000 people were killed in about 100 days, mostly with machetes.

The other alternative for visiting gorillas was Uganda, which has its own chequered history. Dada Idi Amin was an ex-boxer and army commissioned officer. Amin came to power in a coup overthrowing Milton Obote. He promised to abolish Obote's secret police and return Uganda to civilian rule. Ruling as a dictator for eight years, Amin's antics appalled and amused the world, which regarded him as a buffoon. He gave himself grandiose titles: Field Marshall, President for Life, Conqueror of the British Empire and King of Scotland. His self-awarded medals proved too much for his uniform and it tore from the weight. He once challenged Julius Nyerere, president of neighbouring Tanzania, to a boxing match to settle differences. He wished Richard Nixon a 'speedy recovery' following Watergate. He said that Hitler was right to kill 6 million Jews. *Punch*, the British magazine, published a weekly column, pretending to be written by Amin, commenting on global affairs. Amin destroyed the economy, expelling the country's Indian population. He ruled through the army and his private police and security forces. He funded the forces by diverting government spending. He was responsible for the deaths of 100,000–500,000 people – no one is sure of the exact number. Important victims were beheaded and their heads stored in a freezer. When the mood took him, the heads were placed at his dinner table so Amin could 'converse' with the deceased.

In 1991, our fees had inadvertently financed, in part, the horror of Mobutu. Today, it is possible to travel to Uganda and Rwanda to see the gorillas. Dedicated park rangers somehow managed to preserve the habituated gorilla groups. It is impossible to understand their courage and commitment.

Fatehpur Sikri is a huge, sprawling city near Agra, built in the 16th century by Emperor Akbar. Akbar conceived of the city as a utopian centre of scholarship and political power. He desperately wanted a male heir; a Sufi holy man prophesied that he would soon have three. The first of these three sons was Salim, the Emperor Jehangir. The line of succession secured, Akbar moved his royal capital to a brand new city at Sikri to honour the Sufi holy man – Fatehpur, which loosely means 'city of victory'. It was the most magnificent and shortest-lived centre of the Mughal Empire. In 1586, 21 years after construction commenced, Akbar abandoned Fatehpur Sikri to return to Agra. The water supply had dried up.

Fatehpur Sikri is a glorious sight even today. Monumental stairs lead up to the huge gates. There is an enormous congregation courtyard and a copy of the main mosque in Mecca. There are many palaces for the Emperor, his many wives, concubines – Akbar is reputed to have had a harem of 800 women – family, ministers and courtiers. There are formal pavilions where Akbar heard petitions and dispensed justice. There is the pleasure court, the Panch Mahal, a five-storey palace. Akbar spent his evenings listening to music and watching the dancers. In the late afternoon, the complex was suffused in a beautiful, soft dappled light. The stones glowed orange. The guide was telling us the history of Fatehpur Sikri. His storyteller's gift made the place come alive. The conversation turned to politics. He looked at us, summing us up carefully. We talked about modern India, about the freedom struggle. We talked about Netaji Subhash Chandra Bose who formed an ill-advised alliance with the Japanese against the British that was a catalyst for independence. He talked about the rivalries within the Indian independence movement, the ill-conceived partition of India and Pakistan.

We talk about the great ruling dynasties: the Nehrus, the Gandhis. Monarchy disguised as democracy. He mentioned the Shiv Sena – right-wing Neo-Nazi Hindu thugs – who advocate the removal of all non-Hindus from India. They were behind the violence at the Ahyodya Mosque. He was not optimistic about the future. The conversation turned to the great business dynasties: the Birlas, the Tatas. The families parlayed government licences and monopolies into enormous fortunes. Poor people make a marginal living gathering salt that is sold in little packets. Gandhi refused to buy English salt as part of his non-cooperation tactics. People marched to the sea for salt.

The Government is to award a monopoly on salt to a big-business family. He rails against this betrayal of the poor and defenceless. This is the real India rather than the India of 400 years ago in Fatehpur Sikri.

## Final price

I come from a background of non-present-giving. Jade comes from a background of present-giving. We buy small gifts for family and friends. We occasionally buy something for ourselves, or for our house. Sometimes, we even buy our cat, Alice, a present. In a Quito handicraft shop, Jade noticed thick, rough llama-hair cushion covers with simple geometric motifs. The shop cats were sitting on the cushion covers. Jade bought two. Alice sleeps on these covers from halfway across the world.

A present that looked attractive when bought can look shoddy and out of place once transported home. The identical item is available locally. You console yourself with the thought that your item is authentic and cheaper. Then you discover that it isn't really ebony wood at all. It is cheap wood covered with boot polish. We try to buy small things, such as local fabrics. We try to buy at local handicraft centres that support local artisans and industry. It is not easy.

In 2003, Jade and I were in Johannesburg. It was eight years since our last trip. Jade went shopping returning empty-handed. Things we bought on our previous trip 10 years ago were still available. There was nothing new. The shops assume that most visitors do not return.

'Shopping' took on an entirely different meaning at Plettenberg Bay on South Africa's Cape Coast. 'Plett's' physical beauty is undeniable: the beaches are long and spectacular, the bay is an important refuge for marine life. Dolphins, fur seals and, during winter months, whales are abundant. Plettenberg Bay is a holiday destination for wealthy, white South Africans. Just outside Plettenberg Bay, the black population lives in shantytowns and settlements. We stayed in a gated community five minutes outside the town. To leave the community, you negotiated several gates. The final one was manned by black security guards. We waved at them, they waved back. They never asked us who we were or where we were staying.

One morning, Jade was driving into town to shop. At the boom gate, the security guard approached Jade.

'Are you going into town?'

'Yes.'

'Can you buy me half a loaf of bread?'

'Sliced or unsliced?' She couldn't think of anything else to say.

'Sliced,' he responded and gave her 2 rand (US 40 cents).

She went to the bread counter at the supermarket. There were no sliced, half loaves. The attendant got a loaf and sliced it carefully. Then he counted the slices to create exactly half a loaf. The attendant kept losing count. Finally he managed to get it right. Jade walked out of the supermarket with half a loaf of sliced bread and the change. Returning to the house she gave the bread and change to the security guard. I asked her how her expedition had gone. In her desire to get the bread she had forgotten the rest of her shopping.

Jade and I like shopping for food on holidays. We brave local markets to buy food to break up the monotony of hotel and restaurant meals. We sit with our purchases, get out our Swiss Army knives and make a modest meal for ourselves.

## Travel conversations

Travel requires an entire dialect with its own distinctive syntax. In *Eothen*[21], Alexander Kinglake chronicles a respectable and wealthy Englishman's travels in the Far East. Kinglake records the following dialogue between himself (Traveller) and the Pasha. A dragoman translates the conversation. Traveller: 'Give him my best compliments and say I am delighted to have the honour of seeing him'. Dragoman then translates Pasha's 'His Lordship, this Englishman, Lord of London, Scorner of Ireland, Suppressor of France, has quitted his governments and left his enemies to breathe for a moment, and has crossed the broad waters in strict disguise, with a small but eternally faithful retinue of followers, in order that he might look upon the bright countenance of the Pasha among Pashas – the Pasha of the everlasting Pashalik of Karagholook-oldour'. The florid verbal extravagance of the Pasha's response is perversely reduced to a simple 'You are welcome' for the traveller.

We are sitting on the Meikles Hotel Bus. The Meikles Hotel is an upmarket hotel in Harare, Zimbabwe; the bus provides transfers to and from the airport. It is full of tourists, mainly elderly, retired couples. There is nervous chatter between strangers – travel conversations. One man lost his passport at immigration. How did he get into Zimbabwe without a passport? He only lost the passport for three minutes. An elderly man tells his story: he lost all his film at Sydney airport. He put it on the X-ray machine and left it behind. He had to buy the film again. He pats his bag, reassuring himself that the new film is still there. You make out the disapproving expression on his wife's face. The man has already reached profound conclusions about Africa. This will be, he says, his last trip here. It is too far away. He doesn't know what to do with himself

CHAPTER 5

on a plane for 15 hours. Africa and Harare Airport are dangerous. He turns out to be a judge. We see the couple later in the trip in Botswana. They are now seasoned eco-travellers, well versed in safari travel, conversing in the patois of game viewing. The transformation is as interesting as it is superficial.

In travel conversation, context is everything. You will never see these people again. In an unfamiliar setting, someone who speaks your language is trusted. Rather darkly, Charles Sobhraj used this to gain the trust of young and naïve foreigners travelling on the hippie trail in India/Nepal in the 60s. He is alleged to have drugged, killed and robbed many of them.

Travel conversation has a few staples:

'We are from [insert name of country]. Where are you from?'
'Have you been here before?'
'I was in [name of country].'
'I have heard it is [insert description of location e.g. nice, not nice, dangerous, etc.].'
'Did I tell you what happened to me in [name of country].'
'Isn't it terrible?'

It is useful to have a 'prop'. In Zaire, we met Cindy and Dennis from Boston. Our friendship began with a large fold-out map of Africa. Fully open, the only way to read the map was to lay it on the ground and crawl over it. We were staying at the Paradise Club on Lake Kivu. There was an incident – civil war – going on in Goma, at the other end of Lake Kivu. Dennis wanted to know exactly where Goma was. Jade volunteered her map. Dennis gradually unfurled it like a yacht running up a spinnaker for a downwind run.

'It is a large map,' he said admiringly.

In wildlife lodges, the communal eating arrangements provide conversational opportunities. The couple from Durban in South Africa who run the lodge were disappointed at my unfamiliarity with a curry bootie, apparently a highpoint of Indian cuisine. 'Surely you know it?' Each person tells stories. You listen attentively, then indicate that the story was wonderful and reciprocate with one of your own. The camp hosts have back-up plans: animal and snake stories or a few Indian stories from Durban. It is useful to have a 'conversation piece', such as a device to extract corks that have slipped into the bottle. 'It costs £100, you know.' There are only enough stories for one or two nights, the typical length of stay. We tend to stay longer and sit through the repeats. One day, we hope to be able to offer the 'killer' story: 'There was the time when we came across a pangolin!'

Cultural differences lead to unintentional comedy. An Indian man once cornered some friends travelling in India.

'Australia will be being a hot country,' he asked.

'Yes,' the man from Australia replied.

'There will be being a lot of sunshine; very hot sunshine.'

'Yes.'

'India is having lot of hot sunshine as well. This is why we are dark. Why are Australians not dark? Australians should be having dark skin like Indians, no?'

The Australian man had no response.

A European woman asked a South American Indian woman whether she was happy in the jungle. Was the Indian woman happy with her simple life within nature away from the stress and pressure of cities and modern industrial life? The Indian woman was confused. The concepts were probably alien to her.

She answered, 'Yes'.

It was the expected answer.

The true answer would be, 'No, I am not happy. I might once have been content in my life. I knew no other world. Then, the Europeans came. They raped the women. They stole our lands. They introduced diseases that killed us. The survivors were enslaved. Most of them died. You destroyed the land that we had lived off. You confined us to parts that suited you. You left when there was nothing left to interest you. You left a ravaged country with no ability to rule and make its way in the modern world. We were enslaved again. We depend on your money and skills. Now, you come to visit us. You ask us "Am I happy?" No, I am not happy. I do not like having to play a simple native woman dressed in a grass skirt. I do not like standing half naked so you can take our photographs. We hate doing this for dollars, most of which we do not see in any case. I would like to have a home, clean water and sewerage. I would like my family and children to have proper medical treatment so most of my people do not die before they are 40. I would like my children to be educated to have a chance at a better life. Our way of life is over. You destroyed it a long time ago when you came here. No, I am not happy.'

## Postcards from faraway places

The beauty of the wild places and animals leaves an indelible mark. We come to see the natural history. More often than not, people are less relevant, unless they are facilitating our adventure. But the places and people that you meet and see fleetingly also leave their mark. Each encounter remains with you and sometimes haunts you over time in unexpected ways. They are the rewards and burdens of all travel.

I am alone in the hotel limousine taking me to the airport in an Asian city. The car is air-conditioned. It is about 30°C (86°F) outside. The car pulls up at the last traffic light before the airport expressway. The elevated expressway ensures that you do not see the slums that you once saw on your way to the airport. At the traffic light there is a girl. She is seven or eight years old. She carries small plastic bags of fruit juice and ice. She walks from car to car offering them for sale. She moves towards a car and holds up the bags. If there is no interest then she moves quickly to the next, trying to cover as many cars as possible. In this heat the bags do not stay cold for long. She has a bag around her neck for change. Everything about this child is businesslike. She is not begging. She wants to work to eke out a living. She is now near me. I want to buy one of her bags. I am not thirsty. I can't drink the water. It is polluted. I just want to buy something from her. I don't have any local money. Our eyes meet. I sadly shake my head. She registers my response. She moves quickly to the next car, a look of grim determination on her face. Her desire to make her way in the world is clear. She is the same age as our niece. She should be in school. She should not have to do this. The light changes. The car moves forward. I do not see her again.

Travellers go through Isiolo in northern Kenya on their way to the arid wilderness. It is home to the colourful Samburu, Turkana and Boran tribes. Isiolo is known for its brass, copper and aluminium and steel jewellery. We refuel at Isiolo on our way to Samburu. Local men instantly besiege the car trying to sell the jewellery. Many hands are thrust into the car. Our driver has gone off to pay for the petrol. The aggressive throng of men frightens our fellow travellers. The American is agitated and getting aggressive. I smile and try to talk calmly to the men. We don't want anything at the moment. No one can hear me in the bedlam. I make eye contact with a boy – maybe 15 or 16 years old. The boy has an angry look.

'They come to see animals. They treat us like animals.' There is rage in his voice.

We travel back through Isiolo a few days later. The scene repeats itself. I want to buy some jewellery as presents. The sellers engulf us. I see the boy. He probably does not remember me. I beckon him. Somehow he makes his way through the throng. He shows us bracelets – intertwined aluminium and steel. I pick out some. He names a price. We bargain briefly. My heart isn't in it. The driver is on his way back to the car. We agree a price. The transaction is concluded. The boy looks at me directly. For an instant an open joyous smile breaks out on his face.

We travel to Bukavu from Bujumbura in Burundi. We actually drive from Burundi into Rwanda, which we are supposed to avoid. Our destination is the town of Cyangugu in Rwanda where we cross over into Zaire. Bukavu is about 3 kilometres (2.1 miles) from Cyangugu. A wooden bridge across a stream marks the border.

In 1994, Rwanda's genocidal civil war between the Tutsis and Hutus erupted. I saw the bridge at Cyangugu again on television. On the Rwandan side there was a very large crowd. They were Rwandan Tutsis fleeing the war and the advancing Hutu Interhamwe – 'those who kill together'. Thousands of Tutsis were already dead. Men, women and children were gathered at the bridge. They were terrified and exhausted, their only possessions the clothes that they stood in. Some could barely stand. Zaire had closed the border, unable to cope with the refugees. Complex negotiations were going on to open it up again. As days went by the crowds at the bridge grew – a seething, unruly mass of desperate humanity. The Interhamwe were behind the refugees. The television pictures mercilessly captured the look of hopelessness and despair on the faces of these people. I remember the bridge. I remember crossing it. I remember placid and beautiful Lake Kivu. We had seen the gorillas here. It was one of our greatest most unforgettable experiences. I find it hard now to separate my memories of the gorillas and the images of the crowds.

# CHAPTER 6

## 'Fata Morgana': The Hope And Reality Of Eco-tourism

*...We drove through the villages to the entrance of the park. The villagers looked at us listlessly. We were about to spend their lifetime's earnings in a single day to see mountain gorillas...*

# CHAPTER 6

## Fata Morgana

The interplay between humans and the natural world is complex. People have relied on nature's bounty for their survival. Nature provides inspiration for the best in human endeavour. Yet, human activity increasingly places intolerable stresses on the natural world. Examples of this ambiguous relationship are found everywhere.

In Hong Kong there is the Yuen Po Street Bird Garden market. It started in Hong Lok Street, where owners gathered informally to display their songbirds, and bird lovers came to hear them sing. It evolved into a market where people bought and sold songbirds, and, in the mid-1990s, the market moved to Yuen Po Street.

You hear it before you see it: the songs of the birds above and throughout the few old, narrow streets that the market is based around. There are some surviving red lacquered gates in the old Chinese style. Old men sit in vests and open slippers, sipping tea or passing the time of day. In the main they sit next to the ornate cages that contain their birds. Some of the cages are uncovered, displaying the captive birds. The cages are positioned near to those of other birds, in an effort to encourage singing, as the birds follow their instincts to attract mates. Their songs are in vain. I saw finches, larks and thrushes, a few brightly plumed macaws. I recognised a sulphur-crested cockatoo from Australia. There was something sad and plaintive in the songs. The birds sang of their lost freedom, about captivity and isolation. I thought about the ones that I had seen in the wild. I couldn't bear the sight of these caged birds.

Also in Hong Kong are the traditional Chinese medicine shops: a counter with scales and a mortar and pestle; shelves crowded with large glass jars filled with dried animal or plant matter. The jars contain plants: ginseng, mushrooms, orchids and tree bark. There are numerous animal parts, usually dried internal organs and whole or powdered bones. There are dried crabs, squid, cuttlefish, octopus, seahorses, dried whole lizards and the fallopian tubes of female frogs. There is snake venom and blood, dried snakeskin and snake organs, such as gall bladders. There are deer and antelopes' antlers, horns, feet, tails, bones and penises. There are bat faeces. There are the pelts of hedgehogs and the genitals of seals. There are the bones of rare snow leopards. There are the bones and penises of tigers. There are rhinoceros horns. There are jars with fresh bile milked from bears. There are the scales of pangolins. Hedgehog pelts are a cure for rheumatism. Bear bile treats gallstones and other gall-bladder conditions. Dried seahorses promote youthful appearance. Many of the ingredients promote sexual arousal. Dogs' kidneys and the genitals of reptiles and mammals are aphrodisiacs.

Many of the species are protected. Hunting them is illegal. The Convention on International Trade in Endangered Species (CITES) makes it illegal to trade in the body parts of protected species. The Chinese Endangered Species Scientific Commission produced a report based on a survey of the largest Chinese traditional medicine manufacturers. The manufacturer's purchases included 1,600 tons of rat snakes, 500 tons of geckos, 6,000 tons of flying squirrel faeces, 200 tons of pangolin scales and 25 tons of leopard bones. One manufacturer alone used 10 tons of snake gall bladders. A snake seller in a Chinese province indicated that she could supply immediately without notice one ton of dried rat snakes from her stock. Another trader indicated that he turned over 60 tons of dried sea horses annually.

Plants such as orchids and liquorice and certain trees have been totally wiped out in China. Trade in animal parts has decimated populations. In central Asia the population of the saiga antelope has been reduced by over 95% in 10 years (from over one million to 30,000 and falling). Animal-rights groups report that over 7,000 bears are held captive in China to be 'milked' daily for their bile. I wonder how many pangolins are killed for their body parts every year?

I visited Tokyo's famed Tsukiji fish market around 5.00am. It is the size of several football fields. There were hundreds of species. There were dead whole fish, fillets, fish roe and the internal organs of fish. There were live fish and crustaceans. There was a section dedicated to tuna – a Japanese delicacy. Boxes were laid out in neat lines on the floor, each containing a single large tuna. Someone had scrawled in Japanese on each of the boxes. The silver back of the fish and its dorsal fin were visible. The boxes were filled with ice. The whole area was covered in a white, misty condensation. The boxes stretched in every direction – box after box after box. They resembled coffins for each of the slaughtered tuna. How long had the fish taken to reach their size? How long could the slaughter continue?

In the history of the planet, many species have become extinct. Human beings have contributed greatly to the extinction of species. Extinction is in an everyday expression: 'as dead as a dodo'. The dodo is the best known of all extinct species, but the most abundant bird thought to have existed was the passenger pigeon. Passenger pigeons made up about 40% of all birds in North America. They gathered in massive flocks. The sun would be blocked out when these flocks flew past and their passing could take hours. Their droppings fell like snow. Early settlers hunted these pigeons – a seemingly limitless resource. The winner in a hunting competition killed 30,000 of the species. By the 1870s, the huge flocks had disappeared. The last wild passenger pigeon was shot in 1900 in Ohio. The last captive bird died on 1 September 1914 in Cincinnati Zoo.[22]

CHAPTER 6

In 1844, the great auk, a large aquatic penguin-like bird, became extinct.[23] Jacques Cartier, a French explorer, discovered the major breeding colony on Funk Island in Newfoundland. Explorers, sailors and fishermen captured and killed the birds to provision their boats or to use as fish bait. In the end the great auks were only found on the rocky stacks off Iceland. One rocky stack – Geirfulasker – sank in volcanic activity in 1830. The few surviving great auks ended up on the nearby island of Edley. It was there on 3rd June 1844 that the last of them was killed.[24]

'...A party of sailors landed, having been sent by a collector to check if any of the birds remained. They spotted a pair, standing head and shoulders above the masses of smaller sea birds. Legend has it that the female was brooding an egg, a last hope for the future of the species. The great auks made a desperate attempt to reach the safety of the water, but one was trapped between some rocks, while the other was seized just a few metres from the edge of the sea. Both were clubbed to death. The egg, it is believed, was crushed beneath a sailor's boot.'

Stuffed animals, skins, skeletons, eggs and pictures are all that remain of countless species that once existed on this planet.

Human beings have long regarded nature as an inexhaustible resource to be plundered relentlessly. Yet the natural world is also deeply idealized by human beings. Edward Wilson, the famed biologist, even coined a term for this relationship, *biophilia* – an innate passion for nature. Eco-tourism is often offered up as one of the ways in which human beings can reach a new accommodation with the natural world. The 'conservation' movement has gained prominence. 'Biodiversity' and 'sustainable development' have become part of the language. My English teacher taught me to care about language, about the precise meaning of each word. In the modern world there is 'spin', the use of words to create illusions or falsity. Eco-tourism is a Fata Morgana, a mirage or an illusion. As Kurt Vonnegut described it, Fata Morgana is, 'a mirage named after Morgan Le Fay, a fairy who lived at the bottom of a lake. It was famous for appearing in the Strait of Messina, between Calabria and Sicily. Fata Morgana was poetic crap, in short.'[25]

## Puritan and paranoid conservation

David Attenborough has, over the decades, become synonymous with documentary programmes on natural history, the inspiration for many eco-adventures. Despite deeply felt and serious concerns about the environment, he adopts a neutral and objective approach. The beauty and splendour of nature, if communicated properly, would persuade the audience of the importance of preserving natural habitats and the plants and animals that existed within them. In the late 1990s, Attenborough made a series for the BBC – *State of the Planet* – explicitly focused on the threats to the natural world and to the survival of many habitats, plants and animals. These were:

OVER-HARVESTING: The over-exploitation of species, including hunting and fishing to a level that reduces their ability to survive as a viable population.
DESTRUCTION OF NATURAL HABITATS: Human encroachment on wilderness and loss of natural habitats from growth of human populations and the need for land and resources resulting in the destruction of animal and plant species.
INTRODUCTION OF FOREIGN SPECIES: the introduction of animals and plants that compete with and ultimately gain ascendancy over endemic species, leading to their extinction.
ENVIRONMENTAL CHANGE: The environmental impact of human activity (changes in air and water quality, release of toxic substances, climate change) that affect the ability of plants and animals to survive.
ISLANDIZATION: the creation of isolated habitats where animal and plant life is unable to survive because of the loss of genetic diversity or inability to connect with other vital parts of the eco-system necessary for its existence.

But there are dissenting voices. A leading figure of the rejectionist movement is Bjørn Lomborg, Director of Environmental Assessment at the Institute of Copenhagen, Denmark. In a book,[26] several articles, speeches and interviews, Dr Lomborg, a statistician, challenges the prospect of environmental disaster. In 2003, he visited Australia and gave a series of talks and interviews arguing that statistical analysis supports the proposition that the environment is improving. Narrowly based theory on natural limits to growth and resources did not take into account technological progress and innovation. Schemes like the Kyoto protocol were inherently flawed on a cost-benefit basis.

Dr Lomborg's detractors argue that he is not qualified to draw the conclusions he does in a scientific field outside his own. Other scientists have come to a different conclusion using similar statistical data.[27] Being found guilty of 'scientific dishonesty' in Denmark helped Dr Lomborg's notoriety, although he was subsequently exonerated.[28] He attracts the ire of environmentalists and the support of development lobbies.

In Australia, columnists claimed that the conservation movement preferred guilt to Dr Lomborg's 'common sense'. An Australian government minister's office issued a press release stating that Dr Lomborg 'spoke a lot of sense' but cautioned that 'what works in one country doesn't necessarily work in another'. He was heckled for not being radical enough as he had accepted that climate change and carbon dioxide levels are linked. Dr Lomborg was newsworthy because he took the opposite view to the now traditional conservation view. Conservation was yesterday's story. Dr Lomborg had positioned himself in the right 'space'. He had the right amount of 'spin' and 'angle' on the subject. The world couldn't get enough of it. Fellow scientists wallowed in self-piteous obscurity.

The question of whether the environment is being degraded irreversibly still remains. Scientists have helpfully coined a phrase for this phase of natural history: The Sixth Extinction[29]. Edward Wilson noted that we know very little: if natural history were a library of books, we have not even finished the first chapter of the first book. Species were being lost before we could even turn a page.[30]

In Costa Rica there is a mite that lives in specific flowers. When the flowers bloom, hummingbirds come to feed on the nectar. The mites move into the bird's nostril at 12 body lengths per second, a speed comparable to that of a cheetah, the fastest land animal. When the hummingbird reaches another suitable flower, the mites move onto it and take up residence. Each plant species has a different mite. Each organism has hidden links to others. Human activity that affects one species will affect many others through complex relationships.

On the day I was writing this, a small news story recorded that the last wild-born crested ibis died in captivity in Japan. The crested ibis was a stately bird, snowy white with pink-tinged feathers. The bird had a red face and a prominent sloping black beak. It was once common in rice fields. Its decline was due to industrial development, deforestation and pesticides that destroyed its habitats and food supply. The bird is idealized in Japanese art and by traditional scroll painters.

## Desolation row

In the course of our journeys, we have witnessed first hand each of the threats to the natural world that Attenborough identified. The destruction of the natural word is depressing.

The ecology of Alaska and Canada is dependent on the annual salmon runs. Millions of salmon gather in the rich waters of the north Pacific after being at sea for many years. The adults return to the streams they came from, and it is here they will spawn and die. We saw the rivers of fish making their way upstream. They were a bright red, their mouths grotesquely distorted into savage hooked shapes with protruding teeth. We watched them pairing off to mate. On the gravel bed of the stream we could see salmon eggs.

The spawning salmon are central to the entire ecology. The bears and other wildlife rely on this brief summer bounty to store fat reserves for the cold winter. The salmon runs were in severe decline. The fishing fleets use advanced technology to locate the shoals of gathering salmon and sophisticated trawling techniques to catch them. On the Kenai Peninsula, during the fishing season, fishermen line entire rivers. Lines frequently tangle, and tempers reach boiling point in 'combat fishing'. How many salmon survive the combined assault of the fishing fleet and the recreational fishermen? Fishing guides talked about 'meat fishermen'. The aim of most recreational fishermen was to catch the biggest fish and as much of them as possible. The guides puzzled as to what happens to 100 kilograms (220 pounds) of salmon frozen, vacuum-packed and sent home. The cost far exceeds that of buying it at a local supermarket. Most of it spoils and is thrown out.

In the Galapagos Islands, there is a 20 nautical mile territorial limit around the islands. Fernandina, the most western of the Galapagos Islands, is famed for its flightless cormorants and marine iguanas. On any day west of Fernandina and just outside the legal limit you see fishing boats from Taiwan, China, Korea and Japan extending across the horizon. Scientists have chronicled declining fish stocks and smaller size of fish. Trawling or long-line fishing is highly damaging because of the problem of by-catch (fish that are not commercially valuable and which are discarded). The long line and trawling nets claim dolphins, sea lions, fur seals and sea birds as their victims. The numbers of sea birds killed each year is staggering.

In the Galapagos, the population of sea lions and fur seals were declining due to changing climatic cycles (El Niño and La Niña) and reduced fish stocks. The crew worried about the future of the island's famous wildlife.

In Asia there is huge demand for live fish. Diners exult as a whole dish of prawns writhes in front of them as they are literally boiled to death. There is trade in aquarium fish. Live fish is taken by cyanide fishing. Divers use the poison to stun the fish and catch them for export. Many coral reefs are now oceanic deserts as a result of cyanide and dynamite fishing (depth charges used to harvest fish). The reefs are protected. Fishing is illegal. The local people are poor and have no other way to make a living or to feed themselves. There is no money to police the reefs. Authorities are corrupt and easily bribed.

Even remote oceans are not immune from overfishing. The Patagonian toothfish is a new fish delicacy. Toothfish are large, ugly creatures that are related to the cod, 2 metres (6 feet) in length and over 110 kilograms (250 pounds). Toothfish are found in the deep cold waters (up to 2,500–3,000 metres [1–2 miles] deep) of the Southern Ocean off Antarctica. Their white flesh is soft with a delicate flavour and in high demand in the US, Japan and Europe. Fishermen call them 'white gold'. A single sashimi-grade fish can fetch up to US$1,000. In the United States it is sold as sea bass, in Japan *mero*.

Toothfish are slow growing and live up to 40 years, taking 8–10 years to reach sexual maturity. Their slow rate of reproduction makes them vulnerable to overfishing. The Patagonian toothfish industry was once widely distributed. In the mid-1990s, overfishing meant that the industry moved into the polar regions. The Australian Government controls the exploitation of marine resources in its self-proclaimed 'economic zone' in the Southern Ocean around Heard Island. Licences are sold to 'harvest' toothfish. The licensed catch over seven years is around 17,000 tons. Nobody knows whether the catch level is sustainable. The illegal catch is larger than the legal catch.

In 2003, the Australian navy gave chase to a fishing boat – the Uruguayan registered vessel, the *Viarsa*. The boat was eventually boarded by the Australian and South African navies near South Africa. It is alleged that it was carrying a large load of illegally-caught Patagonian toothfish. The Australian Government's main concern about illegal fishing is that 'Australian resources were being illegally appropriated by unlicensed, non-Australian fishermen.'

Patagonian toothfish are in steep decline.[31] Fishing boats are switching to Antarctic toothfish which is found further south, occurring mainly in an area just off eastern Antarctica, about 1,000 nautical miles south of Heard Island. This is Area 58.4.2 – in theory, a nature reserve.

In the Antarctic, factory ships now harvest krill – tiny shrimp-like crus-taceans at the bottom of the ocean food chain – for human food and aquaculture. All life in the Southern Ocean depends on the krill. Without krill, sea birds, penguins, seals and whales will perish. Scientists are currently researching 'how much krill can be harvested without harming the Antarctic ecosystem.' By the time definite scientific research is completed there will be no ecosystem to protect.

In Alaska, we saw a hunter with a licence to 'take' a brown bear. Natives of Alaska can obtain hunting licenses in a lottery system. Alaskans generally sell these licences for large sums to hunters from the Lower 48 States (the Alaskan term for the rest of the USA). The hunter we saw was holding out for his 'big' bear.

This was in a place where visitors came to see bears. The bears were habituated to human beings, not associating them with danger. The owner of the lodge had been trying to stop the hunting for years. It was rare to see large bears. They had all been killed. The hunter had a high-powered rifle with telescopic sight and was in a boat offshore waiting for a bear to appear. The bear would have no way of knowing that he was there and no chance to escape once exposed. What was the sport in killing a defenceless bear with such a rifle?

In Northern Canada, the native Inuit people get licences to 'take' polar bears. Polar bears are the largest carnivores on earth and have no natural enemies, though their numbers are in decline. The licences are sold through intermediaries to hunters for large sums of money. Sometimes the bear is shot from a helicopter; the term 'hunt' is a misnomer.

In Africa 'bush meat' is traditionally an important source of protein. Local forest-dwelling people have always hunted bush meat with primitive weapons, spears and nets in a sustainable way. The scale of hunting has increased to a commercial enterprise and animals are frequently poached. Affluent Africans demand the now-fashionable bush meat. Timber and tourism play a part in the trade. Roads bring logging crews and new settlers. The roads and transport infrastructure help hunters gain easy access to the forest. Developed countries and international development agencies finance these roads, and own or finance the logging operations. The ready availability of automatic weapons (made and exported by developed nations) fuels the slaughter. The animals poached as part of the bush-meat trade included the great apes,[32] severely endangered and protected species, such as gorillas, chimpanzees and bonobos; elephants, forest antelopes, porcupines, wild pigs and crocodiles are also poached. The scale of this trade is not known. It is a severe threat to local animal populations.

Karl Ammann, a wildlife photographer, published a series of photographs portraying severed gorilla heads and orphaned infant gorillas and chimpanzees. The West insisted that the killing and eating of these animals was equivalent to murder and cannibalism. The apes are closely related to human beings. The media briefly took an interest, but that interest rapidly faded. The bush-meat business continues unabated.

In Asia, the consumption of wild animal meat and organs is widespread. The rarer and more endangered the species, the greater the demand and the greater its supposed power to promote sexual arousal or retard aging. If eco-tourism is 'last chance to see,' then this is 'last chance to taste.'

The rhinoceros population in Africa is under severe threat. Some parks have electric fences to protect the rhinoceroses. In one park each rhinoceros is accompanied at all times by armed guards. The poachers, armed with automatic weapons, just kill the guards as well as the rhinoceros. The poorly paid and ill-equipped guards try valiantly to protect the animal. Many die. The value of a rhinoceros horn is just too high. In Zimbabwe, the authorities took the radical step of cutting off the horns, in order to make the animals valueless to the poachers. Poachers would often track a rhinoceros. When they finally found the animal, the poachers would see that its horn was missing and kill it anyway. They did not want to waste their time, accidentally tracking the same animal again.

The United Nation's CITES Treaty regulates the trade in animal parts. CITES is having little or no success in stopping the trade in protected species.[33] In 2000, CITES, at its 11th Conference held in Paris, established a working group to address 'problems related to the bush-meat trade'. The working group met to 'develop an action plan for future activities'. In 2002, at the 12th CITES conference, the parties 'agreed to continue the activities of the working group and to enhance cooperation with activities on bush meat under the Convention on Biological Diversity.' There are numerous 'plans' but rarely any action.

No one can tell us whether pangolins are endangered. Insufficient facts are known about their habits, numbers and distribution to make a definitive judgement. It just seems that very few people have seen them.

## Living together and apart

Eco-travel quickly shows the extent of destruction of natural habitat. Most conservation areas are small and isolated. The Kahuzi-Biega Park in Zaire, where people went to see gorillas, is located high in the Virunga Mountains. The terrain is steep and rugged. Heavily cultivated fields extend right up to the edge of the park, driven by the demands of a large population and the scarcity of arable land. Civil war meant that the boundary was largely irrelevant, with massive encroachment into the park. We drove through the villages to the entrance of the park. The villagers looked at us listlessly. We were about to spend their lifetime's earnings in a single day to see mountain gorillas.

People regularly encroach on the parks. In Nepal, villagers are allowed inside to gather dried grass for thatching. The noise and disturbance make it difficult to see wildlife. In India, political pressures make it hard to relocate villages that are within parks. In Kanha, we were driving at dusk back towards the gate. We suddenly saw a herd of chittal (spotted deer) run towards us. They were being pursued by a pack of dholes. The dholes are large, reddish wild dogs and, like their African relations, superb hunters. A pack of dholes have been known to kill a tiger. We were thrilled. Jade had taken out her camera and was focusing on the dholes with her telephoto lens. Suddenly, I noticed a man and woman on a bicycle. We were quite close to one of the villages within the park. The man dismounted, adjusted his clothing and posed in front of his bicycle. He thought that we wanted his photo.

In Alaska and Canada, there are extensive logging operations within and near national parks. In Canada, logging was permitted very close to the water line resulting in increasing amounts of soil being washed into the streams and rivers. This reduced the clear gravel beds needed by spawning salmon. Ending logging would costs jobs and livelihoods, but everybody expects that logging will be curtailed. Logging companies are redoubling their efforts to take out very large, old growth trees. They use large helicopters to locate the trees. They drop logging crews into the forest to cut them down. The trees are hundreds of years old; some have existed from before the Dark Ages.

Sometimes, human intervention in the environment has catastrophic results. Australia's proudest industrial achievement is the Snowy Mountains Hydro-Electric Scheme (known as the Snowy Scheme). The scheme harnessed the waters of the Murray and Darling Rivers for electricity and irrigation. Australia is a dry continent. There are years of drought when rivers turn into muddy streams. Then there are floods. The scheme's supporters had a vision of a vast agricultural landscape. One politician (Sir Thomas Playford) foresaw that the irrigation system with its 'cheap water' would only lead to development of agriculture that made even greater demands for water.

The Snowy Scheme destroyed the river systems, reducing the flow of the headwaters. The water that was used for irrigation projects created dependence on uncertain rains. It led to planting of crops unsuited to the Australian climate and conditions. The extra water used in irrigation increased the salinity of the land disastrously. It is an ecological catastrophe. The endemic species of the area were finely adapted to the natural water cycle of the river. The river's rich ecosystems are now destroyed. The water birds are mostly gone. The murray cod, a large endemic fish, once abundant, has all but disappeared. It is now a rare, expensive delicacy on gourmet menus. The river is now dominated by an introduced species – European carp. The landscape is covered in salt scalds.

Introduced species are a major problem in Australia. At the end of the last ice age, the rising sea levels cut the Australian continent off from Asia. Indigenous animals evolved to meet the specific challenges of the environment. After Captain James Cook arrived in Australia, the new English colony developed rapidly. The new arrivals introduced animals and plants not endemic to the continent.

Domestic cats that were brought over became feral and preyed on native species not adapted to them. An animal activist (Dr John Walmsley), committed to the preservation of native species, wears the skin of a dead feral cat on his head. He believes fervently that cats have exterminated many native Australian animals. Dr Tim Flannery, on the other hand, argues that there is little evidence that cats caused an environmental catastrophe for native Australian mammals and marsupials.[34] He argues that cats predated European settlement. In a touch of political theatre he argues that 'cats are the Arabs of the animal world'[35].

# CHAPTER 6

The cane toad was introduced to Australia from its native Hawaii in 1935 to counter the scarab beetle found in the cane-growing districts of Queensland. The cane toad took over the landscape, destroying native species. It is highly poisonous, secreting a toxin that is lethal to animals and even to humans. Cane toads have moved into relative pristine forest areas and are moving into populous southern states. The only hope is a new ice age. Toads do not like colder climates. Perhaps the alternative is to convince Eastern herbalists of the medicinal properties of the toad in promoting sexual arousal or retarding ageing.

Attempts to control introduced species have encountered problems. The myxomatosis virus was introduced to control the rabbit population. The virus also proved fatal to many native species, while, over time, the rabbits developed a resistance to the virus. Scientists developed alternative methods of eradication such as the calice virus. They assured a sceptical public that it was 'safe'. The virus is now also affecting native species. The interplay between native and introduced species is subtle. Many wild species do not have any immunity to common diseases carried by domestic animals. In Africa, the transmission of diseases like distemper from domestic dogs is one cause of the precipitous decline in wild dog numbers.

Sometimes, the human impact is more immediate. In Seward in Alaska, we took a cruise on Prince William Sound. Towering snow-covered mountains and glaciers frame the sound. The ocean is rich in fish stocks. It is home to various sea birds and aquatic mammals (whales, seals and sea otters). The waters are also an important sea lane. Large tankers carry Alaskan crude to refineries further south.

On 24 March 1989 the *Exxon Valdez* ran aground on a well-marked reef. The accident caused 11 million gallons of oil to leak into Prince William Sound. The spilled oil affected about 2,100 kilometres (1,300 miles) of shoreline. Death estimates include 250,000 sea birds, 2,800 sea otters, 300 harbour seals, 150 bald eagles and 22 orca whales. Billions of fish and intertidal plants and animals were destroyed.

When we were there in 2001, there was no immediate evidence that the oil spill had taken place. But weathered oil remains trapped beneath rocks, in the subsurface and on the deep ocean bed. It has entered the food chain. Even low concentrations of hydrocarbons are harmful. Despite the massive clean-up, fish stocks have not recovered. The numbers of sea birds and aquatic animals are well below levels before the oil spill. Only two of the 28 species affected by the spill have 'recovered'.

Traces of numerous pollutants (such as heavy metals, for example) have been found in the icebound confines of Svalbard in Norway, just south of the Arctic. It was considered free of pollution. Winds and currents have introduced pollutants to this part of the world. Researchers have noticed genetic abnormalities including hermaphrodism among the polar bears. In the polar areas, global warming in the form of higher temperatures and melting ice caps is already affecting bird and animal life. In the Arctic, in recent years, the sea ice has failed to form in some years. Polar bears need the ice to travel out to sea to hunt seals building fat reserves for the rest of the year. Many bears have starved to death.

In late 2003, a study suggested that the use by navy ships of powerful sonar systems might cause mass whale stranding. The study pointed to how the underwater noise pollution created by human activity may affect marine life. The US Navy immediately disputed the findings, as it had not participated in the studies. It insists that sonar has no or negligible effects on marine life. Conservation movements in California used legal action to temporarily stop the US Navy developing far-reaching low frequency sonar systems. The decision was a small victory for the environmentalists. It allowed the US Navy to test the system in Asiatic waters because deeper waters minimized the impact of the sonar. The prohibition did not apply in cases of 'war' and, undoubtedly, the new sonar systems will be required in the 'war' of the 'willing' against 'terrorism' and to ensure 'homeland security'.

Eco-tourist destinations are oases in the middle of a developed land-scape. These islands redefine the term 'wilderness'. They are no longer wild areas beyond human occupation and reach where nature rules. They are sharply delineated areas surrounded by human presence. These islands are fragile places whose tenuous survival is entirely dependent on human restraint. There are also threats from within. Loss of genetic diversity amongst isolated populations results in inbreeding and genetic problems. Many South African game parks and reserves are artificial. The size dictates that the populations must be carefully controlled. The number of top preda-tors that sit on top of the food chain must be limited, exacerbating the lack of genetic diversity.

In one private game reserve, the owners decided to introduce eland, a large cow-like antelope. They acquired them at great cost from another reserve, where there were no large predators. Several generations of predator-free existence had dulled the elands' instincts. The elands ignored the lions. The lions were puzzled, surprised at the lack of fear and the failure of these animals to flee. Eventually, the lions, driven by hunger, attacked. The elands did not move. Those that remained did not adapt. The lions killed and ate all of them.

The concentration of species into small areas increases the risk of extinc-tion. Fierce bush fires in 2002 destroyed a large part of a national park near Canberra, Australia's capital. It was one of the last areas where the beautiful coroboree frog is found. Scientists had invested heavily in a captive-breeding programme to reverse the decline of this unique amphibian. The bush fires accelerated the end of this species.

The impact of human activity is often difficult to understand.

The Aleutian Islands sit at the convergence of two rich marine eco-systems: the North Pacific and the Bering Sea. The plankton-rich cold waters support a large quantity of marine life, which in turn support varied bird and animal life as well as a large fishing industry. Many hallmark species have almost disappeared: the population of northern fur seals is down 50%; stellar sea lions are down 80%; sea otters are down 75%. Conservationists blame the commercial fishing industry. Others blame contamination of the ocean by chemicals. Scientists speculate that rising sea temperatures change fish species – the 'junk food' theory. Pollock numbers have risen relative to fattier capelin and herring. Sea lions and fur seals favour fattier fish. The decline in capelin and herring affects the predator populations.

Paul Estes, a US Geological Survey scientist, suggests a complex relationship between humans, whales, sea otters and sea urchins.[36] The decline in northern fur seals, stellar sea lions and sea otters is the result of a long chain reaction. After World War Two, the Japanese and Russian whaling fleets killed 500,000 great whales in the North Pacific before the whaling moratorium was implemented. Orcas traditionally prey on great whales. Deprived of this prey by whaling, orca turned to other food sources. An orca needs a lot of sea lions or seals to make up the calorific equivalent of a whale. The sea lion and seal populations had not recovered from centuries of hunting for fur and meat, and the orcas further reduced these populations. In the 1980s, the orcas were forced to adapt again. They switched to sea otters. Sea otters are even smaller than sea lions or fur seals. The sea otter population is down by 90% in some areas. Estes arrived at his theory after connecting unrelated data – the fall in population of sea lions/seals/sea otters, the increasing numbers of sea urchins (a favourite sea otter food) and observing an orca attack a sea otter. The increase in sea urchins now threatens the underwater kelp forest that is essential to fish stocks and the wider eco-system.

In America's Yellowstone National Park, wolves have been reintroduced. Biologists have begun to understand the important role played by them in the park's eco-system.[37] They keep the elk population in check by thinning out the herds of the old and the weak. The presence of wolves also keeps the elk herds moving, which allows the grasslands to regenerate, improving the habitat of small animals and birds as a consequence. Wolf kills frequently provide food for grizzly bears, coyotes, raptors and other scavenging birds. Local farmers and ranchers are angry and bitter. Elk hunters are unhappy about having to compete with wolves.

## Shallow and deep conservation

In Sydney, a man dressed as a koala frequently confronts you at traffic lights. He carries a collection bucket claiming to collect for the conservation movement. The collectors collect on a commission basis (they keep half the contribution) or are scam artists. Works such as Rachel Carson's *Silent Spring* inspired the conservation movement. Common, once abundant species were disappearing. The damage to the environment by chemicals such as DDT (dichlorodiphenyltrichloroethane) was becoming understood. Scientists and ordinary people became aware of threats to the environment.

Ernst Haeckel, a German biologist, created the word 'ecology' in 1866. Historically, interest focused on documenting and recording the natural world, collecting specimens and studying species. Nature was superabundant and resilient. It did not need conservation. In the early 1970s, a succession of stories looking at threatened species focused attention on the threat to bio-diversity. Charismatic individuals publicized the cause of endangered species: Jane Goodall, working with chimpanzees; Dian Fossey with mountain gorillas; Birute Galdikas with orang-utans. Gifted documentary makers, such as David Attenborough, and wildlife photographers communicated their stories to a broad audience. In the December 1965 issue of *National Geographic* there is an extraordinary photo: Jane Goodall reaches out to a tiny young Tanzanian chimpanzee, nicknamed Flint. Its power to move still astonishes.

Gradually the conservation movement took shape. For example, in 1973, the Endangered Species Act was passed in the USA. In 1975 the CITES Treaty, banning trade in endangered species, became effective.

Modern ecological thinking has two divergent elements.[38] The first group consists of the resource ecologists. They take an anthropocentric view that seeks to limit human use of natural resources. Human beings have a responsibility to secure the well-being of humans, and that must be balanced against an obligation towards the natural world. The resource ecologist views nature as a resource. Preservation is driven by the desire to allow sustainable exploitation.

The second group consists of the radical ecologists.[39] It rejects an anthropocentric view of the world. These ecologists seek a fundamental change in the role of humans in the natural world. Any effort to transform nature sets humans above nature. They see development as negative. Preservation of nature is to return human existence into the web of life in a harmonious way. Radical ecology, in its purest form, rejects conservation as it presupposes a role for humans in shaping and controlling the natural environment.

The dominant strain is resource ecology. Government policy and public opinion supports shallow ecology. It is the Realpolitik of the conservation movement.

In Germany, the Green Party has been a significant part of the body politic since the 1980s. The German Greens have been in governing coalitions (with the Social Democrats) in recent years. In Australia, the Green Party has emerged as a significant minor party with political influence at local, state and federal levels. The movement now encompasses social-justice issues. Environmental and conservation issues are part of a wider focus. The Green parties use the turgid business-school speak of modern politics: manifestos, goals, targets, assets, systems, value maximization, resource management and sustainable economic development.

For radical ecologists and even some resource ecologists, the modern conservation movement is a betrayal of the environmental cause, a 'sell out'. The evolution of the conservation movement into Green political parties is re-absorption of the radical will into a safe, conformist and mainstream political reality. Disenchanted, environmental fundamentalists focus on animal rights, militant vegetarianism. Green parties are refuges for disaffected voters and disparate failed constituencies: Stalinists, Trotskyites, anarchists, post-modernists, roundheads. No sooner had it arrived than the conservation movement lost its way. Conservation efforts became the foundation of a political legacy.

The major achievement of conservationists is the preservation of wilderness areas. In 1872 the US Congress set aside 2.1 million acres of wilderness as Yellowstone National Park. In recent years many such parks have been created around the world, some through international pressure, including designation as World Heritage sites. Saving parts of the landscape does not save biodiversity. It preserves islands of wilderness from human development. The conservation movement has not confronted over-exploitation, habitat destruction, introduced species, environmental pollution and islandization in a cohesive way. Preservation of a few species is promoted. Cute and charismatic animals get the money. This does little for actual biodiversity.[40]

Reduction of greenhouse-gas emissions has encouraged alternative sources of energy. Conservationists enthusiastically supported wind power. In the USA, wind farms destroy thousands of birds, due to them flying into the giant propellers. Conservationists now campaign to have wind farms abandoned. Support for conservation is concentrated in the developed nations of North America, western Europe and Australia and New Zealand. There is limited awareness of, or support for, environmental causes in developing countries. This is the North–South divide. The developed countries (the North) having exploited resources in the past at the detriment of the environment now want to prevent the developing nations (the South) exploiting their resources. It is a plot to keep these countries from developing. Only

Western countries can afford to support conservation. They have access to wealth, food and resources. They have choices. In the developing world, poor people cannot afford the sentimentality and nostalgia that is conservation. People in these regions are hungry, lack clean water and sanitation. They fear disease. They have no choice. The typical conservationist wants to save gorillas from extinction. The typical woman in Rwanda wants to feed her family or stop her child dying from preventable diseases. Inability to clear forests for farming or killing for bush meat is not comprehensible to her. You tell her of the benefits of protection of habitat, biodiversity, tourism and the money it will bring. All that will be too little far too late for her and her children. Conservation and nature is not a luxury she can afford. Conservation does not deal with the fundamental inequities of life.

Conservation is a new form of exploitation of the environment. We need to save horseshoe crabs as their blood can detect contamination in drugs and medical equipment. Some frogs secrete fluids that have antibiotic properties. The new compounds may treat bacterial infections increasingly resistant to known antibiotics. Sea sponges are studied as a possible source of an anti-cancer drug. Squalamine, a natural steroid in the liver of the dogfish shark, has potential for treating cancer.

Preservation of nature allows the 'secrets' in 'nature's infinite book' to be unlocked. Scientists fret that extinction robs them of the ability to discover the properties and uses of many species. There is no moral responsibility, no respect for the right of nature to exist in and for itself. Conservation organizations and NGOs are large businesses with million-dollar revenues, speaking the language of business. In 2003, Durban in South Africa hosted 3,000 delegates from around the world, who were attending the Fifth World Parks Congress. Delegates spent 10 days in five-star hotels and took field trips to luxury tourist lodges. Nelson Mandela, Queen Noor and a host of famous celebrities attended and heard uplifting speeches.

The UN and International Union for the Conservation of Nature (an NGO that examines endangered species and natural habitats) published a report showing that fully 12% of the world's land surface is now officially protected. The target of 10% (set a decade ago in Caracas) had been exceeded. The business-plan objectives were satisfied. Nature had been saved. Many parks are token gestures. In developing countries, many parks are abandoned to poachers, soldiers, looters and human habitation. Mozambique's Gorogosa National Park is littered with land mines from the civil war. The Chinese Environment Minister boasted that 15% of the country was national parks. Puzzlingly, he admitted that China's 'weak and inconsistent' management and a lack of resources meant that 'serious damage' had been done to the environment. Elephant Family (another NGO) examined efforts of 21 NGOs in 10 countries to save the Asian elephant.[41] They spent US$4 million on conservation efforts, a small fraction of the money allocated to them. Ordinary people sit in their homes in the developed world trying 'to make a difference'. Businesses use 'conservation' to promote products. Firms tout natural products: 'No animals were harmed in making this product'; 'This product is dolphin-friendly'.

Eco-tourism makes up a growing proportion of the US$35 billion travel industry.[42] Eco-tourism is conservation's handmaiden. If something is worth conserving, then it must be seen. US politicians use a similar argument: it is fine to drill in the Arctic Wildlife Reserve as nobody goes there. Tourists and visitors generate revenue to maintain or to compensate people displaced from the areas preserved. Tourism provides jobs. Eco-tourism allows conservation to pay its way in the age of economic rationalism.

In South America, the best guardians of the rainforest are isolated Indian tribes who have no contact with civilization. They have killed intruders in order to defend their ancient lands; they tenaciously preserve their way of life and the pristine forests that support it. Once we come into contact with these tribes, their way of life is destroyed and, as a result, the destruction of the forest is hastened.

In Kenya, tourist vehicles have damaged some grasslands irreversibly, affecting the once-rich herbivore life and the predators who rely on it. In Namibia, some visitors in a four-wheel drive vehicle drove onto the Etosha Pan, oblivious to the damage.

In Australia, a great conservation battle saved Fraser Island – one of the world's largest sand islands. Now protected and a World Heritage site, Fraser Island is a popular tourist destination. Activity of four-wheel drive vehicles on its white sandy beaches causes serious erosion. Camping on the island damages the eco-system. The island is home to a population of dingoes, a wild-dog species indigenous to Australia. Visitors feed the wild dingoes despite warnings. There have been a number of dingo attacks; the victims are often children; the dingoes are destroyed.

America's love affair with Yellowstone National Park is killing the park through the impact of too many visitors.

Eco-tourism is the final step in the conversion of nature into a consumable item. It is a consumption choice that defines us as a separate group that travels to novel destinations (affluence), supports conservation causes (social and environmental awareness) and purchases eco-friendly products (moral superiority). Pierre Bourdieu, the French sociologist, remarked that taste is first and foremost distaste, the disgust and visceral distaste of others. Paul Erhlich, the economist, remarked that 'nature bats lasts'. Human beings seem capable only of 'shallow' ecology.

Conservation and nature often conjure up fantasies of romantic landscapes and exotic creatures, haunting memories of remarkable experiences. It often seems irrelevant that real animals and plants inhabit this landscape. Conservation is the final exercise of human ascendancy and power over nature. Tim Flannery, an internationally recognized scientist, observed that the concept of preserving areas in national parks smacked of a falsehood: 'the belief that land was "ours" to carve up according to our inclinations.'[43]

Flannery challenges the proposition that whaling is morally wrong. Campaigners against whaling argue that whales are sentient beings like humans. Flannery has a different perspective arguing that they belong to a diverse order of mammals. Some are tiny-brained filter feeders like the blue whales who are aquatic vacuum cleaners' and whose 'intellectual power' is 'slight'. Others, such as orcas and dolphins are large-brained hunters with 'demonstrable intelligence'. Sustainable harvesting of the smaller-brained filter feeders is perfectly acceptable.[44] Flannery does not see any contradiction or irony in the proposition that humans have the right to select which species live or die.

Conservation requires acceptance by human beings of the claim of other creatures on the planet. This implies respect in dealing with the natural world. Human beings seem unable or unwilling to implement that proposition. In 2003, Gerhard Schulz, a German photographer, was awarded the *BG Wildlife Photographer of the Year* award. The winning photograph is of a gorilla and a child taken in Miami's Metrozoo. The gorilla is seated in his enclosure behind glass. The child, a visitor to the zoo, is reflected in the glass. The child admires the primate so closely related to him in the chain of evolution. The gorilla is contemplative. There is a sadness and resignation in his expression. He is a prisoner far from his African home. His species, once abundant, is near extinction. There is no place in this world for him and his kind. The only existence that the human race can afford this magnificent giant, no less a creation than man, is an object of curiosity and display in a zoo.

## The conservation 'game'

Conservation has become an elaborate game. In 1999 we visited India and Nepal. We spent a lot of time in four places – Royal Bardia in Nepal, Kanha in central India, Ranthambore in Rajasthan and Corbett in northern India. These parks had, we were told, significant tiger populations. Tigers proved elusive. We saw two tigers in Ranthambore. We saw one tiger in the cruel staged theatre of the 'Tiger Show' at Kanha. We only saw females. We never saw a male. Where were the tigers? The tiger is the conservation movement's great success. 'Project Tiger' is a model for conservation efforts elsewhere in the world, but in the parks guides told us that the numbers of tigers were much lower than official figures, and falling. So what was going on?

Highly adaptable, tigers once existed in every kind of habitat – from swamps to rainforests, scrub lands to lower mountain slopes. They have few natural predators. The decline in their populations coincided with the arrival of humans. The growth in agriculture resulted in loss of habitat and they were also hunted. My mother told me about the hunt, or *shikar*, as it was known. The hunters would be on *machans* (an elevated platform usually on a tree) or on elephant-back. Beaters would fan out with drums and cymbals to drive the terrified tiger towards the hunters. When the exhausted, frightened animal emerged from the forest, the men shot it with high calibre, powerful rifles. This was the bravery and skill of the hunter, the pleasure of the hunt.

By the late 1960s there was general acceptance that, without drastic action, the tiger would soon be extinct in the wild. There was international pressure. The world was eager to preserve this hallmark species. Project Tiger included the total prohibition of hunting and the setting up of a number of national parks to preserve the tiger's natural habitat. In the late 1980s, Project Tiger was proclaimed a success. Tiger numbers had risen 'officially' to above 4,000 from less than 2,000. Project Tiger was also instrumental, the Government claimed, in preserving the wider eco-system. Many other species had also been 'saved'.

But where were the tigers? Tiger numbers are determined using a census based on park staff recording a tiger's pugmark. Each tiger has a unique paw print that is recognizable by an expert. Tiger's pugmarks are difficult to tell apart. They are affected by the surface (sand or mud) and speed of movement. Dr Ullas Karnath conducted an experiment. He presented tiger census operators with 33 pugmarks taken from four captive tigers: they identified between 6–33 tigers.[45]

While the tiger census overstates the true numbers, the authorities refuse to use relatively simple, accurate and scientific techniques such as camera traps, where an infrared device triggers a camera when an animal passes. Each tiger has unique markings, stripes and facial marks, allowing for more reliable figures.

Official estimates of tiger populations do not tally with other scientific evidence. Tigers need a certain habitat area. They need a certain number of prey animals to sustain them. The census figures for some reserves are far greater than is possible. Tiger populations tend to remain reasonably stable after attaining saturation density. The census statistics show continuous and rapid increases.

Ranthambhore is the story of the efforts to save the tiger.[46] It is also the story of Fateh Singh Rathore. He came to Ranthambhore as a young man. In 1960 he helped organize the *shikar* for Queen Elizabeth and Prince Philip. In the 1970s he returned to the park, a convert to conservation. Ranthambhore was a Project Tiger park. Fateh Singh Rathore stopped the villagers grazing cattle in the park. He repaired the dams to keep water in the lakes. He built roads and started patrols. In 1974 he moved the villagers into a new village with improved facilities outside the park. The villagers were compensated under a government scheme. Ranthambhore began to recover. The forest and animals started to come back. Fateh Singh Rathore was succeeding in 'returning Ranthambhore to its original state'.

Fateh Singh Rathore left in 1987. In the 1990s, the tiger population in Ranthambhore collapsed. There were no more than 8–12 tigers left in the park when we visited in 1999. The official figure was 40. The decline is from illegal poaching for bones, skin, teeth, claws and penises. The park administration is inactive. Poachers are not caught or prosecuted. There are few patrols. It is not a question of resources or funding – both of which have increased substantially. The word 'game' is used to signify wildlife. It also means a sport, hobby or deception. Project Tiger is, in part, a game – a deception.

In India we met many of the lodge managers and owners. Project Tiger had mobilized a lot of money from the Indian Government and international sources. The funds were for habitat protection, prevention of poaching and stopping illegal smuggling in tiger parts. It was also to assist with training and work with local communities to raise awareness of conservation issues. The funds are channelled through lodge owners and associated interests. They have built nice offices and appointed themselves to important sounding posts with impressive salaries. It was unclear how much of the money actually finds its way to actual conservation projects directed at preserving the tiger population. Ill-equipped and poorly paid guards are unable or unwilling to patrol the park or catch poachers. Some conspire with poachers to supplement their meagre incomes.

The reason for the inflated census numbers was quite clear: local and international sponsors demanded success. The tiger had to be saved. They were providing a lot of money towards this end. Increasing tiger populations ensured funds kept flowing. Dramatic improvements and the occasional crisis were the perfect formula for maximizing donor support. These were the rules of the game.

At Ranthambhore we were out one afternoon with Salim. On the way back to the park entrance, we heard the alarm calls. Langur monkeys barked repeatedly.

'Come, let's go,' Salim said.

A young tigress was sitting on the side of an incline. She was pale, lighter in colour than the other tigers, with a beautiful oval face. The tigress watched the visitors without interest. She yawned, got up and walked down the path. Thin, almost slight, she walked past us languidly towards the forest. Then she was gone, merging into the twilight. She is probably one of the last of her kind in Ranthambhore.

At Corbett, Shiva drove us into a part of the park where visitors didn't normally go. A pair of pine martens ran across the road. The yellow stripes on their throats were visible. We heard them chattering in the thick woods. We reached a cliff top overlooking a valley. On the other side, there was an illegal logging camp. A fire was burning. There are many such camps within the park. Shiva said that the park authorities had probably been bribed. There was the poaching of tigers within the park – rich businessmen paid to be flown in by helicopter to shoot them. One had been caught but got off with a fine. We did not see any tigers in the park while we were there. The official census was 100 tigers; the guides told us the numbers were far lower.

## Last chance to see

In 1991 we travelled to Africa to see the mountain gorillas. We had booked two treks in the Kahuzi-Biega Park to see them. A sighting was assured. I wanted to be certain. We were travelling a very long distance. On the first morning Jade and I were apprehensive, unsure of what to expect. At the park entrance, rangers and trackers met us and we drove into the forest. The rangers and trackers start near where the gorillas were seen the previous day. They track them using signs: broken bamboo saplings (the plant is a favourite gorilla food); broken branches and twigs; gorilla beds, crude platforms made from twigs and leaves in trees. The trackers look for gorilla faeces that allow accurate estimates of when they were there.

On the first day, the tracking took two hours along narrow forest paths. The ground is hilly, muddy and wet. We only had ordinary sneakers, not yet having acquired the accessories of eco-travel. Our feet often slipped. Once, Jade's foot was encased in mud up to her ankle. She pulled her foot out gingerly with the help of the ranger. She worried that her shoe would come off as she tried to extricate her foot.

The ranger grinned. 'You must get a little muddy, it is a jungle.'

That evening at the lodge, there was a businessman from Belgium. He had been coming to Zaire for years.

'The guides make the tourists walk around a while,' he said. 'They know where the gorillas are. They just want the tourists to get a jungle experience.'

We saw two separate gorilla families. Each family is headed by a silver-back (the term comes from the white hair on the back of an adult male). A fully developed adult male is around 250 kilograms (600 pounds) and 2 metres (6 feet) tall: up close, a silverback is electrifying. The family consists of a number of females, their young and older juveniles. The first family group we saw was headed by a silverback called Mahesi, a famous gorilla featured on the currency of Zaire. They were feeding. They would stop to eat some bamboo or other shoots. Then, they continued foraging. We kept moving with them. The second day we visited a different family grouping. The silverback was known as Musamuka. The gorillas were resting after a feed. They were grooming each other. The young were playing.

The rules of visitation are simple. You must maintain your distance. You must adopt a submissive pose. Eye contact is forbidden. You must be quiet. If a gorilla charges, you must not run but hold your ground.

The first group included several young gorillas, who were about five or six years of age, and naturally curious. We were standing near a female, while a young gorilla watched us. He decided to give us a demonstration of his strength and abilities. He clambered up a sapling, until he was directly above our heads. The tree swayed under his weight. He released his hands to pound on his chest. Gorillas pound on their chests, producing a soft drumming sound, a signal or communication. Releasing his grip to pound his chest unbalanced him and he tumbled down, ending up on the ground a little way away from us. He looked embarrassed and surprised. I had a smile on my face. He picked himself up and bounded away. The other gorillas took no notice at all.

The group contained two young males. The rangers had named them Lamb Chop and Mint Sauce. They would soon leave the group to start a group of their own. Mint Sauce reclined on his back in a hollow, resting. Jade and I made our way towards him. Jade was taking photos. He was looking at us upside down. He wasn't comfortable. With a grunt, he rolled over. He propped himself on one arm in an approximation of Auguste Rodin's *The Thinker*. He looked directly at us. His gaze was open and inquiring. It was impossible to avoid it. Mint Sauce had clearly not read the rules against eye contact. I looked back at him and our eyes locked for a few seconds – one primate looking at another.

In 1994, Rwanda erupted in civil war. The conflict destabilized the Great Lakes region of Africa and triggered civil war in Zaire (now the Congo), where it continues – the longest running and most murderous conflict in the world. Thousands of people fled into the forests and the park to escape the fighting. The large numbers of refugees necessitated setting up large camps adjacent to the park and forests were cleared for camps and cultivation. Trees were used for fire. Animals, including protected species, were hunted for food. The chaos allowed poachers to operate unimpeded.

The park is rich in a mineral: coltan (colombite-tantalite). It is plentiful in the mountainous terrain and easily extracted. It is the source of tantalum, used in mobile phones, pagers, electronic games, jet engines, car airbags and surgical instruments. The demand for tantalum oxide has grown exponentially and the price has risen. Illegal mining of coltan has always occurred on a small scale in the park. As the price rose, up to 12,000 people poured into the park with picks, shovels and sieves. They could earn US$80 a day, a fortune in a place with an average income of less than US$1 a day (if you are fortunate enough to have a job or land to cultivate).

The park contained 10,000 plant, 220 bird and 131 mammal species and was best known for its gorillas and elephants. By the turn of the millennium, almost all the park's 350 elephants were dead, killed for meat or ivory. Of the park's gorilla population of around 250–300 when we visited in 1991, maybe 100 remain. In 1999 there were perhaps a total of 17,000 gorillas in eastern Zaire. By 2003, the remaining population was less than 1,000. The conflict disrupted the park patrols that monitored the gorillas and deterred poachers. Unpaid and without resources, the rangers tried to protect the remaining gorilla population. Many died in the conflict with rebel soldiers. There is no profound concern about the fate of the gorillas. In 1999 conservation activities resumed to a limited degree under Rwandan Army protection. Rangers and trackers were allowed access to the primates after an absence of some years.

The United Nations has tried to control the trade in illegal coltan. High-profile celebrities publicly support the efforts. A new mining code is being established so users of coltan pay a higher price for illegally mined coltan. But coltan does not come with a 'made in [country]' label. The trade in diamonds used to finance other African wars demonstrates the difficulty in controlling trade in 'blood' minerals. Soon, there will be 'gorilla safe' mobile phones to go with your 'dolphin safe' tuna in your supermarket and your 'non-blood diamonds' at Tiffany's.

In Alaska, John took us out on the boat to a part of Kukak Bay where there were usually bears. A female and two cubs were playing some distance away. We couldn't get any closer with the boat as the tide was out. John suggested that we beach the boat on a nearby gravel beach and walk around on foot to where the bear and cubs were. He knew the bears. It would be fine. Two of the guests stayed behind to fish for salmon. John led four of us in the direction of the bears. It took almost an hour to get to where they had been. They were gone. Disconsolate, we headed back towards the boat. On the way back, John spotted one.

# 'FATA MORGANA': THE HOPE AND REALITY OF ECO-TOURISM

Grizzly bears are large predators, reaching up to 1.5 metres (4 feet) at the shoulder, 3–4 metres (10–12 feet) from nose to tail and weighing up to 600 kilograms (1,500 pounds). The coat varies from light (almost blond) to dark shades of brown and black. The long outer hairs are tipped with white or silver – the grizzled appearance that gives the species its name. The bear has a large hump over the front shoulders, the muscle mass used to power the front limbs. The hump becomes more marked as the bear attains maturity. This bear was not far short of full size. He was grazing on the sedge grass. We stopped and watched him. The bear noticed us. He looked in our direction. Then, he began to walk towards us. The bear had been about 100 metres (300 feet) from us. He was now much closer. We continued to watch him and take photos.

He kept coming towards us and stopped about 50 metres (150 feet) away. Turning a little to one side, the bear rolled his shoulders. The rippling muscles in the prominent shoulder hump were visible.

John said what sounded like, 'Oh, oh.' The bear's behaviour was apparently 'not good.'

I requested clarification.

The rolling of the shoulders was an aggressive posture. The bear was signalling that he was big and strong. I could see that already. The bear resumed walking towards us.

For the first time, John gave us a direct instruction: 'Stay together and look big.'

I wished that as a child I had eaten more cereal and drunk more milk. John did not carry a gun or even bear spray (capsicum spray). There is an Alaskan joke about bear spray. If a bear attacks you spray yourself in the face. That way, you can't see it. The bear was now only about 10 metres (30 feet) from us, and closing. I felt no fear or concern. He looked magnificent in the sunlight. I was absorbed in the sight. The photographers were in ecstasy. The bear was now very close. The ER surgeon with us couldn't focus through his 500mm lens. We were on edge of a stream with a trickle of water. The bear was on the other side. John had a camera tripod in his hand.

The bear slightly changed direction, and walked by us on the other side of the thin flow of water. He crossed the stream slightly behind where we were standing and sat down on the ground. He was now around 3 metres (9 feet) from us. We could see his steely claws clearly. Their tensile strength was obvious. We could see the tousled fur, matted in places, glistening in places, wet from the stream. We were enthralled by the sight of this magnificent animal so close to us. We were now entirely relaxed. The photographers were reeling off photos one after the other. Even John had taken out his camera and was taking shots.

Twenty minutes passed. John indicated that we should leave. We backed off carefully. The bear got up, turning and wandering off along the shoreline. The mountains in the background framed the scene. The sunlight reflected off the ice and snow. The beauty of the moment was sublime. It was an ethereal sight, a timeless scene. I wondered how long the bears had been the Lords of Katmai. I wondered how long the bears of Katmai would reign supreme.

We continue to travel to eco-tourist destinations. We continue to look out, partly in jest and partly in hope, for the elusive pangolin. We would still like to see one. But increasingly I worry that this is pointless if pangolins themselves cease to exist as a species due to hunting or habitat destruction. What would be the point – just to be able to say that we had seen the last pangolin?

## I do not want to live in a world without . . .

In *Preludes*,[48] T.S. Eliot wrote of, 'the notion of some infinitely gentle, infinitely suffering thing.' The words create a haunting image: nature as a sentient being under siege. Since the moment, now so long ago, that I first saw the gorillas in the Virunga Mountains, those words have taken on extra significance. The words speak to me of a world that is at the core of my being. I cannot imagine my life without that world and the creatures that are a part of it.

The Australian continent is very old. The coastline near Sydney consists of towering sandstone cliffs. We often walk along those cliffs. When I think about the age of the cliffs, the forces that shaped them over millions of years, I am struck by the unimportance of my life, the transient nature of human achievements. Indian philosophy calls it *maya* – illusion. The day I wrote this, people demonstrated in Sydney about the preservation of an historic building, but in every part of the globe, people, through their actions, directly or indirectly, are destroying species of plants and animals that have taken millennia to evolve.

A documentary filmmaker made a film about 'grizzly alley' in Alaska. It is famed for congregations of grizzly bears along rivers and streams during the salmon-spawning season. The filmmaker returned to the place to find a bear he knew from previous visits. He had saved it from a hunter. There is a local Native American myth: if you save any living creature then you are responsible for its life. I understand what that means. Our travels have given us a glimpse of the wonders of the natural world. I feel responsible for the creatures that I have seen, the places that I have visited. There is bond transcending space and time between the places and the creatures and me. If I fail to honour them, if I fail to assure their preservation, then I fail them and myself.

In Canada, Knight's Inlet is also famed for grizzly bears. A local Canadian filmmaker shot a piece about the area. Most of the film was shot on the ground amongst bears. He felt no concern or fear. One day, he came upon a female he knew with a new cub. The bear and cub came right up to him. The bear encouraged the cub, who was cautious, to approach the camera and the filmmaker. At one point, the cub sticks his nose right into the lens. I remember his words. He said that he could not conceive a world without the bears. He did not want to live in a world without them. I too cannot conceive a world without the animals, birds, plants and wild places. I too do not want to live in a world without the animals, birds, plants and wild places.

# IN SEARCH OF THE PANGOLIN: REPRISE

In 2001, I was watching a news bulletin. There was a story about pangolins in Vietnam. Hundreds of pangolins had been caught and killed. The dead pangolins were being shipped to China where they were a culinary delicacy and used in traditional medicines. There were countless grey-brown scaly bodies curled up and packed tightly in cardboard boxes. A few captured poachers stood by, hands bound with steel wire. They would have been paid a few hundred dollars for the shipment (a fortune in local terms).

In 2002, I was chatting to a South African woman, Zelda. The conversation was about her holiday. She had been to Botswana.

'You know what? We saw a pangolin.'

'You saw a pangolin?' My voice must have conveyed my disbelief and jealousy.

'Really, I did,' she said.

The camp manager had come across the pangolin while out driving one day. He had never seen one before. He had gone back to the camp and rounded up the guests and staff. It was still there, unconcerned by the attention. It was an experience that we certainly would have cherished.

Paul, another South African, said he had seen one too near Kruger Park.

'You know, some people have actually seen two...'

In Botswana, at a camp near the Khwai River, lucky guests were treated to the spectacle of a leopard playing with a pangolin. The pangolin had rolled itself into a ball for self-protection. So they really do exist.

No, we did not see a pangolin at Ranthambore. In fact, we have not still seen a pangolin. We continue to search. We continue to hope against hope that the wild places and creatures we love so much will survive.

# FOOTNOTES

[1] For example, see Les Beletsky (1998) *Costa Rica: The Ecotravellers' Wildlife Guide*, San Diego, Calif.: Academic Press, p.1.

[2] See Alain de Botton (2002) *The Art of Travel*, London: Penguin, p.9. © Alain de Botton, 2002. Reproduced by permission of Penguin Books Ltd.

[3] Douglas Adams and Mark Carwardine (1992) *Last Chance to See*; New York: Ballantine Books.

[4] See Santo Cilauro, Tom Gleisner, and Rob Stich (2005) *Molvania: A Land Untouched By Modern Dentistry* London: Atlantic Books.

[5] (1938) *The Description of the World* Stoughton, MA: AMS Press.

[6] (1988) *Travels with a Superior Person* London: Pan Macmillan.

[7] Bruce Chatwin (2003) *In Patagonia*; London, Penguin.

[8] (1975) *The Great Railway Bazaar* London: Penguin; (1988) *Riding The Iron Rooster* (1988) London: Penguin; (1979) *The Old Patagonian Express* London: Penguin; (1992) *The Happy Isles of Oceania* London: Penguin.

[9] For example, Peter Matthiessen (1978) *The Snow Leopard* London: Vintage; (1988) *The Cloud Forest* London, Vintage .

[10] See David Attenborough (2002) *Life on Air*, London: BBC Books, p.293.

[11] See David Attenborough (2002) *Life on Air*, London: BBC Books, p.290.

[12] Costa Rica Sun Tours, 'General Guidelines for Travel in Costa Rica,' (April 1994).

[13] (1959) A Rebours London: Penguin Books.

[14] See Alain de Botton (2002) *The Art of Travel*, London: Penguin, p.40. © Alain de Botton, 2002. Reproduced by permission of Penguin Books Ltd.

[15] See Alain de Botton (2002) *The Art of Travel*, London: Penguin, p.57. © Alain de Botton, 2002. Reproduced by permission of Penguin Books Ltd.

[16] Tom Wolfe in his novel *Bonfire of the Vanities* immortalized this special class of New York women; see (1988) *The Bonfire of the Vanities*, London: Picador, p.20.

[17] The trilogy of films are: *First Contact*, *Joe Leahy's Neighbours* and *Black Harvest*.

[18] See Tom Walker (1995) *Alaska's Wildlife*; Graphics Art Centre Publishing Co pp.14, 15.

[19] See 'The Global Menace Of Local Strife' (24th May 2003) *The Economist*, p.26.

[20] See 'The Global Menace of Local Strife' (24th May 2003) *The Economist*, pp.25–27.

[21] (1997) Eothen, Evanston, Il: Northwestern University Press.

# FOOTNOTES

[22] See Tim Flannery and Peter Schouten (2001) *A Gap in Nature*, Melbourne: Text Publishing, p.124. © Tim Flannery, 2001. Reproduced by permission of The Text Publishing Company.

[23] See Tim Flannery and Peter Schouten (2001) *A Gap in Nature*, Melbourne: Text Publishing, p.34. © Tim Flannery, 2001. Reproduced by permission of The Text Publishing Company.

[24] See Tim Flannery and Peter Schouten (2001) *A Gap in Nature;* Melbourne: Text Publishing, p.34. © Tim Flannery, 2001. Reproduced by permission of The Text Publishing Company.

[25] See Kurt Vonnegut Jr. (1963) *Cat's Cradle*, New York: Holt, Rinehart & Winston, p.75.

[26] See Bjørn Lomborg (2001) *The Skeptical Environmentalist*, Cambridge: Cambridge University Press.

[27] See J.R. McNeill (2000) Something New Under the Sun: An Environmental History of the Twentieth Century World, New York: W.W. Norton & Company.

[28] See 'A Reprieve For Free Speech' (20 December 2003) *The Economist*, p.111.

[29] See Virginia Morrell, 'The Sixth Extinction' (February 1999) *National Geographic*, pp.42–59.

[30] See Virginia Morrell, 'The Variety of Life' (February 1999) *National Geographic* p.28.

[31] See Andrew Darby 'Cold Gold' (2 October 2003) The Sydney Morning Herald 14.

[32] See Dale Petersen (2003) *Eating Apes*, Chicago, University of California Press.

[33] See Sara Oldfield (ed.) (2003) *The Trade In Wildlife: Regulation for Conservation*, London: Earthscan.

[34] See Tim Flannery 'Beautiful Lies' in (2003) *Quarterly Essay* Issue 9, pp.1–73.

[35] See Tim Flannery 'Beautiful Lies' in (2003) *Quarterly Essay* Issue 9, p.19.

[36] See 'Alaska Wildlife Refuge' (August 2003) *National Geographic*, pp.79, 82.

[37] See Verlyn Klinkenberg 'Wolf Tracks in the Wilderness' (7 October 2003) *International Herald Tribune*, p.9.

[38] Arne Naess, a Norwegian philosopher, refers to this division as the 'shallow' ecology/'deep' ecology split.

[39] This group is often associated with Ernst Haeckel, a German biologist, who introduced the term *oekologie*, describing the web of life from which the word ecology is derived.

[40] See Tim Flannery 'Beautiful Lies' in (2003) *Quarterly Essay* Issue 9, pp.1–73.

[41] See 'Who Guards The Guardians?' (20th September 2003) *The Economist*, p.79.

[42] Some estimates put this as high as 35%.

# FOOTNOTES

[43] See Tim Flannery 'Beautiful Lies' in (2003) *Quarterly Essay* Issue 9, pp.39, 40.

[44] See Tim Flannery 'Beautiful Lies' in (2003) *Quarterly Essay* Issue 9, pp.43, 44.

[45] See 'How Many Tigers In India?' in Stanley Breeden and Belinda Wright (1996) *Through The Tiger's Eyes*, Berkeley, Ca, Ten Speed Press, pp.134, 135.

[46] See 'The Rise And Fall Of Ranthambhore' in Stanley Breeden and Belinda Wright (1996) *Through The Tiger's Eyes*; Berkeley, Ca, Ten Speed Press, pp.147–53.

[47] T.S. Eliot (1973) *Selected Poems*, London: Faber & Faber, p.24. Reproduced by permission of Faber & Faber.